Andrei Ta

Andrei Tarkovsky

Sean Martin

www.pocketessentials.com

This edition published in 2005 by Pocket Essentials
P.O.Box 394, Harpenden, Herts, AL5 1XJ

Distributed in the USA by Trafalgar Square Publishing, P.O. Box 257, Howe Hill Road,
North Pomfret, Vermont 05053

http://www.pocketessentials.com

A CIP catalogue record for this book is available from the British Library.

ISBN 1 904048 49 8
EAN 978 1 904048 49 7

2 4 6 8 10 9 7 5 3 1

Typeset by Avocet Typeset, Chilton, Aylesbury, Bucks
Printed and bound in Great Britain by Cox & Wyman, Reading, Berks

My discovery of Tarkovsky's first film was like a miracle. Suddenly, I found myself standing at the door of a room, the keys of which had, until then, never been given to me. It was a room I had always wanted to enter and where he was moving freely and fully at ease.

I felt encouraged and stimulated: someone was expressing what I had always wanted to say without knowing how.

Tarkovsky is for me the greatest, the one who invented a new language, true to the nature of film, as it captures life as a reflection, life as a dream.

Ingmar Bergman

Acknowledgements

Thanks are due to The Royal Opera House, Covent Garden; Trond S Trondsen and Jan Bielawski of nostalghia.com; Nick Harding; Olegar Fedoro; Marina Tarkovskaya; André Bennett; Victoria Carolan; Layla Alexander-Garrett; my sister Lois and, for answering my Tarkovsky-related questions of yesteryear, Mark Le Fanu.

Contents

Introduction   11

1:    Life and Times   13
2:    Theory and Practice   26
3:    The Student Films   50
4:    *Ivan's Childhood*   61
5:    *Andrei Rublev*   76
6:    *Solaris*   99
7:    *Mirror*   120
8:    *Stalker*   145
9:    *Nostalgia*   163
10:   *The Sacrifice*   179
11:   Works in Other Media   197

Endnotes   215
Appendix I: Complete Filmography   232
Appendix II: Unrealised Scripts and Projects   236
Suggestions for Further Reading   242
Index   249

Introduction

This book is intended to serve as a short overview of Tarkovsky's work for those unfamiliar with it, or as a stimulus to go back and rewatch the films for those already acquainted with them.

My aim has been to discuss all aspects of Tarkovsky's work, from his full-length films to the lesser-known works for television, radio and stage. Tarkovsky saw himself primarily as a poet and it is a poetic sensibility that pervades all his work, regardless of medium. There are problems, however, in attempting to write about Tarkovsky at all. As Natasha Synessios wrote, 'Most of us still visit the cinema for entertainment, or escapism, not for spiritual sustenance, for revelations and benedictions. Yet those of us who are "Tarkovsky-marked" experience his films in just such religious terms. Analysis is not usually conducive to this type of experience, yet through it one hopes to unravel something of the mysterious and ineffable process of creation.'[1] My approach has therefore been only partially concerned with analysis, as I feel that the inherent mystery of Tarkovsky's films speaks for itself, and the films are, ultimately, not solvable. They are films that change as we do.

Tarkovsky's films could be seen to move through three phases, concentrating successively on History, the Family and a final, more philosophical phase, which I have labelled the

Triptych. Obviously, these distinctions are somewhat arbitrary: *The Sacrifice*, for instance – the third part of the Triptych – could also be seen as a portrait of a dysfunctional family, while *Mirror* is as much about history as it is the family. Others may be inclined to feel that Tarkovsky's work falls neatly into two sections, with *Mirror* marking the end of the first period, or still others may feel that his work is one homogenous whole.

In giving a production history and brief discussion of each film – intended more to provoke reflection rather than to try to explain what the films mean – I have also added sections on the autobiographical elements of each. Tarkovsky's life and work are inextricably entwined. As Peter Green observed, the subjects of his films – childhood, war, a yearning for belief, the complexities of family life, nostalgia for home, exile and death – are also 'stations in his own life. There is a rare congruence between subject and object that goes beyond the usual autobiographical parallels artists draw in their work.'[2]

Of course, no book, including this one, can replace seeing the actual films, preferably on the big screen, and it is my hope that, if this book inspires the reader to go back to Tarkovsky's films and to watch them with both an open and an active mind, then it will have served its purpose. Natasha Synessios's words about *Mirror* are valid for the whole of Tarkovsky's work: 'when all is said and done, this film works on the heart and soul, not the mind; it is with them, first and foremost, that we must approach it.'[3]

Life and Times

Andrei Tarkovsky (1932–86) was a part of the generation of Soviet filmmakers that emerged during the Khrushchev Thaw years, which also saw the emergence of such directors as Otar Iosseliani, Sergei Parajanov and Andrei Mikhalkov-Konchalovsky. Tarkovsky made only seven full-length films, yet this slender oeuvre has established him as the most important and well-known Russian director since Eisenstein. Although Tarkovsky's reputation continues to grow, especially in North America, where initial critical reaction was decidedly cooler than in Europe,[4] his genius was recognised within his own lifetime by Jean-Paul Sartre, who championed Tarkovsky's first feature, *Ivan's Childhood*, and Ingmar Bergman, who regarded Tarkovsky as 'the greatest of them all'.[5] Tarkovsky's work has been admired by directors as diverse as Bergman, Victor Erice, Terry Gilliam, Peter Greenaway, Krzysztof Kieślowski and Lars von Trier. In its Ten Best Films of All Time poll in 1982, *Sight and Sound* critics voted Tarkovsky's second feature, *Andrei Rublev*, as runner-up, a remarkable achievement since the film had only been released in the UK in 1973, making it the youngest film on the list by far.

Tarkovsky's films are slow, dreamlike searches for faith and redemption, and it comes as no surprise to learn that, during his years in the Soviet Union, he was often criticised for 'mysticism' and his continued failure to tackle subjects in a style more acceptable to socialist realism. And yet Tarkovsky and his films were very much a product of the Soviet system, which ironically allowed directors a great deal of freedom to express themselves. Before we move on to examine Tarkovsky's films, writings and works in other media, it is instructive to explore briefly the Soviet film industry as it was when Tarkovsky was working within it and Tarkovsky's own biography, as both played an important part in making Tarkovsky's films what they are.

Tarkovsky's Early Years

Andrei Arsenevich Tarkovsky was born on 4 April 1932 in the village of Zavrazhie, which lies just outside the town of Yurievets on the banks of the Volga in the Ivanovo region about 60 miles north of Moscow. The family were literary: his paternal grandfather, Alexander (1860–1920), was a poet who had been a member of the People's Freedom Movement, which espoused culture and learning for all; as a result, he was banished by the Tsar for his liberal views. Tarkovsky's father was the poet Arseny Tarkovsky, who was born in the Ukrainian city of Kirovograd (then Elizavetgrad) in 1907. He attended the Moscow Literary Institute during the late 1920s, where he met Maria Ivanovna Vishnakova. They subsequently married and had two children, Andrei and his sister, Marina (born 1934). Tarkovsky senior had yet to be published and so, to support the family, worked away from home as a translator. The family moved to Moscow in 1935, where Tarkovsky's mother took a job as a proofreader at the First State Printing House. Tarkovsky's father left the family in 1937 to live with another woman, although he continued to support his family financially and to visit on birthdays and other important occasions. Tarkovsky began his schooling in Moscow in 1939, but with the Nazi invasion of Russia two years later, was evacuated with his mother and sister back to Yurievets, where they remained for two years. Although the family were confirmed Muscovites, Tarkovsky's early life in the country, both before the family moved to Moscow and during his time as an evacuee, would leave an indelible impression on him which he would later portray in *Mirror*.

Tarkovsky claimed that his mother groomed him from childhood to be an artist, making sure that he was exposed to art and literature from an early age (though given both Arseny's and Maria Ivanovna's literary predilections, it would have been difficult for the young Tarkovsky to have avoided books and works of art). To further this end, Tarkovsky studied music for seven years, as well as having three years of art lessons at the 1905 Academy.

Tarkovsky seems to have resented his mother's attempts to foster in him a sense that he was an artist-in-waiting, and, as a result, rebelled by hanging out with kids his mother didn't approve of, playing football and acting tough. However, despite his rebelliousness, he did love books, and was apparently only quiet when reading.[6] At school, he was an average pupil, a 'dreamer more than thinker'.[7] It was perhaps his lack of academic aptitude that made Tarkovsky realise that he might indeed become an artist one day, perhaps as a composer, painter or writer. Although as a boy and teenager, the young Tarkovsky 'caused his mother a lot of worry'[8] – in addition to his difficult behaviour, he also suffered from tuberculosis – he was always to write in later life of his high regard for her, although this would seem to be, in part, a retrospective judgment.

His relationship with his father was likewise complex. Tarkovsky detested Antonina, his father's second wife, and can have only felt something like relief when she died unexpectedly in 1940. Arseny joined the Red Army as a war journalist and was sent to the Front, where he lost a leg. Tarkovsky's memories of the war revolved around waiting for it to end and for his father to come home. When Arseny did return home, as a decorated war hero (he received the Order of the Red Star), he did not rejoin his first family; indeed, he did not even go to meet the young Andrei when he and his sister returned to Moscow from their time as evacuees in Yurievets. But despite this apparent callousness, Tarkovsky held his father in high regard and, as a teenager, seems to have been closer to his father than his mother, spending what time he could with him, discussing books, listening to Arseny read his own poetry and sampling his father's extensive record collection (Bach was to become a favourite). The teenage Tarkovsky seems to have regarded his mother as the more guilty party with regard to the break-up of the marriage, which again may go some way to explain why he would want to spend so much time with his father at this stage of his life.[9]

In 1951, Tarkovsky enrolled in the School of Oriental Languages to study Arabic; he had been interested in the East since an early age (perhaps as a result of hearing stories about his family's supposed origins among the Daghestani nobility during the reign of Ivan the Terrible).[10] However, he did not finish his course due to concussing himself in the gym one day, and he found employment instead on a geological expedition to Siberia, where he spent a year (1953–4) prospecting the remote Turuchansk region for mineral deposits. That Tarkovsky ended up on this expedition may not have been entirely his own doing: his lack of aptitude for serious academic study had been a continuing worry for the family, and it seems that, after the incident in the gym, Tarkovsky's mother intervened and virtually exiled the would-be director to the East, to prevent him wasting away among Moscow's *stilyaga*, the dandified Russian equivalent of the Beat Generation.

Despite being summarily sent away, Tarkovsky thrived in Siberia. He walked many hundreds of miles along the River Kureika, where he spent a lot of time drawing and thinking. It is not recorded how successful he was as an employee of the expedition, but as he didn't get fired, we can assume that he passed muster. But the expedition did not ignite in him the desire to be a geologist. Rather, alone with nature – and himself – for the first lengthy period since his days as an evacuee in Yurievets, he resolved to become a film director. Maya Turovskaya notes that Tarkovsky's 'spiritual baggage was acquired during his none-too-happy childhood and was little affected by subsequent external influences'.[11] Likewise, his year in the Siberian *taiga* would serve as a dramatic base-line for nearly all his subsequent work. Nature is ever present in his films – often celebrated, always mysterious – as is the lone protagonist, struggling to come to terms with his own life and the world around – and within – him.

Upon returning from Siberia, Tarkovsky applied for a place at the prestigious All-Union State Institute of Cinematography, VGIK. That year (1954), there were around 500 applicants for only 15 places. Tarkovsky was among those chosen, and he began studies under the veteran director, Mikhail Romm (1901–71). Romm appeared to be tempera-mentally at the opposite end of the spectrum to Tarkovsky. He was known chiefly for his films of the 1930s, such as *Lenin in October* (1937) and *Lenin in 1918* (1939), both of which firmly toed the Party line. Given that, and combined with Tarkovsky's less than inspiring academic record up to that time, one could be forgiven for assuming that his time at VGIK was not to be a success. Yet Romm was a brilliant and unorthodox teacher, and unorthodoxy was precisely what Tarkovsky needed. Romm believed that one could not be taught to be a director, but had to learn to think for oneself and develop an individual voice.

During his time at VGIK, Tarkovsky and his fellow students studied all aspects of filmmaking, watching the classics of Soviet cinema and taking part in workshops in which they would demonstrate their technical ability. This even included acting: Tarkovsky's fellow student and friend, Alexander Gordon, remembers him giving a superb performance as the aging Prince Bolkonsky when Romm got the students to perform scenes from *War and Peace* during their third year at VGIK.[12] Tarkovsky saw many classics from outside the Soviet Union, including *Citizen Kane*, the films of John Ford and William Wyler, and the works of the fathers of the French New Wave, Jean Renoir and Jean Vigo. Tarkovsky developed a personal pantheon that included Bergman, Bunuel, Mizoguchi and Kurosawa, Fellini and Antonioni. The only Soviet director who made it into his pantheon was Dovzhenko, although he was good friends with the Georgian director Sergei Parajanov, whom he regarded as 'a genius in everything'. He also spoke highly of Iosseliani and, on occasion, of Boris Barnet. But above them all was the towering figure of Robert Bresson, whom Tarkovsky regarded as the ultimate film artist.

Whilst at VGIK, Tarkovsky co-directed two shorts, *The Killers* (1956) and *There Will Be No Leave Today* (1959), which are discussed in the 'Student Films' chapter. He also saw *Hamlet* on stage for the first time (the Paul Scofield production). In 1957, he married fellow student, Irma Rausch, with whom he had a son, Arseny (Senka), who was born in 1962.

Tarkovsky's Professional Career

Tarkovsky's life and career after VGIK are perhaps better known. A year after making *There Will Be No Leave Today*, he completed his studies and made his award-winning diploma film, *The Steamroller and the Violin*, which won first prize at the New York Student Film Festival in 1961. It was an auspicious time for new filmmakers to be emerging in the Soviet Union. The Soviet film industry was undergoing something of a renaissance; the resultant surge in production from the mid-fifties on would bode well for Tarkovsky and his generation. Films such as *The Cranes are Flying* and *The Ballad of a Soldier* caused an international sensation, and Tarkovsky would become the new star in the firmament of this Soviet New Wave.

Tarkovsky shot his first full-length film, *Ivan's Childhood*, in 1961. At the film's first screening in Moscow in March 1962, Mikhail Romm famously declared 'Remember the name: Tarkovsky.'[13] They would prove to be prophetic words: the film won the Golden Lion at Venice later that year and was championed in the West by no less than Jean-Paul Sartre, who praised it as 'Socialist surrealism'.[14] Tarkovsky was instantly recognised in the West as a major director; Ingmar Bergman would later write that his discovery of *Ivan's Childhood* was 'like a miracle' and that 'Tarkovsky is for me the greatest, the one who invented a new language, true to the nature of film, as it captures life as a reflection, life as a dream.'[15] As Tarkovsky began work on what would become his second feature, *Andrei Rublev*, his standing was at its high-water mark in Moscow. He would never enjoy such a position again in his homeland.

Andrei Rublev was to be the beginning of the end for Tarkovsky in the Soviet Union. Although completed in

1966, it was not released until 1971 on the grounds that it was too naturalistic, unpatriotic and, perhaps worst of all in the eyes of the authorities, 'mystical'. The film was first screened at the Cannes Film Festival in 1969, where it was awarded the FIPRESCI Prize. It was finally released in the West in 1973.

By the time *Andrei Rublev* was released, Tarkovsky had shot his third feature, an adaptation of Stanislaw Lem's novel, *Solaris*. Although the film was part of the seemingly 'safe' genre of science fiction, the shoot was difficult, primarily due to frequent arguments between Tarkovsky and his cameraman, Vadim Yusov, who had shot all of Tarkovsky's films from *The Steamroller and the Violin* onwards. The two men would not work together again, and Tarkovsky asked Georgy Rerberg to shoot his next feature, the autobiographical *Mirror*. *Mirror* is at the heart of Tarkovsky's oeuvre in every way, but was met with official condemnation for being obscure and elitist. Such was the furore surrounding the film, that Tarkovsky briefly considered giving up filmmaking and also began to toy with the idea of making a film in the West.

The last film Tarkovsky would make in the Soviet Union was another venture into science fiction, *Stalker*. The film, based on a novel by Arkady and Boris Strugatsky, marks a turning point in Tarkovsky's work, towards a more pared down and minimalistic style. The film was completed in 1979 and was shown in Cannes to rapturous reviews in 1980. The Polish director Andrzej Wajda felt that, with *Stalker*, Tarkovsky was 'throwing down the gauntlet'.[16] The film heralds the onset of Tarkovsky's late period, which would be rounded out by his last two features, *Nostalgia* (1983) and *The Sacrifice* (1986).

Nostalgia was shot in Italy in the autumn of 1982.

Tarkovsky had first visited the country 20 years earlier, when *Ivan's Childhood* had triumphed at Venice. In the summer of 1976, after the controversy surrounding *Mirror* had left Tarkovsky disillusioned and bitter, he began making notes for what would become *Tempo di Viaggio* (1980), his only documentary. The film was finally shot in the summer of 1979, by which time Tarkovsky and the screenwriter Tonino Guerra, his longtime friend, had had an idea – provisionally entitled 'The End of the World' – that would turn into *Nostalgia*.[17] The screenplay was completed in May 1980; Tarkovsky then spent two years in a bureaucratic quagmire before the film could be made. Soviet officials prevented the film from winning the Palme d'Or at the 1983 Cannes Film Festival, a scandal that enraged Tarkovsky and hardened his resolve that he could no longer continue working in the Soviet Union.[18]

On 10 July 1984, Tarkovsky announced his intention to remain in the West at a press conference in Milan. He had considered defecting in 1981 during a trip to Sweden, but concern for his wife and son prevented him from proceeding. When he finally did make the decision to remain in the West, his son was still in the Soviet Union, and would not be allowed out until January 1986, by which time Tarkovsky had been diagnosed with terminal lung cancer. His final film, *The Sacrifice*, won four prizes at the 1986 Cannes Film Festival, including the Grand Prix and the Special Jury Prize. Tarkovsky was too ill to attend, so his son Andrei Jr collected the prizes on his behalf. Tarkovsky seemed to be in remission during the summer of 1986, but the cancer returned. He died in Paris on 29 December 1986.

Tarkovsky did not live long enough to experience *glasnost*, although he predicted that, after his death, he would be rehabilitated in his homeland. His prediction came true: a major retrospective of his work was held at Dom Kino (the House of Cinema) in the spring of 1987. The following year, the original 205-minute cut of *Andrei Rublev* received its first public screening. An Andrei Tarkovsky Memorial Prize was established in 1989, its first recipient being the legendary animator, Yuri Norstein. In April 1990, Tarkovsky was post-humously awarded the Lenin Prize, the highest form of recognition in the Soviet Union.

Tarkovsky and the Soviet Context

Tarkovsky made five feature films in the Soviet Union between 1962 and 1979. All of them were seen – at least in Western Europe – as major masterpieces, even one of which would have guaranteed their director a place in cinema history. Unlike some directors, such as his close friend Sergei Parajanov (1924–90), who spent a number of years in prison on trumped-up charges and whose career was badly hampered by the authorities, Tarkovsky managed to remain relatively free to pursue his vision, despite the fact that he was not a Party man and his films did not conform to the Socialist Realist norm that the Communist Party champi-oned. This suggests that the Soviet system was not as mono-lithic as we might be tempted to think it was, to say nothing of Tarkovsky's own tenacity. A brief overview of the Soviet film industry will go some way towards helping us to appre-ciate what obstacles a filmmaker in the Soviet Union had to face and how that, in turn, played a part in shaping Tarkovsky's films.

The Soviet film industry, like every other walk of life in the Soviet Union, was heavily centralised. Goskino, a body founded in 1922, oversaw every aspect of filmmaking in the USSR, having the final say on each stage of the production of a film, from script approval, to green-lighting a film's release. All 40 or so studios across the Soviet Union were answerable to Goskino, including the largest studio, Mosfilm in Moscow, where Tarkovsky made all of his Soviet features. During Tarkovsky's career, Goskino was headed first by Alexei Romanov (1963–72) and then by Filip Yermash (1972–86), who would become something of a personal nemesis for Tarkovsky.

Mosfilm, like the other studios, was comprised of various departmental heads, who oversaw their respective areas – such as production, scriptwriting and editing – together with an artistic council made up of Mosfilm top brass, filmmakers and Party officials. This council had the final say in how a film should be distributed, either in Category 1 (wide release in the major cinemas), or Category 2 (limited release in smaller cinemas). Everyone at the studio was answerable to the studio head. In Tarkovsky's time, these were V Surin and then Nilokai Sizov. Although Tarkovsky quickly developed a reputation for being stubborn and refusing to make cuts in his films, as we shall later see Goskino and Mosfilm officials were not necessarily hostile to Tarkovsky just for the sake of it; sometimes Tarkovsky took their feedback on board and made changes to his films accordingly (especially in the case of *Mirror*).

The process of getting a script approved was frequently a long and frustrating one. A project would first be submitted to the editor of the script department at the studio, who would then review it before passing it up the hierarchy. Finally, the script would arrive at the desk of the head of the studio. The studio head could not, however, greenlight a film until the whole process had been repeated at Goskino. Despite these supposedly stringent controls, however, the system was hampered by one major factor: during the mid to late 1950s, the Soviet film industry began expanding at an almost exponential rate, epitomised by the international success of Mikhail Kalatozov's *The Cranes are Flying*, which won the Palme d'Or at Cannes in 1957.

This resurgence owed a lot to the 20th Party Congress in 1956, at which Khrushchev denounced Stalinism, thereby precipitating the 'Thaw' that initiated the most liberal cultural climate in the Soviet Union for 30 years. The film industry thrived as a result. In 1955, 65 features were produced; by the early 1960s, this had risen to over 100 per year. Cinemas likewise doubled in number, from 59,000 in 1955 to 118,000 in 1965. Aside from Kalatozov, other directors rose to prominence between the late fifties and mid sixties, such as Elem Klimov, Larissa Shepitko and Andrei Mikhalkov-Konchalovsky, and the only two Soviet directors Tarkovsky professed to admire, Otar Iosseliani and Sergei Parajanov.

The very success of the Soviet film industry meant, ironically, that theory (i.e., ideology) was not always practice. Industry personnel were overworked, deadlines had to be met, and scripts and films had to be approved. Once a script had been approved, a director such as Tarkovsky, who enjoyed an international reputation, would face very little, if any, interference from either Mosfilm or Goskino during shooting. Problems usually set in when Tarkovsky submitted a film for approval. Discussions would be held, cuts would be demanded, complaints would be lodged. As Tarkovsky often rewrote his scripts while shooting them (especially in the cases of *Mirror* and *Stalker*), this stage would often be fraught.

Tarkovsky would sometimes submit edits of his films that he knew were too long, so that when calls came for cuts, he would then cut the parts he was dissatisfied with, and could thus show that he had complied with requests to shorten the film. Although Alexei Romanov personally screened every film submitted for approval to Goskino, his successor, Filip Yermash, often approved films for release without even seeing them. However, as Tarkovsky was regarded abroad as the most important Soviet director then working, all of his films were subject to a great deal of scrutiny and debate before – and after – they were released.

All of Tarkovsky's Soviet features were released in Category 2, with the exception of *Solaris*. He felt bitter about this and came to feel that he was being persecuted. This sense of persecution intensified as his career in the Soviet Union progressed, until it became one of the chief reasons why he decided to remain in the West after completing *Nostalgia*. Ironically, while Tarkovsky did indeed battle relentlessly to get his films made according to his wishes, in some respects he enjoyed privileges not extended to other directors, some of whom resented what they saw as Tarkovsky's 'special treatment'. He travelled a good deal throughout the 1970s, for example often accepting invitations to appear at film festivals, sometimes even participating in jury activities (such as at Locarno in 1972, when he was president of the jury). Compared with his friend Parajanov, who was imprisoned between 1974–7 and then again briefly in the early 1980s, Tarkovsky's situation might have been difficult and ultimately impossible in the late 70s and early 80s, but at least he remained at liberty to pursue his vision.

Theory and Practice

Tarkovsky's films contain a number of recurring themes and visual motifs, as well as narrative and stylistic devices that will be examined in this chapter. We will also look at his theories of the art of cinema, which he wrote about at length in his book, *Sculpting in Time* (1984). It should be noted that Tarkovsky was adamantly opposed to interpretation; instead, he urged his audiences simply to watch his films. When asked why there was so much rain in his films, Tarkovsky would reply that it was always raining in Russia. Be that as it may, it must also be noted that rain, for example, might have another possible function in the films, such as cleansing or blessing. The Polish director Krzysztof Kieślowski explained that if a cigarette lighter in a film doesn't work, it means it doesn't work and nothing else. But on the rare occasion that a film-maker can get it to mean something else, then they have achieved a miracle. 'Only one director in the world has managed to achieve that miracle in the last few years,' he notes, 'and that's Tarkovsky.'[19]

But before we examine Tarkovsky's work in terms of its thematic and poetic content, it is instructive to be reminded of his working methods, aspects of which make his achievement all the more remarkable.

ANDREI TARKOVSKY

Working Methods: Development

With the exception of *Ivan's Childhood*, on which he was a
hired-hand director, Tarkovsky initiated all of his projects
himself. How he chose what would be his next film was a
mysterious process that he did not fully understand. He notes
in his diary, 'It is obviously a most mysterious, imperceptible
process. It carries on independently of ourselves, in the
subconscious, crystallising on the walls of the soul.'[20] (The
diaries furthermore attest to the fact that Tarkovsky continually entertained ideas about many projects, only a handful
of which he actually managed to realise – *see* Appendix II.)
But, for Tarkovsky, a project usually began with a feeling for
'the inner state, the distinctive inner tension of the scenes to
be filmed, and the psychology of the characters.'[21]

Once the 'inner state' had been glimpsed, Tarkovsky
would then pitch his idea to a potential screenwriting collaborator. He regarded screenwriting as a separate discipline
from literature. 'I do not understand why anyone with
literary talent should ever want to be a scriptwriter,' he
declares in *Sculpting in Time*, his reasons being that a script
will inevitably change during the course of development,
shooting and postproduction. The script should only be
treated as a blueprint for the film: 'If a scenario is a brilliant
piece of literature, then it is far better that it should remain
as prose.'[22]

Tarkovsky worked with a co-writer on all of his films, bar
The Sacrifice, which he wrote alone. Vladimir Akimov, a
screenwriter who knew him (but never worked with him),
believed that Tarkovsky essentially used his co-writer as a
sounding board on which to test new ideas, and also as
someone who would ensure that good scenes were not cut
on a whim,[23] as one notable feature of Tarkovsky's working

27

method was its organic nature: scripts and films would be constantly changing as Tarkovsky's understanding grew as to what each scene or film required.

Andrei Mikhalkov-Konchalovsky was Tarkovsky's first collaborator, with whom he co-wrote *The Steamroller and the Violin*, *Ivan's Childhood* and *Andrei Rublev*.[24] On the first two of these, they shared the writing more or less equally, although on *Ivan's Childhood*, their work was to modify an existing script to make it conform to Tarkovsky's conception of the film. Tarkovsky apparently began writing *Andrei Rublev* on his own, but called Mikhalkov-Konchalovsky in for later drafts. Mikhalkov-Konchalovsky noted that Tarkovsky would always work from his intuition, which would frequently exasperate him. During work on *Andrei Rublev*, the two of them decamped to Georgia for a writing retreat. In a break from working on the script, they went out for a walk, hoping to resolve their current impasse, but Tarkovsky, rather than telling his collaborator what he wanted, began talking about the buds on the trees that they were walking past. Mikhalkov-Konchalovsky later accused Tarkovsky of being pretentious, and the two men parted company. (The feeling, it has to be said, was mutual.)

Tarkovsky had a much better working relationship with Alexander Misharin, with whom he wrote *Mirror*. Tarkovsky knew some of the episodes he wanted, but he and Misharin first talked at length about what they remembered of their childhoods in order to arrive at the others. Once this process was complete, they wrote scenes individually and would meet every day to read what they had written. Working like this, they wrote the script in two weeks. Before and during shooting, the script was then rewritten on a daily basis, with Misharin feeling that 'Tarkovsky knew what he wanted but was unable to articulate it.'[25] Unusually for a writer, Misharin was also consulted about the edit, and would sometimes sit in with Tarkovsky and the film's editor, Ludmila Feiginova.[26]

Tarkovsky's intuitive approach resulted in tense and stormy relationships with authors whose work he adapted, namely Vladimir Bogomolov (*Ivan's Childhood*), Stanislaw Lem (*Solaris*) and the Strugatsky brothers (*Stalker*). The dream sequences in *Ivan's Childhood*, which were one of the things Bogomolov objected to, were present in the script as soon as Tarkovsky started work on the film, which again suggests that he knew what he wanted from the beginning. Similarly, his approach to adapting *Solaris*, which he did with Friedrich Gorenstein, was to make the material his own, rather than trying to film Lem's novel as it was written. Lem was furious that the Earth scenes were in the film (in the first draft three-quarters of the action took place on Earth), and was also displeased that Tarkovsky did not seem to be interested in the theme of the novel, that of the progress of science and knowledge, but instead supplied his own, revolving around familial concerns and his love of nature.

On *Stalker*, Tarkovsky was actually collaborating with the authors of the original novel, but a broadly analogous situation arose when Arkady Strugatsky, frustrated by the endless rewrites and Tarkovsky's vagueness about what he wanted, suggested dropping the science fiction element of the story. Tarkovsky immediately beamed 'like a cat that has eaten its owner's parrot',[27] and admitted this was what he had been wanting for a long time but had not wanted to offend the brothers by suggesting it.

Working Methods: Production

From *Andrei Rublev* onwards, Tarkovsky was in complete control once shooting had started, with no external interference. He was fanatically involved in all aspects of production, having the last word on set design, costume and choice of location. Although some saw this as dictatorial behaviour, Tarkovsky viewed it as part of the director's job. In the documentary *Directed by Andrei Tarkovsky*, his second wife and widow Larissa quotes from his diary: 'Never trouble anyone else with what you can do yourself.'[28]

Tarkovsky was also highly selective about which actors he would use. He preferred to use the same actors as often as possible, and built up a company of actors whom he would use again and again, including Nikolai Grinko, Anatoly Solonitsyn, Irma Rausch, Stefan Krylov, Nikolai Burlyaev, Yuri Nazarov, Sos Sarkissian, Olga Kizilova, Tamara Ogorodnikova, Oleg Yankovsky, Erland Josephson and Margarita Terekhova. He favoured the same approach with his crew, and in addition to his collaborations with Vadim Yusov, Tarkovsky also developed long standing relationships with composers Vyacheslav Ovchinnikov and Eduard Artemyev, costume designer Nelly Fomina, editor Ludmila Feiginova, sound recordists Inna Zelentsova and Semyon Litvinov, make-up artist Vera Rudina, assistant director Masha Chugunova and musical director Emil Kachaturian.

Although some of his shoots were a purgatorial experience for all concerned (especially *Stalker*), nearly everyone who worked with him admired him and some professed an almost fanatical loyalty to him. Once his collaborators had earned Tarkovsky's trust, he would welcome suggestions from them provided that they stayed within the overall framework he had established. Tarkovsky himself would frequently diverge from the script, and his films, despite looking carefully thought out, are in fact partially the result of improvisation on set. Because time was not so pressing a factor as it was when he came to work in the West, he would often halt filming for a few days in order to solve a problem, rehearse or wait for props to arrive. With intense rehearsals and a strong intuition of what he wanted (even if he was not able to articulate himself clearly), Tarkovsky was able to get what he wanted usually in only one or two takes. Given that many of his takes are lengthy and involve careful choreography, this is little short of remarkable. At Mosfilm, he was known as 'One-Take Tarkovsky'.

Tarkovsky's closest relationship during shooting was always with his director of photography. That the visual style of his films was essentially Tarkovsky's own is borne out by the fact that, after his collaboration with Vadim Yusov ended with *Solaris*, each subsequent film was shot by a different cameraman: Georgy Rerberg (*Mirror*); Alexander Knyazhinsky (*Stalker*); Giuseppe Lanci (*Nostalgia*); and Sven Nykvist (*The Sacrifice*). For Knyazhinsky, Tarkovsky was one of the few directors who understood film as being, above all else, essentially a visual medium (as opposed to a dramatic medium, like theatre) and remembers Tarkovsky saying that 'if they got the images right, the film was sure to be a success'.[29] Lanci admitted that working with Tarkovsky was a 'most enriching' experience, and felt that, in order to shoot the film according to Tarkovsky's vision, he had to try to enter Tarkovsky's poetic world more and more each day, until Lanci '[felt] as he did, to think as he did. And it was a tremendous experience, unrepeatable... working with him one could risk anything... he was always nearby to give you courage, to give you strength to achieve the objectives that the film required.'[30]

Working Methods: Post-Production

Ludmila Feiginova cut all of Tarkovsky's Soviet features, with the exception of *Ivan's Childhood*, on which she was an assistant. As there were rarely more than one or two takes to choose from, her job was mainly to decide where to begin and end each individual shot. Tarkovsky also hardly ever shot scenes that didn't make it into the final film, the main exception being the 'mirror room' from *Solaris*.[31] Feiginova's other main task was to determine – in conjunction with Tarkovsky himself – how to shorten scenes. This played a big part in appeasing the authorities, in that if they demanded cuts, Tarkovsky would cut something and then say that he had shortened the film, hoping that the authorities would not notice that things they objected to were still in the film. As with his collaborators during the actual shooting, Tarkovsky allowed Feiginova to contribute ideas. Indeed, some of her suggestions were inspired, such as the moving of the stuttering boy scene to the beginning of *Mirror*, or the moving of the speech by Stalker's wife from the bar to the flat, where, instead of addressing the three men, she now appears to address the audience directly. Feiginova was also present at the mixing and dubbing of Tarkovsky's Soviet films.

In the West, Tarkovsky's main editing problems concerned the fact that he wasn't allowed to start cutting until the film had been shot, which had been contrary to his practice in the Soviet Union. 'Practical considerations, such as lack of time for rehearsal, also meant that Tarkovsky went beyond his usual one or two takes when working in the West, but, given that he was covering his scenes in much the same way as in the Soviet Union, the editorial decisions involved on *Nostalgia* and *The Sacrifice* were very much the same.'

Tarkovsky's relationship with composers was as unorthodox as the rest of his working practice. Usually, a composer would be called in to score a film once it had been shot, which is what happened with Vyacheslav Ovchinnikov when he worked on *The Steamroller and the Violin* and *Ivan's*

Childhood. However, when Tarkovsky started work on *Andrei Rublev*, he asked Ovchinnikov to compose some music for the Kulikovo Field battle scene while the script was still being written. As it turned out, the scene wasn't shot, and Tarkovsky used some of the music in the epilogue without consulting Ovchinnikov first. The inevitable row meant that the two men would not work together again.

Ovchinnikov's replacement was Eduard Artemyev, whom Tarkovsky met while he was preparing *Solaris*. Tarkovsky was interested in Artemyev's electronic music, believing that it was the way to dispense with a conventional score altogether, which he felt that films did not really need. As a result, much of the music Artemyev composed for Tarkovsky has an abstract, ambient quality to it. The main exceptions are arrangements of the Bach prelude used in *Solaris*, and the opening theme of *Stalker*, which is an amalgam of plainchant and Indian music. Tarkovsky felt that music in films was best used as a refrain, which, when repeated throughout a film, would '[open] up the possibility of a *new*, transfigured impression of the same material... The meaning... is not changed, but the [film] takes on a new colouring... Perception is deepened.'[32]

Tarkovsky believed that sounds could be as important as music, if not more so, and his soundtracks are rich in natural sounds. In his last two films, he abandoned a conventional score altogether, using instead a collage of classical music and natural sounds. Owe Svensson, the sound designer on *The Sacrifice*, remembers Tarkovsky giving him a list of around 250 sound effects that he wanted for the film. Svensson realised that this would have swamped the film, and proceeded to strip down the list. In the end, they settled on the shepherdess's call as the film's refrain, which is heard whenever something out of the ordinary occurs. Tarkovsky also did not want to hear any birds in the film, apart from swallows. As the film was shot in a bird sanctuary on the Swedish island of Gotland, this proved impossible: 'The noise [was] overwhelming,' Svensson noted, 'it [defied] description.'[33] As a result, the whole film, like all of Tarkovsky's previous films, was post-synched.

In re-recording dialogue, Tarkovsky usually made sure that the actors' breathing was audible in the mix, a subtle effect, but one that almost completely closes the distance between the characters on-screen and the viewer, making the characters' experience tangible to the audience. As with his use of music and sound, Tarkovsky's mixes played their part in deepening the films, rather than explaining them.

Against Interpretation

Tarkovsky was adamantly opposed to any intellectual interpretation of his films. Films in general, and his films in particular, are first and foremost an emotional experience. The viewer does not have to pick up on all of Tarkovsky's references to be able to appreciate and be stimulated by one of his films. Indeed, he would perhaps be more kindly disposed towards viewers who reacted to his work in a totally personal way, rather than someone who over-intellectualised the experience of watching them and what they mean. Tarkovsky's narrative technique aided this process, in that he often put things into his films that were deliberately puzzling. When asked, for instance, about the unexplained reappearance of the Holy Fool at the end of *Andrei Rublev* when she is seen sane and richly dressed, Tarkovsky simply remarked 'Let them make of it what they will.'[34]

Tarkovsky was frequently asked what his films meant, and he would often reply that they meant nothing other than what they were. Rain did not symbolise anything, but was 'typical of the landscape in which I grew up,'[35] while the dog in *Stalker* was 'just a dog',[36] or 'the Zone is a zone'.[37] Tarkovsky drew a distinction between images and symbols, and felt that his films were composed solely of the former. What seems to have annoyed him about the concept of symbolism is that once a person thinks they have understood or explained a symbol, they cease to have an active relationship with it, and the symbol effectively dies. While Tarkovsky was sincere in his beliefs that films did not have symbolic value, he is being somewhat disingenuous, and he even made a number of statements to the contrary. The Zone, he admitted, while being just 'a zone', also symbolised the trials and tribulations of life itself,[38] while the watering of the tree in *The Sacrifice* 'for me is a symbol of faith'.[39]

Given that Tarkovsky's position was at times paradoxical, the following treatments of some of his most frequently used devices, themes and images should be read advisedly. Things *may* be symbolic, they may not; they *may* imply one thing, but could easily mean another. Ultimately, a personal response to the films is of more value than any attempt to explain them.

Speech and Silence

Tarkovsky's use of speech and silence varies depending upon the context. Andrei Rublev and Alexander in *The Sacrifice* take vows of silence but for different reasons. Rublev's silence is a protest against both his own sins and those of the world at large, while Alexander's silence is part of his bargain with God, and an act of faith. Conversely, for the Stutterer (*Mirror*) and Little Man (*The Sacrifice* again), the regaining of speech and articulacy is a sign of hope. But, in general,

Tarkovsky distrusts language or, more specifically, the language of speech and the rational intellect. The speech of poetry, on the other hand, is something in which he does have faith, given the number of times poems are recited in his films. Poetry, for Tarkovsky, is the form of linguistic expression that is as close as we can get to life itself; it is a manifestation of truths beyond language.

Art and the Artist

Tarkovsky's love of painting recurs throughout his work. When his films show art – whether it's Dürer's *Four Horsemen of the Apocalypse* in *Ivan's Childhood*, Breughel's *Hunters in the Snow* in *Solaris* or Leonardo's *Adoration of the Magi* in *The Sacrifice* – they are doing so for a number of reasons. Tarkovsky was acutely aware that cinema is a relatively young art form, and showing paintings in his films is an attempt to ennoble this young and frequently debased form. Paintings also serve to comment on the action or characters. The ambiguous expression Leonardo has captured in his portrait of Ginevra de Benci (shown in *Mirror*) is 'inexpressibly beautiful… and at the same time repulsive', and is introduced into the film in order to 'emphasise… in the actress, Margarita Terekhova, the same capacity to at once enchant and to repel'.[40]

Paintings also influenced Tarkovsky's methods of covering a scene. He speaks of his admiration for Carpaccio in *Sculpting in Time* (*see* the chapter on *Andrei Rublev*), and one of the things that one notices in looking at Carpaccio is his use of a frontal viewpoint, which Tarkovsky uses almost exclusively from his second feature onwards. In his interiors, Carpaccio also places his characters off to one side, with a great deal of empty space around them (such as in his depictions of St Augustine in his study, or of St Ursula), a technique Tarkovsky would come to use more and more, especially from *Stalker* onwards. Tarkovsky spoke of Carpaccio's work being humanistic[41] and, by allying himself visually with the Venetian, he is subtly informing us that his cinema is built upon those same values.

One of Tarkovsky's favourite devices, that of depicting a character in two logically impossible spaces in the same shot, is also derived from paintings, in particular mediaeval saints' lives. The frequent 'still lives' in the films – the tea cups on the table in the rain in *Solaris*, the comb and Bible in *Nostalgia*, the mirror, cup and stereo in *The Sacrifice* to name but three – also echo the painterly device of the *memento mori*, objects which serve to remind the person contemplating the painting that life is transitory. Alternatively, these still lives could be related to Japanese art, which Tarkovsky admired greatly. In the oriental tradition, obviously finite things, such as the corner of a room or the view from a window, represented the infinite. In the context of the films, it could be that Tarkovsky senses a numinous quality in the everyday or forgotten corners of our lives.

Artists recur in Tarkovsky's work from the beginning – in *Ivan's Childhood*, Masha and Kholin talk in reverential tones about writers and painters, a viewpoint that was Tarkovsky's own. Although Tarkovsky's adult artist heroes – Rublev, Alexei, Writer, Gorchakov, Alexander – all experience crises, Tarkovsky sees these characters as being the vital conduits through which humanity expresses itself and will ultimately save itself. The artist, in other words, has a moral obligation to serve others and to play a part in making a better world, a theme Tarkovsky returns to again and again in *Sculpting in Time*.

The Apocalypse

For much of his life, Tarkovsky was preoccupied with the idea of the end of the world, and all of his films contain an element of apocalyptic crisis, either for the characters personally (such as Rublev's horror at both the Tartar atrocities and his own crime, and his subsequent vow of silence and refusal to paint), or for society as a whole (the war in *Ivan's Childhood*, ecological collapse in *Stalker* or nuclear war in *The Sacrifice*). Apocalypse becomes more of a preoccupation in the films after *Mirror*, where the desire to save the world from itself is also linked with the idea of personal rebirth.

This idea is illustrated in his lecture on the Apocalypse given in London in 1984. 'It would be wrong to consider that the Book of Revelation only contains within itself a concept of punishment, of retribution; it seems to me that what it contains above all, is hope. The time is near, yes indeed, for each one of us the time is indeed very, very close at hand. But for all of us together? It is never too late. So yes, the Book of Revelation is a fearful book for each of us individually, but for all of us together, as one, there it is as a book of hope.'[42]

The Holy Fool

Russian literary tradition has a long history of Holy Fools, the most well known of them being Dostoyevsky's Prince Myshkin, the titular hero of *The Idiot*. They are present in most of Tarkovsky's films, beginning with the old man in the ruined house in *Ivan's Childhood*. His successors were the idiot girl in *Andrei Rublev*, the Stalker, Domenico (*Nostalgia*) and Alexander (*The Sacrifice*). All of them are related to an apocalyptic situation (World War II and the Tartar invasions in the first two cases, actual planetary catastrophe in the last three), although it is only his last three films that the Holy Fool becomes a central character. In each case, they are characters of faith who see the true condition of the world, and yearn for its renewal, a renewal that could be signified by motifs as varied as the sunlit childhood dreams of *Ivan's Childhood*, or the simple life lived in harmony with oneself and nature that Domenico calls for in *Nostalgia*. It is only through faith and self-sacrifice that this renewal can take place, but who is willing to listen to the words of a madman? That is the dilemma Tarkovsky offers to us for consideration.

Levitation and Flight

Tarkovsky once remarked that he included levitation in his films 'Simply because the scene[s have] a great power. This way, things can be created that are more filmic, more photogenic.'[43] However, as the two scenes of genuine levitation (in *Mirror* and *The Sacrifice*) both happen above beds, it could be argued that they are metaphors for sexual love and pleasure. Hari's and Kelvin's floating around the library in *Solaris*, while ascribed in the film to weightlessness, is in the same vein, although here, it has a pronouncedly elegiac feel. *Nostalgia* contains implied levitation, in the form of the pregnant Maria lying on Gorchakov's hotel bed. As the lighting mysteriously changes, she appears to be floating just above the bed.

Flight, on the other hand, is not used so uniformly. When Ivan dreams of flying through the treetops in *Ivan's Childhood*, it is a symbol of happiness, or, more specifically, of lost happiness. The balloon flights in *Andrei Rublev* and *Mirror* are linked with the idea of artistic striving (in the former instance) and national striving (in the latter). Both end in failure, but Tarkovsky admires the very attempt itself to reach upwards towards God.

Nature and the Four Elements

'I am... puzzled when I am told that people cannot simply enjoy watching nature,' Tarkovsky wrote.[44] His films are full of shots of the natural world, in particular trees, grass, water (usually in the form of rain, brooks and snow) and wind. Although Tarkovsky's love of nature is an undeniable element for it having such a prominent role in his work, it would seem to have another function. In the films up to and including *Mirror*, nature is fecund and fertile, and Tarkovsky's depiction of it verges on the pantheistic[45] (and possibly even the pagan), although it should be noted that, in the Eastern Church, nature is not seen as fallen, but as something inherently good that is an essential part of the divine plan. Nature is the keeper of secrets and wisdom to which Tarkovsky's characters seem to be oblivious, with the country doctor in *Mirror* being perhaps the sole exception: 'Has it ever occurred to you that plants can feel, know, even comprehend,' he asks Maria. 'They don't run about. Like us who are rushing, fussing, uttering banalities. That's because we don't trust the Nature that's inside us.'

In the later films, nature has become a symbol for the wrong turning that humanity has taken. In *Stalker*, despite the apparent fertility of the Zone, nature is polluted, which is both a literal truth and a metaphor for the spiritual atrophy of the modern world. In *Nostalgia* and *The Sacrifice*, Nature is seemingly abandoned and ignored, although it seems to retain something of its old pantheistic power, and in the latter film, the dead tree becomes a symbol of hope and rebirth.

Fire and water are often seen as being important motifs in Tarkovsky's cinema. Fire traditionally purifies but also destroys, while water washes and cleanses. Although fire is present in every film in the form of candles, bonfires, self-immolation, buildings ablaze and flares, water would seem to be the element with which Tarkovksy felt the most kinship. 'Water is very important,' he said in an interview. '[It] is alive, it has depth, it moves, it changes, it reflects like mirror.'[46] Earth largely appears in the form of mud, which could be interpreted as being the opposite of flight. Where the former has characters flying upwards, mud firmly reminds them that they are inherently earthbound, and it is on Earth that their destinies must be found, and lived out. Air is perhaps the most numinous element for Tarkovsky; it usually occurs in the form of sudden winds that blow up, most memorably in *Mirror* and *Stalker*.

Animals

The role of animals in Tarkovsky's work is analogous to that of Nature herself. Horses and dogs appear most frequently. In *Andrei Rublev*, aside from their practical use as transport, they are a symbol of natural ease, of life without the struggles of ego and intellect (one recalls the horse enjoying a roll near the river bank early on in the film and also the horses eating the apples on the beach in *Ivan's Childhood*). It is this naturalness that the characters in *Solaris* have lost, exemplified by Berton's son being terrified by the stabled horse. In *Nostalgia*, they help unite the concept of Nature with the idea of home and a place of belonging (the horse being seen more than once near the dacha). Paradoxically, horses may also be seen as bringers of death and harbingers of the Apocalypse. In *Andrei Rublev* they bring the Tartar hordes to Vladimir, while in *Ivan's Childhood* we see them in Dürer's engraving carrying the Four Horsemen of the Apocalypse. It is the pale horse that brings death, and pale horses appear in both *Nostalgia* and *The Sacrifice*.[47]

Dogs are also frequently seen in Tarkovsky's films. Although, as we have noted, he claimed that the dog in *Stalker* was 'just a dog', it also acts as a mediator between the worlds of dreaming and waking, as it first appears in what seems to be a dream and then is present in waking reality, and also between the Zone and the world outside it, as it accompanies the men on their journey back. The boxer in *Solaris* likewise appears on Earth, in the home movie and also in Kelvin's room on the station during his delirium, suggesting that it is an integral part of Kelvin's experience of life, but unlike Kelvin himself, appears to be able to negotiate its way safely between the worlds of Earth, memory and the station. In *Nostalgia*, the Alsatian links Gorchakov not only with his memories of home, but also with Domenico and the ritual act that he must perform in the pool.

Dreams

Dreams, memories, visions and reveries are an integral part of Tarkovsky's oeuvre. Traditionally, dreams are heralded by such clichés as watery dissolves and harp music. Tarkovsky, on the other hand, does not inform the viewer of when a dream begins or ends, nor even of who the dreamer is. In the latter films, it also becomes increasingly difficult to tell what is 'dream' and what is 'real'.

Experience for Tarkovsky broadly falls into two categories, the outer world of historical events and the timeless inner world. It is to this latter world that dreams belong. They often illuminate the characters' states of mind: Ivan's visions of the childhood he never had, Kelvin's attempts to make things up with his mother, Gorchakov's longing for home. It could even be argued that the real dramas of Tarkovsky's films are internal, with their concerns being the way in which the internal world affects the external world. In the last three films, this becomes modified to suggest that the internal world must become externalised in order to save the latter.

Wives and Mothers

Women in Tarkovsky's films are generally confined to the roles of wife or mother, and the two are often blurred, as in *Solaris* and *Mirror*, or between wife and lover (or potential lover) as in *Nostalgia* and *The Sacrifice*. The great inner struggles that Tarkovsky's heroes undergo appear to be an exclusively male preserve. Tarkovsky's belief that woman's driving force is 'submission, humiliation in the name of love'[48] seems to place him firmly as an old-fashioned chauvinist of the first order, and his female characters are often dependent upon men – such as Eugenia in *Nostalgia* – or are remote, unreachable figures – Maria in *Nostalgia* or Kelvin's mother in *Solaris*. That women are portrayed in this way is almost certainly due to Tarkovsky's own problematic relationships with women, specifically his mother, his two wives and his stepdaughter. (Significantly, he did not have difficulties with his actresses.)

It would be a mistake, however, to write Tarkovsky off as some sort of unreconstructed dinosaur. Two of his female characters, Hari in *Solaris* and the Stalker's wife (and possibly even daughter too, with her telekinetic powers), are remarkably strong characters. The same could possibly also be said of Maria in *Mirror*, who resourcefully cares for her children during the privations of wartime. Tarkovsky's assertion that a woman's strength comes from her ability to sacrifice herself, which at first may appear to be politically incorrect, is, in fact, his roundabout way of admitting that he admires women because they can do what he himself cannot, give themselves unconditionally in the name of love. 'What is love?' he muses in his diary. 'I don't know.'[49] It should also be noted that some of Tarkovsky's most ardent supporters have been women, such as the critics Maya Turovskaya and Olga Surkova. Had there been something inherently misogynistic about Tarkovsky's films, this support would not have been forthcoming.

Images of Home

Tarkovsky portrays home almost always as a dacha in the country. Although in *Mirror* and *Nostalgia* it is a place that only appears in dreams and to which the hero longs to return, in *Solaris* and *The Sacrifice* it is a place of unresolved familial tensions. As if reflecting dream logic in the former instance and the tangle of family emotions in the latter, the interiors of these dachas are always ambiguously arranged, with rooms seemingly moving around in relation to one another.

Various motifs are associated with home: spilt milk, lace curtains, glass containers, and books recur. The books are always art monographs; we have already noted the role of paintings in Tarkovsky's films. It is highly possible that milk, lace and objects made of glass are in the films not only because Tarkovsky associated them with home, but also because he found them visually fascinating.

Stylistic Devices: The Camera

Tarkovsky rarely blocked his scenes in a conventional way. Whereas traditional film grammar would dictate the use of establishing shots to begin a scene, moving into close-ups and shot–reverse shot for a conversation, Tarkovsky usually employed a restricted vocabulary of camera movements with which to cover his scenes, with increasingly lengthy takes. Tarkovsky's camera will frequently pan around a room, following a character (usually keeping them in the middle of the frame), a device used most frequently in *Andrei Rublev*, *Solaris* and *Mirror*. In *Stalker*, *Nostalgia* and *The Sacrifice*, the pan is replaced by imperceptibly slow zooms. Tracking shots feature in all the films. As with shot length, these tracking shots get longer in the later films, with *Nostalgia* and *The Sacrifice* both featuring tracks of around nine minutes each.

Other favoured devices include placing a character in two logically impossible places within the same shot, such as in the tracking shot in *Nostalgia* that shows Maria and the children twice in the same unbroken take, an effect achieved by simply getting the actors to run around the back of the camera once it has left them to hit new marks in time for the camera to pick them up again in the new space.[50] Tarkovsky was also fond of shooting his actors from behind, or from an oblique angle, such as in the post-credits shot of Maria sitting on the fence in *Mirror*, or the conversation between Gorchakov and Eugenia in the hotel lobby in *Nostalgia*. The camera often simply watches in wide shot as the characters go about their business, which tends to occur in the later films, or follows them through sinuous corridors and walkways, such as in *Andrei Rublev* and *Mirror*. As Tarkovsky's films got increasingly metaphysical and philosophical, so his camera movements became more measured and carefully choreographed.

SEAN MARTIN

Stylistic Devices: Colour

Tarkovsky argued that although the real world obviously
exists in colour, once this is reproduced on-screen the
colours become a distraction if they are simply reproduced
as they are. A film made like this 'will have the same sort of
appeal as the luxuriously illustrated glossy magazine; the
colour photography will be warring against the expressive-
ness of the image'.[51] This use of colour, he felt, was the same
technique as that used by painters; cinema had to find its
own way to use colour. Black and white, while less realistic,
was more truthful, and for this reason Tarkovsky shot *Andrei
Rublev* using this process. The epilogue was in colour to show
that Rublev's life had been transformed by his art (in other
words, Tarkovsky felt it permissible to show 'painterly'
colours).

Tarkovsky was well aware, though, that black and white
was no longer the norm, and decided that the best way
forward was in 'alternating colour and monochrome
sequences, so that the impression made by the complete
spectrum is spaced out, toned down'.[52] In addition to using
monochrome, Tarkovsky also tried to minimise the impact of
colour by using a deliberately restricted colour palette. From
Solaris onwards, all of his films were shot using this method.

Tarkovsky used this concept of alternation in *Solaris* and
Mirror, although the shooting of scenes in black and white
was sometimes a matter of necessity, as he ran out of colour
stock at times on both films. With *Stalker*, Tarkovsky used
sepia-tinted black and white for the world outside the Zone,
and muted colour for the world within it; sepia was also used
in some of the dreams. *Nostalgia* and *The Sacrifice* both share
a consistent use of colour, where black and white is used for
dreams, memories and reveries, and colour for normal

waking reality. (Although in the case of the latter film, this is problematic – *see* the chapter on *The Sacrifice*, below.)

Stylistic Devices: Sound

As with colour, Tarkovsky's use of sound was aimed at attaining 'truth' over 'realism'. His method for achieving this was to abstract certain sounds by not revealing their source (for example, the woman's song in the first episode of *Andrei Rublev*, the whistle or recorder in *Mirror*,[53] the passing trains in *Stalker*, the buzz saw in *Nostalgia* or the shepherdess's calls to her flock in *The Sacrifice*). In this way, sound helps to unify the various dramatic and colour planes of the films (dreaming and waking, colour and monochrome) and also works with them to create an additional mystery that the viewer can experience but not necessarily explain. Put simply, Tarkovsky used sound to create depth. As with his use of camera movements, it is a way of drawing the viewer into the world he has created, and also of ensuring that that world will stay with the viewer long after the film has finished.

Imprinted Time

Tarkovsky's theories about film, and art in general, were published, together with autobiographical reflections, in his book *Sculpting in Time*, which was written in collaboration with the critic Olga Surkova.[54] The book had been gestating for many years in the Soviet Union, until it was finally published in German in 1984 and in English two years later. Tarkovsky saw himself as being part of the great nineteenth-century Russian literary tradition and felt a close affinity with Pushkin, Tolstoy and Dostoyevsky. Tarkovsky wrote that 'art is born wherever there is a timeless and insatiable longing for the spiritual, for the ideal'.[55]

Artists, for Tarkovsky, are servants of the people, sensing their deepest needs, and the works of art that they create exist in order to shape people's souls. The artist is also, according to Pushkin, the servant of the Divine: 'Stand, Prophet, you are my will/Be my witness. Go/Through all seas and lands. With the Word/Burn the hearts of the people.'[56] Adherence to such beliefs places Tarkovsky firmly within the Romantic tradition and makes his views on art somewhat unfashionable in the current critical climate, but, as Nick James argues, this is precisely what makes him still relevant: 'There's still a profound need for the notion of the great artist as film-maker, and nobody fits the profile better than Tarkovsky.'[57]

Tarkovsky also outlines his theories on filmmaking in the book. The first chapter is the earliest, being based on an article first published in 1964, in which Tarkovsky outlined his theory of a form of cinema based entirely on memory. What was to be portrayed on-screen would not be external actions, but the hero's thoughts, dreams and memories. Tarkovsky hoped that by taking this approach, it would be possible to 'achieve something highly significant: the expression, the portrayal, of the hero's individual personality, and the revelation of his interior world'.[58]

Underlying this approach is the use of poetic, not dramatic, logic, as 'poetic reasoning is closer to the laws by which thought develops, and thus to life itself, than is the logic of traditional drama'.[59] Not only was poetry closer to life, but it meant that a film based on poetic principles would involve the spectator in an active role: 'he becomes a participant in the process of discovering life, unsupported by ready-made deductions from the plot or ineluctable pointers by the author'.[60] In other words, Tarkovsky is calling upon his audience to bring their own lives and experience to the film, in order to bring the film most fully to life.

But poetic logic was not the only tool at Tarkovsky's disposal. Time was a concept which preoccupied him for nearly all of his career, both in the wider, historical sense, and also in the immediate sense of the time it takes to watch a film. In *Andrei Rublev*, the closing sequence showing Rublev's work in full colour sweeps away the centuries between his era and that of the viewer, implying that the concerns of Rublev's era are also very much those of our own. But it is in *Mirror*, his most autobiographical film, that Tarkovsky explores time most comprehensively, not just in the historical linear sense, but also in the ways in which the past and the present interact with each other through the prism of human consciousness and conscience.

It was in the 'narrower' sense of the running time of a film, however, that Tarkovsky's ideas about time reached their most radical. He believed that time was the essential building block of cinema, and he stands diametrically opposed to Eisenstein's theory of montage, which holds that a film is made in the editing room. Tarkovsky proposed that if a take is lengthened, boredom naturally sets in for the audience. But if the take is extended even further, something else arises: curiosity. Tarkovsky is essentially proposing giving the audience time to inhabit the world that the take is showing us, not to *watch* it, but to *look* at it, to explore it. Tarkovsky's films are experiential and phenomenological in that they see the world from eye level, and move through it at walking pace. This is not something arbitrary, but something that Tarkovsky believed would open up new possibilities both for the filmmaker and the audience, where the dreams, memories and experience of both would meet in the experience of going to the cinema. A film, therefore, is not an escape from life, but a deepening of it.

The Student Films

The Killers (1956)

Alternate Title(s): None
Russian Title: *Ubijtsi*
Production Company: VGIK
Directors: Andrei Tarkovsky, Alexander Gordon, Marika Beiku
Screenplay: Andrei Tarkovsky & Alexander Gordon, based on the short story by Ernest Hemingway
Directors of Photography: Alfredo Alvares, Alexander Rybin
Directing Instructor: Mikhail Romm
Cinematography Instructor: AV Galperin
Cast: Yuli Fait (Nick Adams), Alexander Gordon (George, the café owner), Valentin Vinogradov (Al), Vadim Novikov (Max), Yuri Dubrovin (first customer), Andrei Tarkovsky (second customer, 'whistling' customer), Vassily Shukshin (Ole Andreson)
Running Time: 19 mins
Shot: Autumn 1956
First Screening: 1956 (VGIK)
Release in West: 2003 (DVD release)

Storyline

Two men in overcoats – Al and Max – enter a café. George, the waiter, takes their orders. They intimidate George and the sole customer, Nick Adams, by disparagingly calling them 'bright boys'. Al and Max's food is brought out. They order the cook to come out. He does so, and Al leads him and Nick into the kitchen. George asks Max what's going on.

Al, sitting in the kitchen by the serving hatch, tells Max to move, enabling him to see the door better. Al is holding a machine gun. Max tells George that they are going to kill a Swede, and asks him if he knows Ole Andreson. George replies that he does, that he comes in to eat at 6pm. The clock behind the bar shows 5.40pm. George asks Max why they want to kill Andreson. Max replies, 'to oblige a friend'.

Al tells Max to shut up, that he talks too much, and that he's got the cook and Nick bound and gagged. George wants to know what will happen to them 'afterwards'. Max doesn't give him a straight answer.

A customer enters. He is told that the cook has gone out for half an hour, and leaves.

They wait. Another man is seen outside. Al cocks his gun. The man comes in. It is not Andreson. He orders sandwiches to go and whistles a tune while George makes the sandwiches in the kitchen.

The customer leaves. A third man enters and is told the cook is ill. He leaves, indignant. Then, seeing that Andreson has not shown up at his usual time, Al and Max leave.

Nick – freed off-screen by George – calls on Andreson to warn him. The Swede seems resigned, saying that he's not left his room all day. Nick offers to call the police. Andreson tells him not to.

Nick returns to the café and reports what happened to

George. He tells George that he's going to leave town, as he can't stand the thought of Andreson lying in his room, waiting to be killed. George tells him not to think about it.

A Bright Boy

The Killers is based on Hemingway's 1927 short story. It was Tarkovsky's idea to adapt the story (Hemingway's collected works having just been published for the first time in the Soviet Union) and marks the first time that VGIK students were allowed to adapt a foreign work. The film was shot largely on just one set at Romm's insistence.

There are a few traces of what would become Tarkovsky's mature style: the action is frequently covered in wide shots; characters are filmed from behind (such as the opening tracking shot of Al and Max walking to the bar and the event around which the story is built – Andreson's murder – happens not only off-screen but, we assume, after the film has ended. However, it should be noted that although Tarkovsky would later employ off-screen events in films such as *Ivan's Childhood* and *Solaris*, here it is more a case of being faithful to Hemingway's story, which ends as the film does. In fact, *The Killers* is Tarkovsky's most faithful adaptation of a literary work. (One could easily imagine Vladimir Bogomolov, Stanislav Lem and the Strugatsky brothers being quite envious of the respect with which Tarkovsky treated Hemingway's work.) The general mood of bleakness and tension as the characters wait for Andreson to arrive at the café foreshadows in embryonic form Tarkovsky's mature work, which frequently takes place in a time of crisis or apocalypse.

Stand-out moments include the visits of the three customers, especially Tarkovsky's own cameo as the second customer. The gangsters get ready to shoot, believing him to be Andreson, but when they realise he is not, they wait on tenterhooks for Tarkovsky's character to leave. His nonchalant whistling 'Lullaby of Birdland'[61] adds much to the tension of the scene. Vadim Novikov as the baby-faced killer Max is also particularly memorable.

Alexander Gordon, who co-directed the film with Tarkovsky and Marika Beiku, noted that although he (Gordon) directed the scene in which Nick visits Andreson (played by fellow student Vassily Shukshin[62]), Tarkovsky and Beiku handled the rest of the action, but 'Andrei was definitely in charge'.[63] *The Killers* is an effective piece, moodily lit and tightly edited. 'Romm praised the film,' Gordon noted. 'And our fellow students like it too.'[64]

There Will Be No Leave Today (1959)

Alternate Title(s): None
Russian Title: *Segodnya Uvolneyiha Ne Budet*
Production Company: VGIK/Russian Television
Directors: Andrei Tarkovsky, Alexander Gordon
Screenplay: Andrei Tarkovsky, Alexander Gordon, based on a story by I Makhov
Directors of Photography: Lev Bunin, Ernst Yakovlev
Music: Y Matskevicha
Art Director: S Peterson
Sound: Oleg Polisonov
Cast: Oleg Borisov, A Alexiev, Pyotr Lyubeshkin, Oleg Mokshantsev, Vladimir Marenkov, Igor Kosukhin, Leonid Kuravlyov, Stanislav Lyubshin, Alexei Smirnov, Nina Golovina, Alexei Dobronravov
Running Time: 45 mins
First Screening: April 1959 (Soviet Television)

Storyline

On a building site in a Russian town,[65] a workman accidentally uncovers a cache of bombs from the Great Patriotic War. Army inspectors arrive, and discover that the cache is larger than previously thought. Army practice dictates that old arsenals should be destroyed on-site by detonation, but they realise that this one is much too big and detonating it could endanger local residents. The inspectors have no option but to order an evacuation.

In a big set piece, the town is evacuated: people leave by bus, bike and cart. The soldiers then carefully move the bombs onto a truck and the whole cache is taken out of town.

One of the bombs looks as though it might explode, so a soldier quickly removes it from the truck. He carries it safely away from the cache before it explodes. For a moment we think he may have been killed in the blast, until he emerges blackened and tattered from the smoke.

The town is repopulated to the strains of stirring Soviet music. The army are treated as heroes as they are reunited with their girlfriends.

Production History

There has long been misunderstanding about *There Will Be No Leave Today*. Mark Le Fanu notes that the film is about the head of a geological expedition waiting on a foggy pier for some papers to be delivered to him, and describes it as 'really only a mood piece'[66] that clearly makes reference to Tarkovsky's time in Siberia. In fact, what Le Fanu is describing is 'a short study', as Maya Turovskaya describes it,[67] called *The Concentrate* (aka *Extract*). From what both writers say of the piece, it would appear that they had actually seen the film, but Tarkovsky's sister Marina confirmed in an interview that the 'short study' was actually a short story that was not filmed by Tarkovsky while he was at VGIK.[68]

Co-directed with Gordon, *There Will Be No Leave Today* was a joint production between VGIK and Russian television (which aired it in April 1959).[69] It is an altogether more ambitious film than *The Killers*, although, like its predecessor, it bears few discernible Tarkovskian fingerprints. It is important mainly for being Tarkovsky's first film to use professional actors – principally the male lead, Oleg Borisov – and for being his first opportunity to shoot on a larger scale than *The Killers* (the evacuation scene being the film's largest set piece). But as Alexander Gordon admits, 'We just chose an easy, uncomplicated script. We did not set out to do a masterpiece, our focus was on learning the elementaries of filmmaking'.[70] Perhaps *Leave*'s most important function was to serve in just this capacity, that of an invaluable learning tool. Moreover, the film, dealing as it does with the Great Patriotic War (or at least an aspect of its aftermath), would serve as an unwitting dry run for *Ivan's Childhood*.

The Steamroller and the Violin (1960)

Alternate Title(s): *The Skating Rink and the Violin*
Russian Title: *Katok I Skripka*
Production Company: Mosfilm (Children's Film Unit)
Production Supervisor: A Karetin
Director: Andrei Tarkovsky
Screenplay: Andrei Tarkovsky & Andrei Mikhalkov-Konchalovsky, S Bakhmetyeva (story)
Director of Photography: Vadim Yusov
Assistant Director: O Gerts

Editor: Lyubov Butuzova
Music: Vyacheslav Ovchinnikov
Musical Direction: Emil Kachaturian
Art Director: Savet Agoyan
Costume: A Martinson
Make-Up: Anna Makasheva
Special Effects: B Pluzhnikov, Albert Rudachenko, V Sevostyanov
Sound: Vladimir Krachkovsky
Cast: Igor Fomchenko (Sasha), Vladimir Zamansky (Sergei), Natalya Arkhangelskaya (Girl), Marina Adzhubei (Mother), Yura Brusev, Slava Borisev, Sasha Vitoslavsky, Sasha Ilin, Kolya Kozarev, Zhenya Klyachkovsky, Igor Kolovikov, Zhenya Fedochenko, Tanya Prokhorova, Antonina Maximova, Ludmila Semyonova, G Zhdanova, M Figner
Running Time: 46 mins
First Screening: Moscow, 1960
First Screening in West: New York Student Film Festival, 1961
Release in West: 2002 (DVD release)
Awards: Best Film, New York Student Film Festival 1961

Storyline

Sasha leaves the flat he shares with his mother to attend his violin lesson. A gang of kids tease him as he exits the building. Sergei, a steamroller driver working nearby, comes to Sasha's rescue.

Walking to his lesson, Sasha pauses in front of a shop window. City scenes are reflected in its prism-like windows.

Sasha waits outside the music room. He leaves an apple for a little girl who is also waiting. He goes into his lesson after a little boy emerges in tears from the music room. The teacher is strict with Sasha, reprimanding him for having too much imagination. Sasha leaves, not noticing that the girl has eaten the apple.

At the building site, a female steamroller driver flirts with Sergei. Sasha, returning home, helps Sergei with some repairs to his steamroller. Sergei gives Sasha a ride on the steamroller, letting him drive it. The gang, watching, are envious.

On their way to lunch, Sasha and Sergei pass a boy who is being bullied. Sasha intervenes and restores the boy's ball to him at the cost of receiving a beating himself.

The gang sneak a look at Sasha's violin, which he has left on the steamroller, but decide to leave it alone.

Sasha objects when Sergei calls him a 'musician' and not a 'worker'. They watch a building being demolished. During a sudden downpour, they become separated.

Over lunch, Sasha plays for Sergei. They arrange to go to the cinema that night. Sasha practises at home, but his mother won't let him go out. Sergei's female colleague finds him waiting at the cinema. With no sign of Sasha, he goes into the cinema with her.

In a dream, Sasha is reunited with Sergei on the asphalt.

Tarkovsky's Calling Card

Tarkovsky's diploma film for VGIK, *The Steamroller and the Violin* (1960), was his first film as sole director. It sets the agenda for what would make his work 'Tarkovskian' in a way that *The Killers* and *There Will Be No Leave Today* did not. The film contains visual motifs that he would later make his own, and, in foreshadowing much of his later practice, also contains plot elements that are directly taken from his own life. *Steamroller* also anticipates the aesthetic that he would develop in numerous articles and interviews before it achieved its final written form in his book, *Sculpting in Time*. Tarkovsky was clearly ambitious with the film: it was twice as long as the average VGIK short, running at 46 minutes, and it was in colour. Although the film marks the beginning of his collaboration with cameraman Vadim Yusov, that was largely due to the fact that Tarkovsky failed to get star cinematographer Sergei Urusevsky, who had shot Kalatozov's *The Cranes are Flying*. *Steamroller* also sees the start of Tarkovsky's collaborations with composer Vyacheslav Ovchinnikov, musical director Emil Kachaturian and special effects artist V Sevostyanov.

In choosing to make a film seen through the eyes of a young boy, Tarkovsky was conforming to standard VGIK practice of the time. Andrei Mikhalkov-Konchalovsky's and Yuli Fait's diploma films (*The Boy and the Dove* and *Streetcar to Other Cities*, respectively) were also films about children. Stylistically, the film contains flashy sequences that were clearly meant to demonstrate Tarkovsky's ability but which he would never use again, such as the scene in which Sasha stops outside the shop window and looks at the reflections in the various mirrors on display. A kaleidoscope of city scenes is shown: trams; buildings; a woman dropping a bag of apples (foreshadowing the apples spilling from the lorry on the beach in *Ivan's Childhood*); a balloon seller (a possible reference to Albert Lamorisse's hugely popular 1956 short, *The Red Balloon*); a little boy with his toy boat; and a clock face. The final shot, of a flock of birds taking off, is perhaps the only Tarkovskian element of the whole sequence. Similarly, although Sasha's final imagining of his meeting with Sergei prefigures the later imagined or dreamt endings of *Ivan's Childhood*, *Solaris*, *Mirror* and *Nostalgia*, we are taken into the sequence by the conventional device of a dissolve and a lush string arrangement on the soundtrack. The handling of the space of the stairwell is likewise fairly ordinary, with the camera seeming to follow an invisible Sasha out of the building.

However, the film does contain a number of other elements that are much more in keeping with what would become Tarkovsky's mature style. Water is perhaps the most obvious, appearing in the film in a glass, as a sudden downpour, puddles, a river and a running tap. Mirrors are used three times: the shop window scene and twice at Sasha's home, where we see his mother reflected in one as she forbids him to go and meet Sergei, and then at the end, when Sasha looks at his own reflection, imagining meeting Sergei. In what is perhaps the most visually Tarkovskian scene, when Sasha plays his violin for Sergei, light reflected in puddles plays on the walls around them, anticipating the use of the same technique in *Nostalgia* by more than two decades. The film is also notable for the performances from the children, especially Igor Fomchenko as Sasha. Tarkovsky was a sensitive director of children, possibly because he was said to have had an essentially childlike nature himself, and he maintained that children always understood his films.

On a thematic level, the film's depiction of the power of art (maybe Sasha is surprised at his own playing for Sergei) and the artist as someone set apart from society harks back more to the nineteenth-century literary tradition of Dostoyevsky and Tolstoy rather than to contemporary Soviet ideology. Tarkovsky would pursue these ideas both in later films – Rublev, Gorchakov and Alexander are all men of arts and letters – and in his thinking. Even a cursory reading of *Sculpting in Time* shows the extent to which Tarkovsky saw himself as part of this tradition: 'Film-making, *like any other artistic authorship*, has to be subject first and foremost to inner demands.'[71] [emphasis added] These 'inner demands' are present in *Steamroller* – if only in sketch form – and would not only shape Tarkovsky's subsequent films, but also the way in which he would call for a new type of image, a new type of film, which would respect its audience by showing them as little as possible.[72] In this way, Tarkovsky hoped to stimulate the viewer into 'filling in the gaps' using their own experience effectively to 'complete' his films.[73]

Autobiographical Elements

Direct autobiography appears in the guise of Sasha having music lessons: Tarkovsky himself had music lessons for seven years when he was a boy. The role of the adults in the film is likewise autobiographical. Sasha's mother is remote, being mainly shown reflected in a mirror, and then only briefly, perhaps echoing the reported aloofness of Tarkovsky's own mother. Maria Ivanovna's concern for her wayward son is spoken by the stern music teacher:[74] 'You've got too much imagination. What'll we do with you?'

But if Sasha's mother is remote, then his father is even more so: he does not appear on-screen at any time, nor is mention made of him in the film. In his place is the steam-roller driver, Sergei, whom Sasha looks up to after Sergei saves him from being bullied by the gang of kids who live in Sasha's building. That the relationship between the artist (Sasha) and the artisan (Sergei) is conventionally Soviet would no doubt have played a part in Tarkovsky achieving full marks upon graduation from VGIK (the film's most obviously 'Soviet' shot is the demolition of the old house to reveal the white tower block behind), but Sergei is undoubtedly a stand-in for Arseny, and the fact that Sasha's planned outing to the cinema with him is thwarted by his mother is perhaps an indication of the ambivalence Tarkovsky felt towards his own mother.

Ivan's Childhood (1962)

HISTORY I

Alternate Title: *My Name is Ivan* (US title)
Russian Title: *Ivanovo Detstvo*
Production Company: Mosfilm
Production Supervisor: G Kuznetsov
Director: Andrei Tarkovsky
Screenplay: Mikhail Papava, Vladimir Bogomolov (and Andrei Tarkovsky & Andrei Mikhalkov-Konchalovsky, uncredited) based on Bogomolov's novella *Ivan*.
Director of Photography: Vadim Yusov
Editor: Georgi Natanson
Music: Vyacheslav Ovchinnikov
Musical Direction: Emil Kachaturian
Art Director: Evgeny Chernyaev
Special Effects: V Sevostyanov, S Mukhin
Military Adviser: G Goncharov
Sound: Inna Zelentsova
Cast: Nikolai Burlyaev (Ivan), Valentin Zubkov (Capt Kholin), Evgeny Zharikov (Lt Galtsev), Stepan Krylov (Cpl Katasonych), V Malyavina (Masha), Nikolai Grinko (Lt-Col Gryaznov), D Milyutenko (Old man with hen), Irina Tarkovskaya (Ivan's Mother), Andrei Mikhalkov-Konchalovsky (Soldier with spectacles), Ivan Savkin,

Vladimir Marenkov, Vera Miturich
Shot: Autumn/Winter 1961
Running Time: 95 mins
First Screening: Moscow 30 January 1962 (Rough cut)/March 1962 (Finished)
USSR Release: 1962
First Screening in West: Venice Film Festival, September 1962
Release in West: 1963
Awards: Golden Lion, Venice Film Festival 1962; Best Director, San Francisco Film Festival 1962

Storyline

A rural idyll shows 12-year-old Ivan delighting in nature and flying over it. He tells his mother that he has heard a cuckoo. A sudden burst of gunfire. Ivan wakes up; we realise what we have just seen is a dream. Ivan leaves the old windmill where he has been hiding and makes his way across a barren landscape. The credits roll over him wading across a river.

Ivan reports to a military outpost. Lt Galtsev refuses to believe that Ivan is an agent. A phone call, though, confirms that Ivan is a Russian agent (he is a scout). Ivan writes his report, and then sleeps.

Dream #2: Ivan and his mother are looking down a well. Ivan then appears to be at the bottom of the well. Ivan's mother is killed.

Ivan wakes to greet Capt Kholin, who is a sort of father figure to him. They go to their HQ, where Lt-Col Gryaznov tells Ivan he wants to send him to military school. Ivan threatens to run away.

Ivan talks to a deranged old man in the ruins of the man's

house. He has lost his wife at the hands of the Nazis.
Gryaznov arrives and takes Ivan away.

Galtsev chides Masha, a young nurse, witnessed by
Kholin. Kholin tries to woo Masha in a birch grove. Masha
returns to Galtsev.

Kholin and Cpl Katasonych plot to retrieve the bodies of
two scouts who have been executed by the Nazis and left on
the other side of the river. Galtsev needles Kholin over his
interest in Masha.

Ivan studies a reproduction of Dürer's *The Four Horsemen
of the Apocalypse*, and tells Galtsev that the figure of Death
reminds him of a German he saw, and also that Germans
can't have writers, because they burn books.

Galtsev, Kholin and Katasonych discuss how to retrieve
the bodies of the scouts. They listen to an old Chaliapin
record, 'Masha May Not Cross the River'.

The men select a boat for the expedition and discuss the
possibility that one of them adopt Ivan. We learn that Ivan's
mother and sister were killed by the Nazis and that his father
died in military service.

In a dream-like waking sequence, Ivan acts out a fantasy
of killing Germans. Galtsev again tries to persuade Ivan to
attend military academy, but Ivan rejects the idea.

Dream #3: Ivan and a little girl (who may be his dead
sister) are on a truck laden with apples. He offers the girl an
apple. She refuses. The truck drives onto a beach, spilling
apples in its wake. Horses eat the apples off the sand.

Kholin and Galtsev set off with Ivan in a canoe, after
learning that Katasonych has been killed. They drop Ivan off
to start his next mission, then collect the bodies of the two
scouts.

Kholin listens to the Chaliapin record again. Masha appears
for the last time. Galtsev tells her he is sending her away.

Newsreel footage of the Soviet army in Berlin, 1945. We see the burnt bodies of Goebbels and his wife, and those of their six young children; the Germans signing the instrument of surrender; more dead Nazis and their families.

Galtsev is overseeing an operation to sort through Nazi paperwork. He imagines a conversation with Kholin, who has been killed offscreen. Galtsev discovers Ivan's file: it confirms that Ivan was captured and executed.

Dream #4: Ivan and his friends are playing hide and seek on a beach. Ivan's mother watches over them. Ivan races his sister towards a dead tree. As Ivan reaches the tree, the screen fades to black.

Production History

Ivan's Childhood, or *Ivan* as it was initially called, began shooting in the autumn of 1960, under the direction of Eduard Abalov, a director and actor of Tarkovsky's generation. However, the material shot was deemed unsatisfactory and the production had closed down by the end of the year. Abalov's footage was written off, with Mosfilm seeking a new director. On 16 June 1961, Tarkovsky was confirmed as the new director; he was asked to submit his shooting script by the end of the month.

Although he was allowed to choose his cameraman (Yusov) and also his young star, Nikolai Burlyaev, Tarkovsky inherited Abalov's script, co-written by the original novella's author, Vladimir Bogomolov (1924–2003). Even while Abalov had been working on the film, there had been disagreements about the script; at one point, it even had a happy ending, with Ivan surviving the war and getting married. Bogomolov, who had himself been a scout during the war, objected, and a more downbeat ending was written.

Once Tarkovsky came on board, he immediately proposed inserting the four dream sequences, which Bogomolov also objected to, as he did the love-story element centring around the character of the young nurse, Masha.

Shooting began in the autumn at Kanev, on the Dnieper, where the events of the story really took place. Despite bad weather, filming was completed by 18 January 1962. Tarkovsky, as would become his practice, had begun editing while shooting, and the first cut was screened at Mosfilm on 30 January 1962. He worked throughout the following month on fine-tuning and, on 3 March, the film was approved. Despite the fact that Bogomolov was still protesting about the dream sequences and what he felt were inconsistencies in the handling of military detail, Tarkovsky received praise for bringing the film in 24,000 Roubles under budget, and the film became something of a talking point at a seminar called 'The Language of Cinema', held at the Filmmakers' Union later that month.

The film was first shown in the West at the Venice Film Festival in September 1962, where it caused a sensation and won the festival's top honour, the Golden Lion (shared with Valerio Zurlini's *Family Diary*). Tarkovsky became famous overnight. While the Italian Communist Party newspaper, *Unita*, attacked the film for being petit bourgeois, no less a figure than Jean-Paul Sartre championed the film, praising its 'socialist surrealism'.[75] Back home, Tarkovsky fared less well. As Evgeny Zharikov, who played Galtsev, recalls 'In our country, the film was shown on a limited basis [i.e. Category 2] because Khrushchev, on seeing it, said "We never used children like that in the war." And it was enough for the film to be almost not mentioned, to be almost not shown, to be hushed up in general. And the whole world ran it as a masterpiece.'[76]

A Qualifying Examination

Tarkovsky spoke of *Ivan's Childhood* as his 'qualifying examination' to see 'whether or not I had it in me to be a director'.[77] While Tarkovsky's mature style is not yet evident, it contains numerous elements that would reappear in his later films, and it would therefore be a mistake to see the film as mere prentice work. After all, it won the Golden Lion at Venice and launched his career overnight. It would be instructive to examine the film in this light, to see what *Ivan's Childhood* contains that Tarkovsky later did and did not do.

Ivan's Childhood is a war film in which we do not see any fighting. This is not so much Tarkovsky trying to make a revisionist film, but merely a reflection of Bogomolov's original story. Although we see the end of one mission at the beginning of the film and the start of what will be Ivan's last mission at the end, the film is largely concerned with what happens between missions, away from the Front Line. In doing so, Tarkovsky is establishing a basic dramatic structure which will recur in nearly all his subsequent work: Rublev, if not waiting, exists in a world in which he cannot move forward until a crisis or defining moment occurs (the casting of the bell); Kelvin is largely shown not working (the recording and sending of his encephalogram, two of *Solaris*'s key plot points, happen offscreen); Alexander in *The Sacrifice* says that he has felt as if he has been waiting for 'this moment' (that is, nuclear war) all of his life.

The film's central trio of characters – Ivan, Capt Kholin and Lt Galtsev – is the first in a succession of such trios: Rublev, Daniel, Kirill; Kelvin, Snaut, Sartorius; Stalker, Professor, Writer. Like their later counterparts, the three characters in *Ivan* spend the film wrestling with one major theme, in this case, responsibility: Ivan feels that it is his duty to go back to the Front to continue his mission of vengeance; Kholin feels protective towards the boy as if he were his son (Katasonych and Gryaznov could also be said to form a 'fatherly' trio with Kholin, as both of these characters, while widely separated by rank, are also very close to Ivan); while the young and inexperienced Galtsev has to deal with not only what do to with Ivan, but also his feelings towards the young doctor's assistant, Masha, and his rivalry over her with the older Kholin.

Both waiting and responsibility are inextricably linked to the apocalyptic situation the characters find themselves in. As if to underline this, we see Ivan studying a reproduction of Dürer's *The Four Horsemen of the Apocalypse*, noting that he has seen a German on a motorcycle who looked like one of the horsemen. Apocalypse – whether personal or public – is one of Tarkovsky's recurring themes, and an apocalyptic or crisis state prevails to a greater or lesser degree in all of the later films: the Mongol invasions in *Rublev*; Kelvin's inability to work when faced with his past in *Solaris*; Alexei's apparent recalling of key moments in his life on his deathbed in *Mirror*; the general state of post-industrial and ecological collapse in *Stalker*; Domenico's incarceration of his family and ultimate self-immolation in *Nostalgia*; and the outbreak of nuclear war in *The Sacrifice*.

The end of the world is a theme closely linked to the idea of the establishment of a new world, or a world redeemed. In *Ivan's Childhood*, the only way for Ivan to enter this new world is by fighting to avenge the death of his parents; his tragedy is that he has had no conventional childhood and can have one only in dreams.

The Dream Sequences

The dream sequences were part of Tarkovsky's conception of the film from the very beginning. There are four of them in the film and they serve not only to highlight Ivan's – and Russia's – tragedy, but also to show that, even at this early stage of his career, the world, for Tarkovsky, is simultaneously 'inner' and 'outer' (an idea most fully realised in his last film, *The Sacrifice*).

The first dream shows Ivan running to tell his mother that he has heard a cuckoo. The peaceful, light mood of the dream is shattered by a burst of gunfire. The second shows Ivan seemingly both at the top and then at the bottom of a well, trying to catch a fallen star. The gunfire comes again, but this time his mother is killed. The third dream shows Ivan in the back of a lorry, offering an apple to a little girl of about his own age. He offers her the apple twice and both times she refuses. A sense of impending doom is suggested by the use of a back-projection in negative,[78] and the little girl's ever more serious expression. This is immediately alleviated – if only for a short time – when we see the lorry drive onto a beach, spilling the apples, which grazing horses gladly eat. Ivan and the girl are now smiling. The final dream shows Ivan and his friends playing hide and seek on a beach, but ends ominously with the camera floating into the blackness of the dead tree.

The dreams are all cut against scenes that are generally their opposite: from the joy and flight of the first dream, Tarkovsky cuts to Ivan, resolutely earthbound and hiding in a ruined windmill; the second dream, in which his mother dies, follows a scene in which Ivan is shown sleeping comfortably; the third dream, of the uneaten apples, is preceded by a meal scene; while before the children's games of the fourth dream, we see the bodies of Goebbels' children lying next to the charred corpses of their parents, and Galtsev's imagining Ivan being beheaded.

The dreams also employ devices that would recur in the later films: flight (first dream); Ivan being shown in two logically incompatible spaces (being at the top and bottom of the well); while the fourth dream raises the question of who the dreamer is, as Ivan himself is dead by the time the dream 'happens' (a device later used in *Mirror* and *Nostalgia*). By placing this dream in a logically 'impossible' place in the narrative (logically impossible, that is, if we assume the dreamer to be Ivan), Tarkovsky could be suggesting that it is only in death that the contradictions and paradoxes of this life are resolved.

Narrative, Stylistic and Visual Devices

Ivan's Childhood contains few of the lengthy takes, tracking shots and slow zooms that inform Tarkovsky's mature style. However, it does contain a number of Tarkovsky's other trademark devices that are worth noting here.

The pre-credits sequence is almost a calling card for the mature style: Ivan walks out of frame left and the camera begins to crane up the tree. Ivan is then seen re-entering frame, again from the left, but this time in the middle distance. (When Ivan leaves the windmill, Tarkovsky blocks the scene in the same way: Ivan, on the horizon, walks out of frame left, only to reappear frame left in the foreground a few moments later.) Ivan is then shown rising up into the trees, before flying down to meet his mother in order to tell her that he has heard a cuckoo. Flight recurs, perhaps most memorably in *Solaris* and *Mirror*, as does the figure of the mother; the setting, too – a grove of trees – is something that

Tarkovsky would make his own. Trees are not his only concern, however: just after Ivan has 'landed', the camera tracks right across a rock face, betraying Tarkovsky's interest in natural surfaces and textures. The second dream is prefixed by a similar shot, where the camera moves away from the stove, over some logs towards a bowl of water. These shots are too long to be seen as cutaways in the traditional sense; rather, they could be seen as 'necessary digressions', the way the characters themselves might do if they were pausing for a moment to look around to gauge – or quietly celebrate – the depth and mystery of the world around them.

Ivan's first meeting with Galtsev in the field base likewise bears a number of elements which show that Tarkovsky's mature style is already present, albeit in somewhat embryonic form. The scene, while made up of short takes, is unusually long, as if Tarkovsky were aiming to capture real time flowing through the frame, an idea which was to become a major preoccupation. For most of the scene, Ivan and Galtsev do not face each other, except for moments of confrontation, such as Ivan's attempts to pick up the phone and call HQ himself. Again, characters in the later films spend much of their time facing away from each other, whether it is Andrei Rublev and Theophanes the Greek discussing the last judgment in the birch wood or the three men in *Stalker* bickering amid the puddles and grime of the Zone.

Another device that would become almost a fetish for Tarkovsky was the filming of the head from behind, or from an oblique angle, almost like a classical bust but in reverse. Here, as Ivan begins to write his report, the angle is unusually flat, but the shot still serves the same purpose: it is as if Tarkovsky is showing us that any aspect of the body, whether in motion or at rest, can be worthy of scrutiny and its uniqueness celebrated. As the camera dollies in to the back of Ivan's head, he is busy arranging the seeds and leaves that stand for the German positions, which, while important for the story, take a secondary place at this moment, perhaps suggesting that, for Tarkovsky, Ivan's physical being, his frailty, his boyishness, is as important as the troop movements. It recalls the observation Tarkovsky would later make in *Sculpting in Time*: 'In terms of a person's spiritual experience, what happened to him yesterday may have exactly the same degree of significance as what happened to humanity a thousand years ago.'[79]

Tarkovsky's disregard for conventional plot is evident from the way the story develops immediately after Ivan has written his report and has been reunited with Kholin. We then see Gryaznov on the phone, when Ivan bursts into his office to protest that he is going to be sent to a military school on Gryaznov's orders and threatens to run away. Despite his protests, Ivan appears to acquiesce. This scene is followed by Ivan's meeting with the old man with the hen, the first of Tarkovsky's Holy Fools. It is only when Gryaznov and Kholin appear to collect Ivan do we realise that he has in fact run away rather than be sent to the military school. Tarkovsky would term this 'retrospective understanding', which is to say that the scene only makes sense at its end. The device recurs throughout the film in differing forms: the opening sequence can only be identified as a dream once we see Ivan wake up in the old windmill; after he's been picked up by Gryaznov and Kholin, Ivan mentions two soldiers called Lyakhov and Moroz, but it is only much later in the film that we realise that these are the two men whose bodies have been strung up on the other side of the river, which Galtsev and Kholin rescue at the end of the film; and, more simply, a handheld sequence in the birch grove can be identified as Masha's point of view only when we see her at the end of the shot.

Likewise, Tarkovsky is never clear about precisely what the final mission is: all we know is that Galtsev and Kholin take Ivan across the river in order to retrieve the bodies of Lyakhov and Moroz. The sequence is also further complicated by shots of reflections of the trees in the water, that would at first appear to be a POV shot from the canoe, but the camera then cuts back, twice, to Galtsev, who is standing by a tree, perhaps watching Ivan recede into the twilight, perhaps deep in thought. Given that there is no logical explanation or dramatic function for the reflection shots, it may be that, for Tarkovsky, the reflections in the water are just as important as the story. It could even be that Tarkovsky is suggesting that the reflections are as transient as human life and that nature is more permanent than we are.

Other trademarks dot the film: the door blowing open and shut to reveal the old man with the hen seems to be animate, moving of its own accord; Galtsev stumbling in the trench while talking to Kholin; Galtsev castigating Masha in the field hospital in a shot that follows him as he walks, then picks up Masha, settles on her as Galtsev walks out of shot only to follow him when he walks back in again, until it picks up Kholin (who has just entered) and settles on him, letting Galtsev leave frame once more; the scene in Berlin, slightly reminiscent of *Citizen Kane*, as the Russians sift through Nazi files; and ash raining down in silence as Galtsev has a brief conversation with the dead Kholin.

Ivan's Childhood contains, however, a number of elements that would not recur in any later film: the severe, expressionistic camera angles as Ivan leaves the windmill; the use of back projection; the whip pan that introduces Masha and Kholin in the birch grove; the hand-held sequences (in the first dream, in the birch grove and at the end in the Nazi archive in Berlin); the use of conventional scoring (such as in the scene where Masha wanders happily through the birch grove to the accompaniment of lush strings).

To say that *Ivan's Childhood* pre-empts Tarkovsky's later work in many respects is in no way to diminish the film. It is a major achievement and, had it been Tarkovsky's only film, it would have earned him a place, however modest, in the history of Russian cinema. There are many striking moments that show Tarkovsky's originality and mastery to be already manifest: the dreams; Ivan playing at war; the audacious use of graphic newsreel; and the tracking shots across the surface of the river just after Ivan leaves Kholin and Galtsev for the last time.

Like *The Steamroller and the Violin* before it, *Ivan's Childhood* is more a case of what Tarkovsky could do with the camera and narrative technique, rather than what he would do in later films. Tarkovsky later wrote in *Sculpting in Time* that the completion of *Ivan's Childhood* marked the end of one particular phase in his life. While fêted internationally, Tarkovsky remained something of a pariah at home, yet nobody could have predicted the quantum leap he would take with his next film, *Andrei Rublev*.

'His situation is that of my generation.'

'Were you in the war?' Sasha asks Sergei at one point in *The Steamroller and the Violin*. Sergei nods, but refuses to be drawn further. Had he lived, Ivan would have been Sergei's age and the two characters share with Tarkovsky an approximate birth-date in the early 1930s. Tarkovsky's own experience of the war of course differs from Ivan's: he spent part of it as an evacuee in Yurievets, and all of it waiting, not only for the war to end, but for his father to come home. Arseny, of course, never did come home permanently and Tarkovsky shares with Ivan the sunlit dreams of childhood, before the war, when the family – and happiness – was still complete. As Natasha Synessios notes, 'true childhood was the time before the war'.[80] *Ivan's Childhood* cannot, of course, be viewed as being entirely about some idyllic 'lost time' in the Proustian sense; it is very much about the deprivations that Tarkovsky and his generation suffered. Tarkovsky admitted as much: 'I am in love with the subject. I was his age when the war began. His situation is that of my generation.'[81]

The newsreel sequence at the end of the film speaks for itself: not only is Ivan shown to have died at the hands of the Nazis, but we also see the horror of the Nazis' treatment of their own direct families when we see Goebbels' six children lying dead next to the charred remains of their parents. Direct autobiography appears when Ivan is told by Galtsev that he is going to be sent to the Suvorov military academy after the mission that opens the film, mainly, it seems, on the humanitarian grounds of keeping Ivan alive. Galtsev therefore stands in for the protective father that Tarkovsky himself never knew, although it is ironic that Galtsev is repeating a threat that Tarkovsky's father did actually make in order to instil some discipline into his wayward son. The plan to send the teenage Tarkovsky to Suvorov did not materialise, but, a few years later, his time in Siberia seems to have instilled, if not discipline into the 21-year-old Tarkovsky, then it certainly succeeded in showing him what his destiny would be.

Ivan's Childhood represents Tarkovsky's formative taiga year better than any other of his films. Here we have the young Tarkovsky for the first time able to utilise his experiences on the River Kureika in Siberia, transforming them into haunting images. *Ivan's Childhood* is, like all of his subsequent films, replete with water, but this film in particular is about a river: Ivan has just come back from crossing it at the beginning, while the mission to retrieve the bodies of the two Russian soldiers is likewise back across the same river. Before the final mission across the river, the protagonists listen to an old Chaliapin song, 'Masha May not Cross the River'. During Ivan's final mission, we see, instead of the canoe that bears him across the water, simply the reflection of the trees above. The shot has no dramatic purpose; instead it serves to remind either Ivan or, more likely, the viewer, that the world of nature is unchanging and will survive when wars have been forgotten, or that, in taking place outside of narrative time, Tarkovsky seeks to remind us in this shot that what is important is beyond not only narrative time but also beyond historical time and event as well (war in this case). The calm of the reflective water could represent either Tarkovsky's own memories of the River Kureika, or suggest that human experience is transitory and will one day be forgotten. The opening line of dialogue, 'Mother's there's a cuckoo!', however, comes not from Tarkovsky's time in Siberia, but is one of his earliest memories.[82]

Andrei Rublev (1966/69)

HISTORY II

Original Title: *The Passion According to Andrei* (title of original 205-minute cut)
Production Company: Mosfilm
Production Manager: Tamara Ogorodnikova
Director: Andrei Tarkovsky
Screenplay: Andrei Tarkovsky & Andrei Mikhalkov-Konchalovsky
Director of Photography: Vadim Yusov
Editors: Ludmila Feiginova, O Shevkunenko, Tatyana Yegorycheva
Music: Vyacheslav Ovchinnikov
Art Directors: Evgeny Chernyaev, Ippolit Novoderyozhkin, Sergei Voronkov
Assistant Director: Igor Petrov
Special Effects: V Sevostyanov
Costumes: Lidiya Novi, Maya Abar-Baranovskaya
Make–Up: Vera Rudina, M Aliautdinov, S Barsukov
Sound: Inna Zelentsova
Cast: Anatoly Solonitsyn (Andrei Rublev), Ivan Lapikov (Kirill), Nikolai Grinko (Daniel the Black), Nikolai Sergeyev (Theophanes the Greek), Irina Tarkovskaya (Darotchka, the

Holy Fool), Nikolai Burlyaev (Boriska), Rolan Bykov (Jester), Yuri Nikulin (Patrikey), Mikhail Kononov (Foma), Yuri Nazarov (Grand Duke/His Brother), Stepan Krylov (Bell-founder), Sos Sarkissian (Christ), Bolot Eishelanev (Tartar Chief), Nikolai Glazkov (Efim the balloonist/man in hut/man on horseback), Tamara Ogorodnikova (Mary the Mother of Christ), I Miroshnichenko (Mary Magdalene), N Snegina (Marfa), N Grabbe, B Beishenaliev, B Matisik, A Obukhov, Volodya Titov

Shot: April–November 1965, April–May 1966

Running Time: 185 mins (original cut, *The Passion According to Andrei*, ran 205 mins); first Western prints ran 145 mins

First Screenings: Moscow, December 1966
(190-minute version)
Moscow, February 1969
(185-minute version)
Moscow, April 1988
(205-minute version)

USSR Release: December 1971

First Screening in West: Cannes Film Festival, May 1969

Release in West: 1973 (one print ran in Paris during 1969/70)

Awards: FIPRESCI Prize, Cannes 1969; French Film Critics Association Prize 1969

Storyline

Shots, sequences or titles that occur only in the 205-minute version are placed within square brackets [...].

The opening credits play against the white wall of a monastery. A bell tolls. [The credits play over a black screen.]

A balloonist takes off from a church tower, despite the

efforts of an angry mob that tries to stop him. He sails over the waterlogged landscape, elated to be flying. The balloon (made of animal skins) suddenly loses height and he plummets to his death.

Part One: Episode 1, 'The Jester' (aka 'The Buffoon', 'The Mummers'), [Summer] 1400

[The monks, Andrei Rublev, Kirill and Daniel the Black, leave the Trinity Monastery to seek work as icon painters in Moscow.] They cross a field and are caught in a sudden downpour. They take shelter in a hut, where a jester performs a bawdy song. The Duke's men suddenly arrive and take the jester away. The monks leave.

Episode 2, 'Theophanes the Greek', [Summer–Winter–Spring–Summer] 1405[–1406]

Kirill visits Theophanes in Moscow. Theophanes asks Kirill if he is Andrei Rublev. Kirill says that he knows Rublev, but criticises the younger monk's work. Theophanes asks Kirill to help him paint the Church of the Annunciation (also in Moscow). Kirill replies that he will accept only if Theophanes summons him in front of Rublev and the other monks. Theophanes goes outside to watch an execution.

At the Andronikov Monastery (where the three monks are now living), Kirill is in his cell. A voice-over (by Kirill?) reads from Ecclesiastes XII when the young apprentice Foma rushes in to tell him that the Duke's messenger has arrived. He goes out to find that it is Rublev, and not himself, who has been summoned to work in Moscow. [In the 205-minute cut, these two sequences are reversed.] Kirill is ordered to leave the monastery. He storms off, beating his dog to death when it tries to follow him.

Episode 3, 'The Passion According to Andrei', 1406

[In the 205-minute cut, this is not a separate episode, but the second half of Episode 2.] Rublev and Foma are walking in the woods. Rublev castigates his pupil for laziness and untruthfulness. Theophanes, sitting nearby with his feet in an anthill, also condemns the boy, and then argues with Rublev. Rublev thinks that people are worthy of mercy, but Theophanes is dismissive, stressing that time is cyclical and that if Christ were to return, he would be crucified a second time. There then follows the 'Russian Calvary' sequence, in which the Russian Christ is crucified in a snowy winter landscape. Rublev's voice-over speaks of the sufferings of the Russian people.

Episode 4 [3], 'The Holiday' (aka The Celebration), [Spring] 1408

Andrei, Daniel, Foma and their group are en route to Vladimir. Making camp on a riverbank, Andrei wanders into the woods and inadvertently witnesses a pagan festival. He is captured and tied up in a mock crucifixion, but a pagan girl releases him. She kisses him and he tries to flee. The following morning, Rublev returns to the camp, claiming that he got lost in the forest. The Duke's men chase some pagans out of the woods, including the woman who freed Andrei. She escapes from the men and swims across the river. Rublev averts his gaze from her.

SEAN MARTIN

Episode 5 [4], 'The Last Judgment', [Summer] 1408

Rublev's team are now in the cathedral at Vladimir, but no
work has started. Out in the fields, Rublev tells Daniel that
he can't paint The Last Judgment, as he doesn't want to
frighten people. Back in the cathedral, Rublev admits he
doesn't know what to do. Foma announces that he is quit-
ting to work elsewhere. A dreamlike flashback shows Rublev
at the Duke's new palace, as a voice-over recites 1
Corinthians 13. As he plays with the Duke's small daughter,
a group of stonemasons quit to work for the Duke's brother.
A party of the Duke's men catches up with them in a wood
and blinds them all, except for the young boy, Sergei, who is
also part of Rublev's team. We cut back to the cathedral, with
Rublev hurling paint against a wall. He commands Sergei to
read from the scriptures, and, as Sergei does so (Corinthians
again, this time Chapter 11:3–9), a mad woman enters the
cathedral, taking shelter from the rain. She becomes upset at
the smear of paint on the wall. Rublev takes pity on her and
declares that he will make his Last Judgment 'a feast'. He
walks out into the rain. The girl follows him while Rublev's
team look on.

Part Two: Episode 6 [5], 'The Raid', [Autumn] 1408

The Duke's younger brother joins forces with a Tartar army;
together, they sack Vladimir. A series of flashbacks reveals the
Duke's relationship with his twin brother. Rublev and the
idiot girl are taking refuge in the, by now, fully decorated
cathedral. The hordes break in, but Rublev saves the girl
from being raped by killing her attacker with an axe.

In the subsequent desolation of the cathedral, Rublev, in
a dreamlike scene, talks to Theophanes, who is now dead.

80

Rublev tells him he will give up both painting as a protest against the evil of the times and speech to atone for his crime of murder. Snow begins to fall through the ruined roof of the cathedral.

Episode 7, 'The Silence' [6 The Charity/Love], [Winter] 1412

Rublev and the idiot girl are at the Andronikov Monastery outside Moscow. The Tartars arrive. They take the girl away, to Rublev's mute protests.

Kirill reappears, now blind, begging to be readmitted to the fold. The abbot agrees (they already appear to be sheltering some of the blind stonemasons), but charges Kirill with the task of writing out the scriptures 15 times.

Episode 8 [7], 'The Bell', [Spring–Summer–Autumn–Winter–Spring] 1423–4

The Duke's men enquire after the bell-caster by asking his son, Boriska. Boriska replies that his father is dead and that only he now knows the secret of bell-casting. The duke's men decide to take Boriska with them. Boriska starts work with a team of initially reluctant older workers, embarking on a long search for the right kind of clay.

The mute Rublev observes Boriska and his team at work. The jester reappears, and accuses Rublev of betraying him to the Duke's men back in 1400. Kirill intervenes, later confessing to Rublev that it was he who had betrayed the jester and that he had always been jealous of Rublev's talent.

The bell is unveiled before the Duke and his entourage and is rung triumphantly. The idiot girl reappears, leading a horse. She is now sane and well-dressed. Boriska confesses to

Rublev that he never knew the secret of bell-casting. Rublev finally breaks his vow of silence to console Boriska and tells him[83] that the two of them will work together, with Rublev painting icons and Boriska casting bells.

Epilogue

The film cuts to colour, showing a series of close-ups of Rublev's icons. The paintings shown are details of *The Trinity*, *The Transfiguration*, *The Entry into Jerusalem*, *The Nativity*, *The Raising of Lazarus*, *The Baptism of Christ*, *The Annunciation* and *The Saviour in the Wood*. Finally, we see four horses [in colour], grazing in a meadow in the rain.

Production History

The Soviet Union celebrated the six-hundredth anniversary of the birth of the great icon painter and national hero, Andrei Rublev, in 1960.[84] Tarkovsky apparently got the idea to make *Andrei Rublev* from his friend, the actor Vasily Livanov, who saw himself in the title role. Tarkovsky drew up a proposal with Andrei Mikhalkov-Konchalovsky, and submitted it in 1961, before he started work on *Ivan's Childhood*. Due to other commitments, Livanov did not become involved in the project (which he later regretted),[85] but Tarkovsky pursued it doggedly, even when there was pressure on him after the success of *Ivan's Childhood* to make something else (in particular a film based on Leonid Leonov's 1961 story *The Escape of Mr McKinley*).[86]

A contract was signed for *Andrei Rublev* in 1962, the treatment approved in December 1963 and the script published in the official film journal, *Iskusstvo Kino*, over two issues in 1964. This step was taken apparently in the name of drumming up support for a project that was already proving to be controversial. It was debated not only at Mosfilm and Goskino, but also among historians, academics, ordinary readers and party apparatchiks. The ploy certainly seemed to have helped, as the project was given the go-ahead in June, with pre-production beginning in September.

Tarkovsky was forced to drop a number of key scenes, as he had not been given enough money (the budget was around one million Roubles). The main casualties were: an opening scene depicting the Battle of Kulikovo, the first major Russian defeat of the Tartars in 1380; an episode called 'The Hunt', in which the Grand Duke's younger brother goes on a swan-killing spree (one of the dead swans does appear in the film, discovered by Foma in the birch wood); a flashback to the Tartar siege of Moscow, in which the women sacrificed their long hair; and the 'Famine' episode, which was to show the Holy Fool regaining her wits after giving birth to her child by the Tartar chieftain.

The film was shot between April and November 1965, at which point bad weather forced the film to close down. The remaining scenes were shot in April and May of 1966. Despite the large scale of the film, the shoot ran smoothly, with a number of reports attesting to the good atmosphere on set. The film was ready by August, when permission for its release, known as the *akt*, was signed. At this stage, it was known as *The Passion According to Andrei*, and ran 205 minutes.

This is where the film's troubles really began. For some reason, the official film industry premiere did not happen immediately. The delay may well have been caused by a number of people objecting to the film's length, its graphic cruelty and the somewhat nebulous charge of 'naturalism'. By November, Tarkovsky had shortened the film by 15 minutes and it was presumably this 190-minute version that was screened at Dom Kino in December 1966. 'Never had such a teeming, complex, crowded panorama of medieval Russian life been seen on Soviet screens', wrote the critic Maya Turovskaya. She also noted that the audience was 'stunned' by the film.[87] Nevertheless, there were still calls for further cuts, but Tarkovsky refused to make the film any shorter. He also complained to Romanov, the head of Goskino, that he had still not received the *akt* for the film's release, despite the fact that it had been signed. The film was unofficially shelved, with no one on either side prepared to make any further compromises.

Word that Tarkovsky was working on another film had leaked out into the West. The selection committee of the Venice Film Festival, where *Ivan's Childhood* had been screened, wanted the film for the 1966 Festival. A request was made to Goskino, but the committee was told that the film had not yet been finished, which at that time (March 1966) was true. The following year, both Cannes and Venice tried to get the film, but were told variously that it was still not finished, or that there were 'technical difficulties'. The 1968 Cannes Film Festival was cancelled midway through due to the state of near revolution that France was undergoing at the time, and Venice seems to have thrown in the towel. Despite these setbacks, an embarrassing bureaucratic blunder resulted in the film being sold to a Western distribution company representing Columbia, which had the rights to sell it in no fewer than 22 territories outside of the Soviet Union. Cannes tried to get the film again in 1969, this time with the backing of the French Communist Party. Goskino agreed to their request, provided that *Rublev* was shown out of competition, in the last possible screening slot, after all the awards had been given.

1969 proved to be the year of not one, but two premieres for *Andrei Rublev*, and even more turmoil. A second Moscow premiere was held in February, the print now running at 185 minutes (although it remains uncertain as to when exactly Tarkovsky made these further cuts). It would appear that Goskino was coming round to grudgingly accepting the film at last, and may have been preparing to release it as quietly as possible. However, when the film was screened at Cannes, at 4a.m. on the last day of the festival, it was immediately awarded the FIPRESCI (International Critics') Prize, the one award that had not yet been awarded. It was Venice all over again: Tarkovsky had caused another sensation. The Soviet authorities hit the roof.

All plans to release the film quietly and then bury it were now impossible. The film was publicly shown at the Moscow Film Festival in July, where Brezhnev showed his displeasure by walking out halfway through. Goskino pressured Columbia into not releasing the film, which the company agreed to temporarily, and it seems that the film might never have been released at all, were it not for one cinema in Paris, which held on to its print despite visits from KGB agents, who tried cloak and dagger tactics to retrieve it.

The film ran in Paris all through 1970; news of the film's already high reputation quickly spread. French critics named it their Film of the Year, while Ingmar Bergman called it the best film he had ever seen.[88] The film was eventually released – in its 185-minute version – in the Soviet Union in December 1971. In the West, it was cut even further (by distributors, not Tarkovsky), finally appearing in 1973, a full 12 years after Tarkovsky began work on it.

'A Startling, Uncanny Beauty'

Little is known for definite about the life of the historical Andrei Rublev (c.1370–1430). During the 1390s, he was

SEAN MARTIN

thought to have been at the Trinity Monastery, just outside
Moscow. During his time as a monk there, he helped to
decorate the Cathedral of the Dormition in Zvenigorod. By
1400, he was at the Andronikov Monastery in Moscow. In
1405, he decorated the Cathedral of the Annunciation there
together with Theophanes the Greek. 1408 saw Rublev in
Vladimir, where he decorated the Cathedral of the
Dormition. For the last 20 or so years of his life he was back
at the Andronikov Monastery, although he did return at
some point to the Holy Trinity Monastery to paint his most
famous work, *The Old Testament Trinity*.

Given this paucity of material, Tarkovsky and his co-
writer, Andrei Mikhalkov-Konchalovsky, opted to create
largely imagined episodes in Rublev's life that not only dealt
with the role of the artist, but, given that the film takes place
in a formative time for Russia, the film is also, to some
extent, a Russian *Birth of a Nation*. Rublev's lifetime saw the
first stirrings of Russian reunification after nearly 200 years
of Tartar domination. Their hold was broken when the
Muscovite Grand Duke Dmitri Donskoi defeated the Tartars
at the Battle of Kulikovo Field in 1380. While the Tartars
could still be found laying siege to Moscow as late as 1571,
they would never again be in a position to dominate the
Russian people to the extent that they had. The tide had
turned and the work started by Donskoi would be
completed by his great successors, Ivan III, the first Tsar (aka
Ivan the Great) (1462–1505) and Ivan IV (the Terrible)
(1533–84).

Andrei Rublev marks the onset of Tarkovsky's mature style,
here informed by two stylistic innovations that were only
embryonically present in *Ivan's Childhood,* and which would
dominate all of the later films: a lengthy, episodic narrative
and a camera style largely comprised of long tracking shots.

Furthermore, the film is dotted with sequences that are difficult to identify definitely as dreams or memories; indeed, it is often not possible to determine who the dreamer is in each case. The Russian Calvary scene is perhaps the most memorable example: the sequence would appear to be someone's imagining of Christ's return to Earth and his crucifixion a second time (an obvious nod to Dostoyevsky's *Parable of the Grand Inquisitor*, in which Christ returns to Earth and is arrested as a heretic by the Inquisition). But who is imagining these events? Is it Rublev himself? Or his assistant Foma? Theophanes? Perhaps even the film itself? Tarkovsky provides us with no easy answers.

While the film's narrative is episodic, one theme that pervades the whole is that of the relationship of the artist to the society in which he lives. Rublev, his fellow monks Daniel and Kirill, Theophanes, the balloonist, the jester and Boriska all embody different approaches to creativity and to society. The two 'artists' we first see in the film are Efim, the balloonist, and the jester. Efim risks all in trying to rise up towards God (literally), while at the same time needing to overcome his fear and the bigotry and superstition of those who try to stop him taking off. The jester, in contrast, is a man of the people, who, rather than being hounded by ordinary people, is able to make a direct connection with them. His mocking of the rich and powerful backfires, however (he is betrayed by Kirill), and he is led away to face years of torture and imprisonment.

Of the painters in the film, Kirill is untalented, blighted by jealousy and arrogance; he fears God, but does not love his fellow man. Daniel is a conformist who doesn't believe in innovation. While a kinder character than Kirill, his conservatism limits his vision; he will remain forever in the foothills of painting. Theophanes the Greek starts out as seemingly nothing more than a cynical businessman, who, like Kirill, does not love man; his art is there to uphold the spiritual status quo and does not exist to try to inspire people to better themselves or the world around them. It is only later, in the scene where he comes back from the dead to comfort Andrei in the sacked cathedral, that Theophanes is revealed to be an artist of great stature: 'How beautiful all this is,' he remarks of Rublev's icons in the cathedral and warns Andrei that he is committing a 'grave sin' in abandoning painting.

Rublev, in contrast to Kirill and Theophanes, possesses both humility and a love of man (evinced by his voice-over during the Calvary sequence, stressing that people are essentially good and that perhaps Christ came to reconcile God and Man), and puts himself at the service of both God and Man – art, for Rublev, is there to bring the two closer together. Although he becomes increasingly uncertain of the power of art as he is (apparently) seduced by a pagan girl, witnesses more Tartar horrors and ultimately kills a man, his faith is restored by the young bell-founder, Boriska, who works through faith alone: it is only when he reveals to Rublev that his father never imparted the secret of casting to him that Rublev decides to take up painting again.

Rublev and Boriska can be seen as complementary opposites: while both are ultimately men of faith, only Rublev's art is consciously directed towards serving both God and Man. In contrast, the cocky young Boriska's determination to complete work on the bell is largely an attempt to save his own skin. The two characters also have markedly different approaches to their collaborators. When Rublev reprimands his assistant Foma in the wood for eating too much and not telling the truth, he does so gently, almost with humour. It appears that Rublev's concern matures Foma, as he later quits the barely started cathedral in Vladimir, announcing that he's been asked to paint a church in Pafnutievo. In contrast, Boriska frequently behaves quite despotically towards his team, even having one of them whipped at one point to ensure that everyone is reminded of his authority.

Surprisingly, for a film about a painter, Rublev is not shown painting (the nearest we get to seeing him at work is during 'The Last Judgment', where he can be seen cleaning an icon of the triumphant St George). This, and the decision to show Rublev's icons only at the end of the film, were central to Tarkovsky's conception of the film from the very beginning of the project. He wrote in 1962 that 'there will not be a single shot of Rublev painting his icons. He will simply live, and he won't even be present on-screen in all episodes. And the last part of the film (in colour) will be solely devoted to Rublev's icons. We will show them in detail'.[89] This suggests that, for Tarkovsky, to show his hero 'simply living' would be an adequate method of representing the past, a method that also has links to traditional forms of artistic representation: that of landscape painting, mosaics and icons themselves.

Landscape painting makes itself most obviously felt in the Russian Calvary sequence, which has a Breughelesque quality in the way Tarkovsky has arranged his actors within the frame: characters in the background are frequently active, going about their day to day business, ignorant of the drama unfolding nearby, much as they do in Breughel's *The Road to Calvary* (1564). Also drawing from Breughel, Tarkovsky dresses his characters in contemporary costume. The frame teems with life during 'The Raid' (where the influence of Kurosawa can be felt as much as that of Breughel), while 'The Bell' continues to echo the painter with its wide horizons populated by Boriska's team and those who have been called in at the end to help hoist the bell for its inauguration.

Work by nineteenth-century Russian painters also influences the look of the film, especially when Andrei escapes from the pagan village: his reappearance on the banks of the river perhaps owes something to Alexander Ivanov's *The Appearance of Christ to the People* (1837–57) and Ivan Kramskoi's *Christ in the Desert* (1872).

Painting also shapes the narrative itself. Vittore Carpaccio (c.1460–c.1525) was a particular favourite of Tarkovsky's and he writes enthusiastically about the 'startling, uncanny beauty' of the Italian's work in *Sculpting in Time*: 'As you stand before them, you have the disturbing sensation that the inexplicable is about to be explained', a comment which would not be out of place in trying to describe *Andrei Rublev*. But he continues: 'the point is that *each* of the characters in Carpaccio's crowded composition is a centre'.[90] If we approach *Rublev* as a mosaic made up of centres, its apparent lack of a forward dramatic arch becomes irrelevant. As Rublev's journey is an interior one towards a realisation that art must selflessly serve both God and Man, there is, in reality, nowhere for him actually to 'go' physically. This, coupled with the film's measured pace and demanding running time, suggests that Tarkovsky was attempting to make the film timeless: as there is nowhere for Rublev to go, Tarkovsky is inviting us to look around the world he has created, a world which his characters – and his audience – can fully inhabit.

The film is dominated by slow pans and tracking shots, Tarkovsky's camera investigating the glories and terrors, both great and small, of this world. Several techniques that were to become his trademarks appear for the first time, such as his fondness for putting the same character in logically impossible places within the same shot, a technique used to great effect in the conversation between Rublev and Theophanes in the sacked cathedral, where Theophanes walks out of frame right, the camera pans left with Andrei, and Theophanes then reappears not from frame right, where he should logically be, but from frame left.

Another device, that of panning with a character as they walk until the camera picks up the person they are talking to, the camera then following the second person and so on (first used in *Ivan's Childhood* when Galtsev reprimands Masha in the field hospital) appears in *Andrei Rublev* – for example, in Rublev's encounter with the ghostly Theophanes – and would become one of Tarkovsky's basic methods of covering a scene. Andrei's dispute with Theophanes by the edge of the wood is a veritable mini-compendium of Tarkovskian leitmotifs: the characters are frequently framed centrally; they spend large parts of the scene facing away from each other; and the whole scene was shot in one single take. The following sequence, that of the Russian Calvary, is again typical of Tarkovsky's mature style: it would seem to be taking place in the imagination of one of the characters, but, as already noted, we are not given any clues as to whose vision it is.[91]

The world as revealed to us by Tarkovsky's long takes is one in which the daily and the Divine are threaded together in the fabric of life. The frequent conversation between the characters illustrates this apparent dichotomy, such as when Andrei and Daniel disagree about how to paint the Last Judgment; the mention that the young assistant Peter has not seen the Cathedral of the Assumption before; the stonemasons telling Rublev and Daniel about the Duke's reaction to their leaving; Theophanes asking Kirill if he has ever prepared a wall before; and Boriska arguing with his assistants about where to dig the casting pit or which clay to use. All of these daily trivialities, artisan's shop talk, are in sharp contrast with the sacred nature of their work (which is also reflected in the Russian Calvary sequence and the reappearance of the Holy Fool at the end; with her wits now recovered, she exudes a saintly aura as Rublev and Boriska lie in the mud).

Tarkovsky does not, of course, show us Rublev's world solely through dialogue; almost every sequence in the film has an 'uncanny beauty'. After the jester's routine has ended in the first episode, the camera tracks around the hut examining people's faces as they wait for the rain to stop, while an unseen woman intones a wordless melody (perhaps she is the woman to whom Daniel says 'Christ be with you mistress' when they leave?). Here Tarkovsky quietly celebrates ordinary people in an ordinary, but somehow magical, situation. They do not do anything, they simply wait. Tarkovsky returns as often as he can to stillness and silence: the quiet of the pagan village in the early morning; the wood after the stonemasons have been blinded, with milk flowing into the brook; and Andrei and Kirill sheltering from the rain under a tree in the middle of a field, the camera following Andrei's gaze to hold on leaves blowing in the wind. Tarkovsky's use of nature is at once Orthodox (unlike most forms of Western Christianity, the Eastern Orthodox Church regards nature as good, not fallen) and also pantheistic, perhaps even quietly pagan.[92]

These silences in the film are made all the more powerful by what surrounds them. Most notoriously, the film is violent. The violence is both casual and ferocious: Kirill, on his way to see Theophanes, passes a man being tortured to death in the town square, and Theophanes later complains that his young assistants have gone outside 'to see how the ruler will die'. Peter's death from a gaping neck wound is echoed in the saw whose blade undulates horribly next to him. The stonemasons have their eyes gouged out for daring to agree to work for the Grand Prince's brother. During the sack of Vladimir, a horse is killed on-screen and a cow is set alight.

There is also an earthiness to the film, in the form of bawdy humour in the jester's routine (he has a human face painted on his buttocks) and bodily functions (the Holy Fool's first action on entering the cathedral is to urinate on the floor).[93] The contrasts between the sacred nature of icon painting or bell-casting and the tiring, filthy work that creates them is echoed in the slow-motion shots of the sack of Vladimir: the Grand Duke lording over it as the gold is stripped from the church roofs; a pair of geese flying down gracefully over the panicking crowd.

Icons themselves not only appear in the film – in Kirill's cell, in Theophanes' workshop, in Rublev's hands, in the cathedral after it has been sacked and in the epilogue – but also inform the film's overall narrative strategy. As we have discussed in the 'Theory and Practice' chapter, Tarkovsky sought to encourage the viewer to watch his films actively, working out connections for themselves; to be, in effect, a co-creator of the films. This echoes what a number of writers have said of icons. Pavel Florensky (1882–1937), a Russian priest whose work Tarkovsky knew, held that 'The icon requires an active viewer who… works to array the discontinuous image into a meaningful narrative.'[94] The French critic Guy Gauthier, writing about *Rublev*, explained that icons could be seen as windows into eternity, whose beauty was derived from the divine realities that were present within them, but whose inner qualities could only be fully understood by people who were sensitive enough to perceive them.[95]

The Passion According to Andrei and *Andrei Rublev*

Andrei Rublev exists in three versions: two edits done in 1966 and a third first shown in 1969, running 205, 190 and 185 minutes respectively. Of these, the first and third versions are available on DVD, and it is worth briefly examining the main differences between the two, as they reveal how Tarkovsky refined his ideas about the film.

In the 205-minute version, the Prologue adds a shot of Efim being chased across the heath by a mob, making it clearer that his flight has aroused local hostility. (The tracking shot that follows him through the ground floor of the tower is also an alternative take to the 185-minute cut.) After Efim's crash, the horse is seen rolling on its back for longer. It eventually gets up and trots out of frame, leading us into a shot of a horse walking past Efim's prone body on the river-bank. The camera then tracks past Efim to end on the balloon. The 185-minute cut, by contrast, adds a shot of a monastery when Efim is in the air, as if to link the Prologue to the rest of the film, shortens the horse shot and omits the track past Efim's body.

'The Jester' begins in the 205-minute cut with a shot that the recut version omits, showing Andrei, Daniel and Kirill leaving their monastery to go and look for work as icon painters. The scene in the hut is slightly longer in *The Passion*: when the Jester does his second handstand, he reveals that he has a Boyar's face painted on his buttocks; and, following Kirill's comment that 'the Devil sent Jesters', there is a complete 360° pan around the hut's interior.

Episode 2, 'Theophanes the Greek', is the most radically different in its original version. It includes a shot of one of Theophanes' assistants running downstairs carrying a pair of buckets. In response to Theophanes' complaints that his helpers are nowhere to be found, the young man with the buckets explains that the other assistants have all gone outside to watch the torture. Theophanes' hectoring of the mob in the original version takes place well before the end of the scene, unlike in the recut version, where it happens at the end.

When the action cuts to the monastery, the original edit showed Kirill in his cell, and then the arrival of the messenger to summon Andrei, not Kirill, to Moscow to work with the Greek. In the recut, these two sequences are switched and the scene in Kirill's cell is also shortened. When Kirill leaves the monastery, the scene originally concluded with a shot of his dog dying in the snow, followed by a shot of Kirill walking off into the woods. The recut version omits both. The episode then originally continued with the scene of Andrei chastising Foma in the birch wood, but, when he came to recut it, Tarkovsky decided to make this scene the first in a new episode, 'The Passion According to Andrei'. The recut of the scene also removed a long aerial shot, which originally occurred after Foma had lifted the dead swan's wing, perhaps suggesting that Foma was imagining what it is like to fly.

The original version of 'The Holiday' had a longer ending, showing the Duke's men appearing on the riverbank and discussing amongst themselves whether Andrei and his team are the people they're looking for. 'No,' they decide, 'these are strangers.' When they do locate the pagans, Marfa's attempts to escape are covered in two extra shots cut from the 185-minute version, which show her struggling with her persecutors and having her dress ripped off. The original cut also makes it clear that, in this scene, she is played by three different actresses, all the women whom Andrei had encountered during the night.

'The Last Judgment' contains one of the film's most infamous scenes, that of the blinding of the stonemasons; in the recut version, Tarkovsky omits two shots to lessen the horror of the incident. The Holy Fool's first appearance in the cathedral is also toned down: in the original version, her first action upon entering the building was to urinate on the floor. The other biggest change in the recut version of this episode is Tarkovsky's decision to move the flashback of the three monks sheltering under a tree in the middle of a field during a storm to the final episode, where it is cut into the scene of the exhausted Boriska being carried out of the casting pit on a fleece.

'The Raid' is the film's most violent episode and most of the main cuts that Tarkovsky made were to remove the most shocking elements, easily the two most notorious being the on-screen killing of a horse and the immolation of a cow. In the original edit, the horse, after falling down the stairs, tries to get up again, falls and is put out of its misery by a lance to the heart. In the recut version, Tarkovsky cuts away before the animal tries to regain its footing. The burning cow was originally seen running around a yard, kicking its hind legs, but Tarkovsky cut so much out of the scene that you can't actually tell what is on fire, as the cow is almost out of shot in the extreme foreground.[96] Other cuts to the sequence include shortening the Tartars' ride into Vladimir at the beginning of the episode, cutting some of the early massacring and condensing the flashbacks of the Grand Duke and his brother.

The film's penultimate episode was the only one to experience a change of title. Originally known as 'The Charity', it became 'The Silence' in the recut version. Kirill's penitential reappearance at the monastery was also reworked. *The Passion According to Andrei* shows Kirill being led inside, then recognised, and then prostrating himself before the abbot. In the recut, Kirill's arrival is not shown, and we also lose the humour of the gatekeeper being rebuked for being too soft a touch and letting all comers into the monastery (which would explain why the Tartars get in later). The scene is also split into two sections, with the Tartars arriving before the abbot confronts Kirill. The episode originally ended with a tracking shot of the Holy Fool on horseback with the Tartar chieftain as they gallop away from the monastery. The recut omits this.

'The Bell' remained largely unchanged in the shorter version of the film, the several cuts being relatively minor. The main difference, that of the placement of the tree flash-back, has already been noted.

The 'Epilogue' remained the same in both versions of the film, although the final shot of the horses grazing in the rain was originally in colour. In the recut, it is printed in mono-chrome.

The changes to the film do more than merely shorten it and make it less violent. In general, the 185-minute cut focuses more attention on Andrei himself, with other char-acters – notably Kirill, Foma, the Holy Fool, Boriska and Marfa – suffering at the hands of the re-edit. But in cutting parts of scenes in which these characters appear, Tarkovsky also created ambiguities, such as Kirill's unexplained reap-pearance in the monastery in 'The Silence'. Such problems did not appear to bother Tarkovsky, however, and he declared that the 185-minute version was the definitive version of the film. Interestingly, though, when Tarkovsky was trying to get Eduard Artemyev to work with him on *Solaris*, he showed him the original version, suggesting that he may perhaps have regretted cutting the film. But if he did harbour regrets, he never made them public.

A Portrait of the Artist

If *Ivan's Childhood* had been autobiographical at one or so removes, then *Andrei Rublev* would be even more so, but would also serve to reinforce Tarkovsky's own theories about the role of the artist in society – his own role, in other words. Indeed, *Rublev* is a classic case of film-as-metaphor, at least in the way in which it was received in the West after it was screened at Cannes in 1969. Several commentators writing in *Dossier Positif*, the French magazine that championed Tarkovsky from the early stages of his career, felt that in talking about Rublev's travails, Tarkovsky was talking about his own: Michel Ciment saw the film as a 'transparent allegory'[97] of Tarkovsky's own situation in the Soviet Union, while Jacques Demeure saw the film as 'a serene allegory with no apparent connection to historical reality'.[98]

In his own pronouncements on the film, Tarkovsky spoke often of his concern for the role of the artist in society, and how art reflected the aspirations of society as a whole. 'I am interested in the theme of the artist's personality in its relationship to his time,' he wrote in 1962, whilst attempting to get *Rublev* off the ground. 'The artist, on the strength of his natural sensitivity, is the person who perceives his epoch most profoundly and reflects it most fully.'[99] Art and artists recur throughout Tarkovsky's films: from the musical aspirations of little Sasha in *The Steamroller and the Violin* to the retired actor Alexander in *The Sacrifice*. For Tarkovsky, there was no doubt that, although still a young art, cinema was the heir to the older traditions, and that he himself, like Rublev, was in a position to 'perceive his epoch most profoundly and reflect it most fully'.

Solaris (1972)

THE FAMILY I

Alternate Title: None
Production Company: Mosfilm
Production Supervisor: Vyacheslav Tarasov
Director: Andrei Tarkovsky
Screenplay: Andrei Tarkovsky & Friedrich Gorenstein, based on the novel by Stanislaw Lem
Director of Photography: Vadim Yusov
Editor: Ludmila Feiginova
Music: Eduard Artemyev; JS Bach, 'Ich ruf zu dir, Herr Jesus Christ' BWV 639, from *Orgelbüchlein*
Art Director: Mikhail Romadin
Assistant Directors: A Ides, Larissa Tarkovskaya, Maria Chugunova
Special Effects: V Sevostyanov, A Klimenko
Costumes: Nelly Fomina
Make-Up: Vera Rudina
Sound: Semyon Litvinov
Cast: Donatas Banionis (Kris Kelvin), Natalya Bondarchuk (Hari), Yuri Jarvet (Snaut), Anatoly Solonitsyn (Sartorius), Vladislav Dvorzhetsky (Berton), Nikolai Grinko (Kelvin's Father), Sos Sarkissian (Gibarian) Olga Barnet (Kelvin's Mother), Tamara Ogorodnikova (Aunt Anna), Alexander

Misharin (Timolis), Olga Kizilova (Gibarian's visitor), Yulian
Semyonov (Shannon), Georgi Tejkh (Professor Messenger)
Shot: March–December 1971
Running Time: 165 mins
First Screening: Moscow, 30 December 1971 (Rough cut)
USSR Release: 20 March 1972
First Screening in West: Cannes Film Festival, 13 May
1972
Release in West: 1973
Awards: Grand Jury Prize, FIPRESCI Prize, Ecumenical
Jury Prize, Cannes Film Festival; Best Film of the Year,
London Film Festival

Storyline

The credits roll over a black screen to Bach's Prelude 'Ich ruf
zu dir, Herr Jesus Christ'.

Part One

Kris Kelvin is walking in the grounds of his father's dacha,
deep in thought. Berton, a former cosmonaut, arrives. He
talks with Kelvin's father. Kelvin, on the veranda, is caught in
a sudden downpour. On the table in front of him is a still life
of fruit and tea cups. When the rain stops, Kelvin goes inside.

Kelvin, Berton and Kelvin's aunt, Anna, watch Berton's
black and white film of his mission to Solaris and the official
enquiry afterwards. In this film within the film, Berton
claims to have seen a garden form on the surface of the
ocean of Solaris and then a gigantic child, four metres high.
The scientists are sceptical, as is Kelvin when the film ends.

Kelvin has uneasy conversations with both his father and
Berton. Kelvin feels that science should follow its own

course, while Berton claims that knowledge without moral scruples is invalid. Berton storms off; Kelvin's father announces that it's dangerous to send people like Kelvin into space.

Anna is watching a TV programme about Solaris, which reveals that only three scientists remain on the station, Snaut, Sartorius and Gibarian. The programme is interrupted by a videophone call from Berton. He is driving back to the city. He tells Kelvin's father that the child he saw floating above the ocean on Solaris was exactly the same (except for its height) as one of fellow cosmonaut Fechner's children.

Berton continues to drive into the city. We see shots from the car as it travels along tunnels, underpasses and elevated motorways.

Early the following morning, Kelvin burns old papers, including a photo of a young dark-haired woman. Kelvin tells his father that he's taking a home movie with him.

Kelvin flies to Solaris. Upon his arrival, he finds the station to be almost deserted. He locates Snaut, who tells Kelvin that Gibarian has killed himself. Kelvin notices that there seems to be someone asleep in the hammock that Snaut has rigged up in his room.

Kelvin finds an empty room to use as his own and then finds Gibarian's. His room is in complete disarray. A note bearing Kelvin's name is stuck to the video monitor. Kelvin watches Gibarian's last message to him. While he is watching it, he hears someone outside and runs to keep the door shut. Kelvin picks up a gun left lying by the video recorder and leaves, taking Gibarian's tape with him.

He finds Sartorius's room. They have a brief conversation, interrupted by a male dwarf who runs out of Sartorius's room. Sartorius puts him back inside, telling Kelvin that he is too impressionable.

Kelvin looks out of the porthole at the Solaris ocean (one of a number of shots of its ever-changing surface throughout the film), but is distracted by a young girl of about 12 wearing a nightdress who walks past him. He follows her to a cold room, in which is stored Gibarian's frozen body. The girl is nowhere to be seen.

Kelvin returns to Snaut's room. He asks Snaut if there is anyone else on the station. The young girl walks past along the corridor outside. Snaut refuses to answer who – or what – she is. Kelvin accuses Snaut of being afraid.

Back in his room, Kelvin barricades the door and watches the rest of Gibarian's tape. The young girl offers Gibarian a drink, but he pushes her away. Snaut and Sartorius knock on his door, saying they want to help. Gibarian picks up a syringe. He tells Kelvin that what is happening on the station is something to do with conscience. Kelvin lies down and gets some sleep with the gun by his side.

When he wakes up, he has been joined by the dark-haired woman from the photo he burnt on the morning of his departure for Solaris. They kiss. He asks how she knew where he was. She accidentally kicks the gun away. She finds a copy of the photo Kelvin burnt on his last morning on Earth. She asks Kelvin who it is, then catches her reflection in the mirror. She realises it's herself. She tells Kelvin she feels as though she's forgotten something. She asks Kelvin if he loves her; he calls her by her name, Hari, and tells her not to be so stupid. He explains that he has work to do, but she insists on coming with him. He tells her she'll have to put a space suit on. She can't get out of her dress, as it has no zip. Kelvin cuts her out of it, noticing a syringe mark on her arm. He then notices that the boxes he used to barricade the door are still where he put them.

Part Two

Kelvin loads Hari into a small escape rocket and launches it. Returning to his room, he is visited by Snaut, who realises Kelvin has had 'guests'. Kelvin informs him that Hari died ten years ago. Snaut explains that what Kelvin saw was the materialisation of his memory of her, which the ocean obtains by probing their brains to extract 'islands of memory'. He tells Kelvin that Hari will return.

Kelvin wakes in the middle of the night. A new Hari is with him in the room. She joins him in bed. The following morning, Kris leaves his room to try to dispose of the shawl the first Hari left behind. The new Hari panics when she realises she is alone and breaks through the metal door of the bedroom to join him. She is badly cut, but her wounds heal before Kelvin's eyes.

They visit Snaut and Sartorius in Sartorius's lab. Kelvin introduces Hari as his wife. Snaut greets her as if she were human, but Sartorius regards her as a laboratory specimen, fit only to be experimented upon. Kelvin threatens Sartorius if he tries anything.

Kelvin shows Hari the home movie he brought from Earth. It shows Kelvin as a boy, plus Kelvin's father and his dead mother in a snowy, Breughelesque landscape. It ends with shots of the 'real' Hari outside the dacha. Hari claims to be able to remember that Kelvin's mother hated her, which he denies.

Snaut calls by to tell Kelvin that the rate of regeneration seems to be slowing. He proposes sending an encephalogram of Kelvin's thoughts into the ocean. He also invites Kelvin and Hari to his birthday party in the library.

Sometime later, Kelvin wakes. Hari wants to know what happened to the 'real' Hari, as, while Kelvin was sleeping,

Sartorius told her that she had killed herself. Kelvin explains what happened and tells Hari that he loves her.

At the birthday party in the library, Snaut arrives late and asks Kelvin to read a passage from *Don Quixote*. Sartorius proposes a toast to Snaut and science, but Snaut is not interested. He ruminates on their predicament instead and proposes a toast to Gibarian. Kelvin and Sartorius begin to argue. Hari comes to Kelvin's defence, declaring that he has behaved humanly in an inhuman situation. Sartorius tells her that she's not a woman, but Hari retorts that she is becoming human. Sartorius storms off; Kelvin escorts the drunk Snaut back to his room.

Kelvin returns to the library to find Hari contemplating the reproduction of Breughel's *Hunters in the Snow*, which hangs on the library wall. Close-ups of the painting from Hari's point of view follow, with imagined birdcalls and dog barks. Kelvin and Hari float in each other's arms weightlessly around the library as the station changes its orbit.

Hari tries to commit suicide by drinking liquid oxygen, but she comes back to life again. Kelvin tells her he will live with her on the station. She tells him she's afraid. At this point, Kelvin becomes delirious, imagining his mother on the station and then talking with her back in the dacha.

When Kelvin recovers from his fever, Snaut tells him Hari is 'no more': she has been destroyed by Sartorius's annihilator. Snaut reads Kelvin Hari's last letter to him. He also tells Kelvin that the 'guests' have not returned since the encephalogram was sent and that islands are starting to form in the ocean.

In the library, Kelvin and Snaut talk about 'the mysteries of happiness, death and love'. Snaut thinks it's time for Kelvin to return to Earth.

We see Kelvin returning to the dacha. Inside the house, it

is raining. His father seems oblivious to this. He sees Kelvin and goes out to meet him. Kelvin falls to his knees, hugging his father. The camera pulls slowly back to reveal that the whole scene has taken place on an island in the ocean of Solaris.

Production History

Tarkovsky began working on what would become his third feature in the autumn of 1968. Perhaps unwilling to court more controversy while *Andrei Rublev*'s troubles continued to play out around him, he proposed filming Stanislaw Lem's novel *Solaris*, set firmly in the seemingly 'safe' genre of science fiction. He worked on the screenplay with the novelist Friedrich Gorenstein (1932–2002) throughout 1969, but, as with his disagreements with Bogomolov over *Ivan's Childhood*, so Tarkovsky fell out with Lem, although in a more spectacular fashion. Lem disapproved of Tarkovsky's humanism and was outraged by the first draft of the script, which had three-quarters of the action taking place on Earth (in the novel, all of the action takes place on board the space station). Not only that, but Kelvin returned to Earth and his wife, Maria, at the end. Tarkovsky and Gorenstein reworked the script, which eventually had only about a quarter of the story taking place on Earth, which, in the film, became the opening 40 or so minutes and the character of Maria was cut completely.

Despite Lem's continuing protests, the script seems to have been approved in the spring of 1970 and in May Tarkovsky was starting to cast the film. He initially wanted the Swedish actress Bibi Andersson for the role of Hari, the female lead, and also considered his ex-wife, Irma Rausch, for the part.[100] The usual process of committee meetings at both Mosfilm and Goskino dragged the project out through the remainder of the year, with shooting finally starting with the winter scenes (at the dacha and from the home movie) in March 1971. By this time, Tarkovsky had settled on Natalya Bondarchuk, the 20-year-old daughter of the director Sergei Bondarchuk, as Hari.

Filming continued throughout the summer of 1971, with Tarkovsky and Vadim Yusov falling into serious disagreement, mainly about the choice of lenses they should be using: Tarkovsky thought the film should have been shot with a longer lens (50mm), which would have favoured the actors over the sets, while Yusov favoured a 35mm lens, which would have shown off the space station set to better advantage. Tarkovsky was also not seeing eye to eye with his leading man, Donatas Banionis; Banionis simply did not understand what Tarkovsky wanted, a problem exacerbated by Tarkovsky's inability to express himself clearly. The problems continued. On 12 July, Tarkovsky complained to his diary that they'd run out of film stock, but were still nowhere near finished. On 10 August, he wrote that 'work on *Solaris* has been hell. We're behind schedule... Yusov and I are constantly arguing.' The following day he noted, 'Making *Rublev* was a holiday picnic compared with this business.'[101]

In early September, they seem to have run out of colour Kodak stock again, this time necessitating the shooting of certain scenes in black and white, such as the bonfire scene, in which Kelvin burns his papers on the morning of his departure for Solaris.[102] The 'city of the future' sequence, in which Berton drives back into town from the dacha for nearly five minutes of screen time, was shot in Tokyo between 24 September and 10 October, again, partially in black and white to keep costs down. The scenes of Kelvin discovering Gibarian's body were shot as late as 10 December.

The first cut was shown at Mosfilm on 30 December

1971, but, contrary to Tarkovsky's fears, the film was passed. (Some further cutting did, however, take place in early 1972.) It was released as a Category One film in the Soviet Union on 20 March 1972,[103] and was first shown in the West at Cannes on 13 May, with Tarkovsky himself in attendance. The film met with a cooler response than either *Ivan* or *Rublev*, but was still treated with respect and was awarded the Special Jury Prize.

The 'Soviet *2001*'

When *Solaris* was shown at Cannes in 1972, it was hailed as the Soviet 'reply' to Kubrick's *2001: A Space Odyssey*. But the two films could not be more dissimilar: where Kubrick has his camera firmly trained on the cosmos, Tarkovsky looks back towards Earth, and man. There is, however, a link of sorts between the two films, in that Tarkovsky watched *2001* before shooting *Solaris*. He disliked it intensely, finding it 'cold and soulless',[104] and resolved to make his film as different as possible from Kubrick's.

Although Tarkovsky frequently claimed that he didn't like science fiction — such as in one of his conversations with Tonino Guerra in the documentary, *Tempo di Viaggio* — he in fact read quite a lot of it, tending to favour 'soft' SF (in which philosophical and moral issues take precedence over science and spaceships), his favourite being Ray Bradbury.[105] This approach to the genre tells us at once what kind of film *Solaris* would be, and why Tarkovsky had such difficulty shooting it.

Tarkovsky and Lem

That *Solaris* turned out to be a film of quiet dignity and humanism shows that Tarkovsky eventually prevailed over both Stanislaw Lem, who objected to Tarkovsky's deviation from the theme of the novel, that of the nature and limits of human knowledge and values, and Vadim Yusov, with whom Tarkovsky argued constantly about what lens should be used and how much of the space station set should be shown. In the finished film, we only see parts of the station, as Tarkovsky felt that dwelling on the set too much would detract from the characters' predicament.

The film follows the plot of the book quite closely, although, as we have noted, Tarkovsky added the scenes set on Earth – the prologue, the home movie, and the seeming return to the dacha at the end. These are not found in the novel and did not please Lem. The main difference between Tarkovsky and Lem is in their treatment of the relationship between Kelvin and Hari.[106] For Lem, the relationship is mainly a vehicle to allow him to examine what happens when people 'try to stay human in an inhuman situation'.[107] Kelvin comes to realise that the things we hold dear, such as love and forgiveness, mean very little in a universe that seems to be oblivious to such values. Tarkovsky, on the other hand, sees these same values as being intrinsic to our existence, whether we are in a human situation (at home on the Earth) or not (orbiting Solaris).

Furthermore, Tarkovsky's approach to scientific thinking and knowledge was diametrically opposed to Lem's. Lem, in both the original novel and much of his other work, remained, if not cynical about human values, then certainly regarded them as being inferior to a coolly detached, impersonal view of a universe that may be organised along very different lines to what we may imagine. Science, for Lem, was our only real tool for coping with the potential strangeness and unknowability of the universe and any life it may contain. Tarkovsky was in the opposite camp. In his diaries, he quotes Montaigne: 'Our fantasies are worth more than our judgments',[108] which summarises his position pretty well. For Tarkovsky, knowledge and truth were interior and intuitive, whereas for Lem they were deductive and rational, possibly even something wholly other to our experience. While both the novel and the film agree that 'there is something inside us which we don't like to face up to',[109] Tarkovsky and Lem were so fundamentally at odds with each other that they effectively faced in opposite directions.

Tarkovsky and Genre

Tarkovsky's dispute with Lem was, in effect, a clash between Lem's 'hard' science fiction and Tarkovsky's own preference for the 'soft' science fiction of writers like Ray Bradbury. Despite Tarkovsky's enthusiasm for the novel, it is clear that what appealed to him were the themes of the book, which he made his own. Watching Kubrick's 2001 simply furthered his resolve to make a film that could reasonably be described as 'revisionist soft science fiction'. For example, whereas Kubrick's space station is antiseptically clean and tidy, the station in Solaris is as unkempt and dishevelled as its inhabitants. By the time we reach the station, however, we have already experienced perhaps the most radical aspect of Tarkovsky's revisionism both of the novel and the genre: the scenes set on Earth.

In shots similar to one we have already seen in Rublev,[110] Tarkovsky shows us fronds swaying gently under the surface of a pond. We then see Kelvin, standing, deep in thought. He slowly makes his way back to the dacha. A more radical beginning to a film about outer space – which is really a film about inner space – could hardly be imagined. As Mark Le Fanu observes, 'How often do we find such rapt intense stillness in films? No narrative at all for the time being; simply a man, by himself, standing in the presence of nature, *thinking*.'[111] Tarkovsky is hinting that this is really a film about Earth, not space, and our inescapable ties with it.

The dacha, its contents and Kelvin's relationship with his father all continue to lay out themes that Tarkovsky will deal with for the rest of the film. The family relations are somewhat opaque. The dark-haired older woman is not immediately identified as Kelvin's aunt, Anna; all we can say of the little boy is that he is presumably Berton's son or grandson, while the little girl with whom the boy plays is never identified at all. Photographs of Kelvin's mother and Hari can only be identified as such much later in the film when we have seen both women 'in the flesh'.

The layout of the dacha mirrors this confusion. The room where they watch Berton's film seems to be separate from the room with the birdcage and the balloon prints on the wall, but it is never identified as being so, while the room where Kelvin 'meets' his mother in the delirium scene seems to be a conflation of both rooms plus elements from the space station.[112] Furthermore, Tarkovsky also conflates the space and time of two rooms during the conversation that Kelvin has with his father immediately after watching Berton's film. The conversation starts in the room with the TV and then cuts away to the photograph of the woman, whom we later learn is Kelvin's mother. When we cut back to Kelvin and his father, they are now in the room containing the birdcage, plus Kelvin has his leather jacket back on. This is the first of the film's subtle disruptions of objective space and time, which will become more pronounced as the film goes on.

Despite the ambiguity of both the dacha and its occupants, it is clearly a home to which they are devoted. Kelvin's father tells Berton 'I don't like innovation', and the furnishings of the dacha reflect this. We can make out a classical bust, Chinese vases, old prints of balloons on the wall and an old, illustrated edition of *Don Quixote* that later mysteriously reappears on the station. Home is clearly somewhere for Kelvin – and Tarkovsky – that is strongly associated with nature, art and culture.

Tarkovsky and Narrative

If, in the opening minutes of the film, Tarkovsky is modifying the genre to suit his own purposes, he also starts to do something else, namely to introduce small inconsistencies in terms of plot and dramatic action. Most of these are unnoticeable at first, although the fact that we see Berton being driven into the 'City of the Future' for nearly five minutes of screen time suggests that space and time have already become highly subjective, and will become more so once Kelvin arrives at the station. Perhaps this sequence is so long in order to suggest that Berton is ruminating about the problems Kelvin will inevitably face once he get to Solaris; then again, it has its own rhythm and hypnotic beauty as much as the pond at the beginning does. Perhaps Tarkovsky is suggesting that the important journeys we need to make are the ones that take place in everyday 'ordinary' reality.

Berton is related to several other unexplained inconsistencies in the film. The first concerns his film, which lays the ground for the rest of *Solaris*'s handling of narrative. At the end of the film, the bearded academic (called Shannon in the script) announces that 'exploration in this area [i.e., Solaris] will be discontinued'.[113] To judge by Berton's appearance, we could estimate that his film was shot 20 years earlier. Why then, if exploration of Solaris was to be discontinued all those years ago, is Kelvin being sent there to assess whether or not to close down the station? It is a riddle that Tarkovsky leaves unanswered. Berton's film, in fact, gives us clear hints not only about Solaris and what Kelvin will probably find there, but also how Tarkovsky will relay the remainder of the story to us. After viewing Berton's film, in which none of the things he saw over the ocean of Solaris were captured by his camera, Shannon announces, 'This report in no way, or in almost no way, corresponds with reality.' What he is saying, in other words, is that there is a clear distinction between Berton's subjective, inner experience and the so-called objective reality that his camera has caught and that the scientists have assembled to discuss. As *Solaris* progresses, it is less and less concerned with 'corresponding to reality', and more and more engaged in depicting Kelvin's inner world. Furthermore, the disjointed space that the inquiry takes place in is ambiguous and suggests that the remainder of the film will only *appear* to be objective.

Berton's argument with Kelvin at the swing introduces two further aspects of the film that Tarkovsky handles elusively. Kelvin says that his clear goal is to assess whether or not the station should be closed down and possibly to bombard the ocean with heavy radiation as a last resort. When he gets to the station, he discovers Gibarian's film, in which Gibarian also suggests bombarding the ocean with radiation. However, when Kelvin meets with Snaut after he has put the first Hari into the rocket, Snaut tells him that the 'visitors', as Hari and her ilk are called, only started to appear *after* the ocean had been bombarded with radiation.

The other aspect of the meeting at the swing which sets up a further puzzle is Berton's reaction to Kelvin's plan to irradiate the ocean. 'I am not an advocate of knowledge at any price,' he angrily retorts. 'Knowledge is only valid when it's based on morality.' Yet when Kelvin meets Sartorius for the first time, outside the latter's laboratory on the station, he takes a position somewhat similar to Berton's, mocking Sartorius for his talk of 'duty' and 'truth' and calling him 'inhuman'. It is almost as if the ocean were somehow subtly at work, distorting reality and clouding both the judgment and the humanity of the characters.

Hari is a character inextricably linked to both the seeming inconsistencies in the narrative and the idea that knowledge is based on morality. When she first appears, she tells Kelvin that he is 'running around all dishevelled, like Snaut', which begs the question: has she met Snaut already? And if so, how, as she is a product of Kelvin's past and his conscience? Similarly, when Hari tells Kelvin that Sartorius revealed how the real Hari died, how could this meeting have happened if she needs to be with Kelvin all the time?

As with Tarkovsky's two previous films, some of the most important narrative moments happen off-screen, such as the recording and sending of Kelvin's encephalogram and Hari's final meeting with Sartorius. This adds to the sense that perhaps Kelvin does not understand the full import of what is happening to him as the film becomes increasingly seen from his point of view, although Snaut, ever conciliatory, seems to be sympathetic to what Kelvin is going through (although Snaut's visitor is never shown).

Kelvin, perhaps inevitably, is headed for some sort of personal crisis, which starts to manifest when Hari commits suicide by drinking liquid oxygen. This is the second time he has found her dead (the first being on Earth ten years previously), and it seems to push him finally over the edge: from now on, time and space become increasingly unreliable. After Hari resurrects,[114] we next see her and Kelvin in Kelvin's room, but they are wearing different clothes, so it is obviously sometime later, but we have no idea of how much time has elapsed. Kelvin tells Hari he wants to live with her on the station, but he has already agreed to the encephalogram that will destroy her and the other visitors (does he now regret agreeing to record the encephalogram, one wonders?). Kelvin is then shown wandering about in his pyjamas, where he meets Snaut by one of the outer portholes that look down onto the ocean. Snaut tells him that the encephalogram has been sent and appears to be working. Kelvin is then helped back to his room by Snaut and Hari, with his fever worsening: he imagines several Haris in his room, as well as his dead mother and the family dog.

This then leads to a scene in which Kelvin 'meets' his mother in what appears to be the dacha, but a variation of it that includes a number of items of furniture from the station. It is the second of the film's 'endings', the first being the library scene (*see below*), in which Kelvin attempts reconciliation with those he feels he has wronged: Hari and his parents. We know that Kelvin's mother is from the past, as we have only seen her before (outside of the photograph) in the home movie (*again, see below*); although Kelvin's mother behaves kindly towards him, she reproaches him gently for not calling, and for 'leading some sort of strange life'. The scene has a strange poignancy to it, somewhat reminiscent of the scene between Andrei and the ghost of Theophanes in *Andrei Rublev*. But in the former film, Theophanes seems to visit Andrei in order to console him at a moment of crisis; in *Solaris*, there is little comfort or reconciliation between Kelvin and his mother. That appears to happen in the 'final' ending, that of Kelvin's apparent return to Earth, where he visits the dacha. We return to a recapitulated version of the film's opening, although now it is winter. Kelvin falls to his knees in front of his father and hugs him. As the camera pulls up and away from the house to reveal that it is on an island in the ocean of Solaris, Kelvin's appears to have learnt to love and forgive. It is the final narrative riddle in a film whose richness would be the less without them. Is Tarkovsky trying to suggest that, however objective and solid the world seems, the real dramas take place on the subjective level where we are all continually confronting our own 'visitors'?

The Earth

But *Solaris* is not only a film whose narrative texture is riddled with such quietly disconcerting conundrums. The library scene, the first of the film's 'endings', is the film's moral – and perhaps dramatic – centre of gravity. The library is a repository of all that's good on earth: art, literature, culture and nature (in the form of paintings of it). It is a conscious echo of the dacha.

Kelvin, Hari and Sartorius wait for Snaut in the library to celebrate his birthday. When he arrives, an hour and a half late, he is drunk and even more dishevelled than usual (the arm of his suit has been torn). Sartorius proposes a toast to his colleague and to science, but Snaut rebukes him, declaring that 'man needs man' and that exploring space is a waste of time. We don't know what to do in the cosmos, because we don't know what to do with our home planet. That they can't deal with their visitors – their consciences – is the root of their problems on the station. In short, Snaut echoes Montaigne's dictum that we go outside of ourselves, because we do not know what is within us.[115] If there is anyone on the station who *does* know what is within us, it is Hari, and that is love.

Her increasing self-awareness is revealed in two scenes that rank among Tarkovsky's finest. The home movie shows her the 'real' Hari for the first and only time. After shots of

Kelvin's mother and father, and Kelvin himself as a boy, Hari is seen outside the dacha. She waves (presumably it is Kelvin who is filming her). In a closer shot, she turns to the camera and gives the faintest hint of a smile. The sadness in her expression speaks volumes: she has learnt the lessons of love, that it can be painful, but with the pain comes self-knowledge. The second scene shows her studying the reproduction on Breughel's *Hunters in the Snow* that hangs in the library. As her gaze explores the painting, we hear earthly sounds birdsong, dogs, distant voices as if Breughel's world has suddenly become animate. It may be a vicarious taste of life on Earth, but it seems to be enough for her.

The birthday party ends in stalemate. Sartorius denies Hari's humanity, Snaut waxes lyrical and quotes *Don Quixote*. At one point, he kisses Hari's hand, as if to acknowledge the seeming hopelessness of their situation. Kelvin is the only one among them to treat Hari as human and, as if to demonstrate his attachment to her, falls on his knees in front of her. Kneeling in Tarkovsky is usually associated with the idea of humility and the possibility that a character may grow and be redeemed. Kelvin's kneeling in the library is the apotheosis of his own journey. In one gesture, he acknowledges his own failings and begs forgiveness. That Sartorius immediately shouts for him to 'Get up!' only makes Kelvin's gesture the more powerful.

Kelvin's father's warning that 'It's dangerous to send people like you [Kelvin] into space' could be taken as a gloomy prediction that human beings will destroy the ecology of other worlds as much as they have done on the Earth. But when he continues to admonish his son, he uses the words 'Everything there is too fragile. Yes, fragile!' Perhaps this is Tarkovsky's way of saying that not only is nature fragile when confronted with a science that has no moral basis with which to restrain it, but that we ourselves are fragile, and are made more so in the process of exploring space, which is little more than a displacement activity for the real work of exploring ourselves. *Solaris* is Tarkovsky's testimony to the need to explore inner space while there is still time.

'I dreamed about her again last night.'

Despite the genre and epic scale of the film, *Solaris* is Tarkovsky's first major foray into autobiography. That he also began work on *Mirror* in 1968 suggests that both films were water drawn from the same well. Perhaps, after articulating his role as a filmmaker in *Andrei Rublev*, Tarkovsky now turned his attention to what exactly an artist working in the cinema should be addressing. After the features of the 1960s, which concerned themselves primarily with Russia's history and the fate of those experiencing it from within, Tarkovsky's first two films of the 1970s – while not ignorant of history, especially *Mirror* – are first and foremost films about family relationships.

Solaris is more autobiographical than may at first appear to be the case. Tarkovsky's first marriage to Irma Rausch ended in 1965 during the production of *Andrei Rublev*, when he left her for Larissa Kizilova. Tarkovsky and Larissa got married in 1970, when *Solaris* was in pre-production; later that year, she gave birth to Tarkovsky's second son, Andrei Jr. Tarkovsky noted in his diary at the start of production the following spring that he was still troubled by the failure of his first marriage: 'I dreamed about her [Irma Rausch] again last night – my heart was really painful.'[116] In one of the film's most powerful moments, the birthday party in the library, Kelvin falls to his knees in front of Hari and clings to her helplessly. In his treatment of Kelvin's relationship to Hari, Tarkovsky is eulogising his marriage to Rausch. At one point, Tarkovsky even wanted Rausch to play the role of Hari,[117] which would have made the film much more confessional, almost on a par with the later *Mirror*.

Tarkovsky's regrets over his first marriage are linked to his relationship with his parents. 'They blame me for [my divorcing] Ira, I can feel that,' he notes in his diary.[118] In the same entry, he analyses his feelings for his mother and father: 'It's patently clear that I have a complex about my parents. I don't feel adult when I'm with them. And I don't think they consider me adult either. Our relations are somehow tortured, complicated, unspoken. It's not straightforward, any of it. I love them dearly, but I've never felt at ease with them, or their equal. I think they're shy of me too, even though they love me.' A little later, he muses 'Whose fault is it? Theirs, or perhaps mine. Everybody's, up to a point.'[119] After reminding himself that he does indeed love his parents, his sister Marina and eldest son Arseny (Senka, his child by Rausch), he berates himself: 'A stupor comes over me and I can't utter my feelings [for them]. My love is not active, somehow.'[120]

Kelvin spends much of *Solaris* in a similar stupor. He is prickly with his father in the scene just after they have watched Berton's movie; his father admits 'We don't talk much, you and I,' to which Kelvin responds 'I'm glad to hear you say that, albeit on the last day [before Kelvin's departure for Solaris].' The conversation is conducted in what would become a familiar device, namely Kelvin and his father frequently facing away from one another while talking. At the film's end, Kelvin returns to what appears to be Earth and falls to his knees in front of his father in the doorway of the dacha, much as he had done with Hari on the space station. Kelvin is returning home to seek forgiveness; to underscore the point, Tarkovsky quotes Rembrandt's painting *The Return of the Prodigal Son*.[121]

Kelvin's relationship to his mother in the film is not so prominent, mainly because she is only identified as his mother in the scene towards the end of the film, when Kelvin is delirious. We have learnt prior to this from Kelvin showing the home movie to Hari that the blonde woman in the film is his mother, and that she died before he and Hari met. Hari immediately disputes Kelvin's claim, saying that she remembers his mother, who hated her. Kelvin is clearly pained to recall the hostilities between the two women, and tells Hari what happened between him and the 'real' Hari back on Earth ten years previously. Although Kelvin's mother is obviously 'distant' – a criticism often made of Tarkovsky's own mother[122] – due to her death, when she does finally appear in a dialogue scene in the film (the 'delirium' scene), she is gentle and nurturing towards her son, washing his arm and asking him 'Why do you hurt us?' Evidently, Kelvin dreams of her during his illness because she can give him what Hari – either the real Hari, or her neutrino copies on board the station – cannot. Indeed, Kelvin's mother behaves almost like a lover towards him in this scene, heightening its ambiguity. The blurring of the wife/mother roles – a device which Tarkovsky would use in later films – perhaps owes its origin to the fact that Irma Rausch bore a striking physical resemblance to Maria Ivanovna.[123]

It is these familial strains that give *Solaris* its humanity at the same time as being one of the principal sources of the film's gentle melancholy. Yet, in attempting to deal with the ongoing problem of his relationship with his parents and the ghost of his first marriage, Tarkovsky produced a film of deep pathos and power. But *Solaris* did not exorcise all of Tarkovsky's demons; that would be the task of his next film, *Mirror*.

Mirror (1974)

THE FAMILY II

Alternate Titles: *A White, White Day* (working title); *Confession* (Original screenplay title); *The Mirror*

Russian Title: *Zerkalo*

Production Company: Mosfilm, Unit 4

Producer: Erik Waisberg

Director: Andrei Tarkovsky

Screenplay: Andrei Tarkovsky & Alexander Misharin

Director of Photography: Georgy Rerberg

Editor: Ludmila Feiginova

Assistant Directors: Larissa Tarkovskaya, V Karchekno, Maria Chugunova

Art Director: Nikolai Dvigubsky

Special Effects: Yuri Potapov

Costumes: Nelly Fomina

Make-Up: Vera Rudina

Music: Eduard Artemyev; JS Bach: 'Das alte Jahr vergangen ist' BWV 614, from *Orgelbüchlein*, *St John Passion* BWV 245, No.1, 'Herr, unser Herscher', No. 33, 'Und siehe da, der Vorhang im Tempel zeriß'; Pergolesi: *Stabat Mater* 'Quando corpus morietur'; Purcell: *The Indian Queen* 'They tell us that your mighty powers'

Sound: Semyon Litvinov

Narrator (Alexei): Innokenti Smoktunovsky. Arseny Tarkovsky's poems read by the author.

Cast: Margarita Terekhova (Maria, Alexei's mother/Natalya, Alexei's wife), Maria Tarkovskaya (Alexei's mother as an old woman), Ignat Daniltsev (Ignat/Alexei at 12), Philip Yankovsky (Alexei aged five), Oleg Yankovsky (Alexei's Father), Nikolai Grinko (Ivan Gavrilovich, male colleague at printers), Alla Demidova (Lisa), Yuri Nazarov (Military instructor), Anatoly Solonitsyn (country doctor), Larissa Tarkovskaya (Nadezhda Petrovna, the rich doctor's wife), Tamara Ogorodnikova (woman in Pushkin & deathbed/sickbed scene), Olga Kizilova (redhead), Alexander Misharin (doctor in deathbed/sickbed scene), Yuri Sventikov (Asafiev, the orphan), T Reshetnikova, E del Bosque, L Correcher, A Gutierrez, D Garcia, T Pames, Teresa del Bosque, Tatiana del Bosque (Spanish twins), Andrei Tarkovsky (Alexei on his deathbed/sickbed) (uncredited)

Shot: July 1973–March 1974

Running Time: 106 mins

First Screening: Moscow 1974 (Industry screening)

USSR Release: April 1975

First Screening in West: Paris, January 1978

Release in West: 1978

Awards: Best film of the Year, French Critics' Association, 1978

Storyline

Twelve-year-old Ignat turns on the television. He watches a programme in which a boy who stutters badly is cured by hypnotism. The hypnotist gets him to repeat his name and then say 'I can speak.'

The opening credits roll over a black screen to Bach's

prelude 'Das alte Jahr vergangen ist.'

Maria, Alexei's mother, is sitting on a fence outside the dacha. A voice-over by Alexei informs us that she is waiting for her husband – Alexei's father – to return home from the war. A country doctor passes by and flirts with her. A mysterious wind gets up as he departs.

Maria and the children are seen inside the dacha as Arseny Tarkovsky's poem 'First Meetings' is read in voice-over by the poet himself. Maria summons the children outside: the barn is on fire.

The first dream: a wind blows along the edge, or out of, the forest; Maria washes her hair as plaster falls from the ceiling. She catches her reflection in a mirror, but it is not herself as she is that she sees, but herself as an old woman. An unidentified character warms their hand against a fire.

Alexei speaks to his mother on the phone. She tells him that Liza, with whom she worked at the printing works, has died. As the camera moves through the seemingly empty flat, a French poster for *Andrei Rublev* can be seen.

Maria runs through the rain to the printing works. She learns that the mistake she saw has somehow not gone to press, much to her relief. The poem 'From morning on I waited yesterday' is read in voice-over. Liza accuses Maria of being just like Maria Timofeyevna from Dostoyevsky's *The Devils*. Maria flees to the shower block.

In the flat, Alexei and Natalya are arguing. He tells her that she looks like his mother, and we see a shot of Maria walking towards the dacha. Back in the flat, Alexei urges Natalya to remarry. It is then revealed that some Spanish friends are in the next room. Alexei asks Natalya to intervene before the reminiscences cause an argument.

We then cut to newsreel from the time of the Spanish Civil War – a bullfight, children being evacuated. This is followed by the Soviet balloon ascent of 1934 and the aviator Chkalov's return to Moscow after his flight across the North Pole (1937). Pergolesi's *Stabat Mater* can be heard on the soundtrack.

The 12-year-old Alexei[124] looks through a Leonardo monograph.

Ignat helps his mother to pick up coins when she drops her purse. He tells her that he feels as though he has been there before. After his mother leaves, a mysterious woman and her maid appear in the flat. The woman gets Ignat to read Pushkin's 1836 letter to the philosopher Chaadayev[125] about Russia's role and destiny. The woman vanishes, leaving only a heat mark from her cup of tea on the table to attest to her presence.

Ignat's grandmother (Maria) calls at the flat, but strangely fails to recognise Ignat. Alexei telephones. He asks Ignat if he knows any girls and then tells him that he was in love when he was Ignat's age.

We then see the object of the young Alexei's affections, a teenage redhead with chapped lips, walking through a snowy landscape as Purcell's *Indian Queen* plays on the soundtrack. Nearby, Alexei and boys his age are being given shooting lessons at a firing range. One of the boys, an orphan called Asafiev, throws a grenade onto the range. The instructor throws himself onto the grenade. It is revealed to be a dummy.

Newsreel footage shows the Red Army crossing Lake Sivash in the Crimea in 1943. The poem 'Life, Life' is read in voice-over.

Asafiev reaches the top of the hill above the firing range.

Further newsreel shows the tanks rolling in to liberate Prague in 1945; the body of Hitler's double; fireworks in Moscow; the mushroom cloud rising over Hiroshima.

A small bird lands on Asafiev's head.

More newsreel shows Mao's Cultural Revolution in China, and the Sino-Russian border conflict on Damansky Island in 1969.

The young Alexei is looking at the Leonardo monograph again. Maria chops wood. The father returns home from the Front. Alexei and his sister Marina run into his arms. Bach's *St John Passion* can be heard on the soundtrack as we cut to Leonardo's Portrait of Ginevra de Benci.

In the flat, Alexei and Natalya discuss who should have custody of Ignat. Outside, Ignat sets fire to the bush in the courtyard.

The second dream: the forest is agitated by the wind again; Alexei as a small boy tries to enter the dacha; Maria chops wood in an outhouse.

Alexei as a 12-year-old accompanies Maria as she tries to sell her earrings to a rich doctor's wife. Alexei thinks of the redhead while he waits; it is revealed that it is she who was warming her hand against the fire. The doctor's wife shows Maria her new baby. She then asks Maria to kill a cock, which she herself can't do as she is pregnant again. Maria kills the bird. We then see her and her husband, Alexei's father. It is revealed that she is levitating over their bed. Maria is then shown fleeing from the doctor's house without taking payment for the earrings. The poem 'Eurydice' is read in voice-over as Maria and Alexei walk along a riverbank.

This leads into the third dream: the wind comes out of the forest again; the five-year-old Alexei enters the dacha; he is seen holding a jug full of milk amid lace hangings and then swimming as Maria washes clothes.

In what appears to be the modern-day flat, a doctor and the two women from the Pushkin scene discuss Alexei's state of health. From his bed, Alexei tells them to leave him alone and releases a small bird into the air.

At the dacha Alexei's father asks Maria if she wants a boy or a girl. Maria thinks for a moment, looking away. Maria as an old woman is seen leading the two small children across a field as the opening of Bach's *St John Passion* plays on the soundtrack.

The music finishes, and the camera slowly tracks further and further into the woods. Fade to black.

Production History

Like Tarkovsky's other most celebrated film, *Andrei Rublev*, *Mirror* had a long and convoluted history between conception, shooting and eventual release. Tarkovsky wrote that, prior to shooting *Mirror*, he had been haunted by a recurring dream: 'I only know that I kept dreaming the same dream about the house where I was born. I dreamed... as if I was walking into it, or rather, not into it but around it all the time. These dreams were terribly real, although I knew even then that I was only dreaming... I believed that this feeling carried some material sense, something very important, for why should a dream pursue a man so?'[126] Tarkovsky spent a number of years trying to grapple with these dreams and give them coherent form.

The earliest scenes – some of the mother's scenes and the firing range – were written in 1964, while Tarkovsky was preparing *Andrei Rublev*.[127] Tarkovsky at the time was apparently thinking of writing a novella about his childhood experiences, centring around the shell-shocked military instructor who memorably survived into the final film. When Tarkovsky and his co-author, Alexander Misharin, first proposed the project to Mosfilm in late 1967, the figure of Tarkovsky's mother had become the person around whom the film would be built. Tarkovsky and Misharin wrote the first draft of the script in February 1968 while staying at the film-makers' retreat at Repino. Central to the script was an inter-view with Tarkovsky's mother, to be filmed with a hidden camera, in which she would be asked various questions covering topics as diverse as the war, her memories of her own mother, art, the meaning of life, feminism, boxing and UFOs. Mosfilm, however, turned the project down and, by the autumn, Tarkovsky had begun working on *Solaris* instead.

The project, however, refused to leave Tarkovsky alone, and, in 1970, he published some of his recollections as a short story entitled *A White Day*. This offended Misharin, despite the fact that the story was comprised of material written before their writing stint in early 1968, and the two men were not on speaking terms for a long while thereafter. The publication of the story may have prompted Grigory Chukrai, the head of Mosfilm's experimental fourth unit, to ask Tarkovsky for the script. Although he was about to start work on *Solaris*, Tarkovsky felt *A White Day* dogging him almost constantly: 'Whatever happens, I must make *The White Day*... I think constantly about [it]... If only I had finished *Solaris*, and it isn't even started.'[128] By the summer of 1971, while he was bogged down in the seemingly interminable problems of *Solaris*, Tarkovsky was discussing *A White Day* with Chukrai and dreaming ever more strongly of shooting it: 'I so want to make *The White Day*',[129] 'I want to start work on a new picture [i.e. *The White Day/Mirror*]. I'm fed up with *Solaris*'.[130]

His diary contains frequent further references to the project throughout the remainder of 1971 and into 1972. By September of that year, the project was heading for a start date and the film finally got the go-ahead six months later, possibly due to what appears to have been a slight thaw during the early days in office of the new head of Goskino,

Filip Yermash, who told Tarkovsky 'You can film whatever you want.'[131] Tarkovsky's intimations that he was about to make a film of tremendous personal – and possibly artistic – importance are revealed in a diary entry for 23 March 1973, when he wrote 'the time has come when I am ready to make the most important work of my life'.[132] Permission to develop the shooting script – effectively greenlighting the film – was given three days later.

Filming started in July 1973, with the outdoor summer scenes at the dacha.[133] Progress was slow, with only 22 minutes of footage being shot in the first six weeks. Tarkovsky received an angry telegram from Mosfilm, chastising him for his lack of progress, but their censure seems to have had no effect on the work rate. A significant factor in this state of affairs was Tarkovsky's constant rewriting of the script. There was never a single draft that everyone worked from: Tarkovsky brought scraps of paper to the set every day on which he had written what he wanted to shoot that day.

Tarkovsky did not see any of the rushes until September, when he returned to Moscow after a break in filming. Although he remained dissatisfied with some of the material, he was open to suggestions made by bosses and colleagues at the studio. Two significant things changed at this stage: the interview with Tarkovsky's mother was dropped (it was never shot) and Margarita Terekhova's performance as Maria, Alexei's mother in the childhood scenes, was so well received that Tarkovsky wrote some new scenes for her as Alexei's estranged wife Natalya in the present-day scenes. Filming resumed in November and lasted until the following March. Almost the last thing to be shot was the scene with the curing of the stuttering boy.

Editing presented numerous major problems. Given the lack of a firm script, the film metamorphosed into around 20 different versions. Tarkovsky was not happy with any of them, at one stage calling the film 'shit' in his work diary. The film's title acted as a barometer of Tarkovsky's frequent changes of mind: back in 1968, it had been called *Confession*, which was then changed to *A White, White Day* (which was the title used on the clapperboard during shooting), but Tarkovsky didn't like these, finding them 'pretentious' and 'limp'. He considered *Redemption* ('a bit flat'), *Why Are You Standing So Far Away?* was 'better, but obscure' and *Martyrology*, which was his favourite for a time, although he noted that 'nobody knows what it means, and when they find out, they won't allow it'.[134] Tarkovsky first refers to the film as *Mirror* in March 1974,[135] when editing was getting under way.

Various edits were screened at Mosfilm between March and July, with the film's running time dropping from 130 to 106 minutes. But Tarkovsky and his editor, Ludmila Feiginova, were doing much more than merely tightening the edit. Episodes migrated from one end of the film to the other: the opening scene with the stuttering boy, for instance, was originally in the middle until Feiginova realised it would work well as an opening, acting almost like an epigraph. The film met with a hugely divided response from Tarkovsky's colleagues. He was asked to make clear distinctions between the past and the present, between dreams and memories, and to 'relieve the entire film of mysticism'.[136] By August, Tarkovsky was refusing to make any more changes, feeling that the film had finally gelled.

Kremnev, the new head of the fourth unit, called the film a work of art, but these supportive voices were few and far between. The official position on the film was that it was 'an obvious artistic failure'.[137] It was released quietly in April 1975, with Goskino making every effort to thwart the film's distribution abroad: Cannes asked for the film twice (in 1974 and again the following year), but were turned down without explanation, possibly because the festival director – who had seen the film in Moscow – had guaranteed that Tarkovsky would be given the Palme d'Or for *Mirror*, which would be a major embarrassment for Goskino. Its first screening in the West was not until January 1978, when a premiere was held in Paris. It was voted the Best Film of the Year and there was even talk of an Oscar nomination. 'Not that I want it,' Tarkovsky remarked in his diary, 'but it would be one in the eye for that idiot Yermash.'[138]

Tarkovsky was so outraged at the treatment the film received that he contemplated giving up making films altogether, but was reassured by the remarkable number of letters from ordinary people who had seen the film. Some were admittedly baffled by it, but others wrote about how much the film had touched them. 'Thank you for *Mirror*,' one woman from Gorky wrote, whose letter is perhaps the most poignant of all the ones that Tarkovsky quotes in *Sculpting in Time*. 'My childhood was like that… only how did you know about it?… in that dark cinema, looking at a piece of canvas lit up by your talent, I felt for the first time in my life that I was not alone.'[139]

Filming the Soul

Tarkovsky's desire to make a film based entirely on a character's memory and inner world goes back, as we have seen, to 1964. 'It occurred to me… that from these properties of memory a new working principle could be developed, on which an extraordinarily interesting film might be built… It would be the story of [the hero's] thoughts, memories and dreams… without his appearing at all.'[140] While Tarkovsky was waiting for *Mirror* to get the go-ahead, he noted in his

129

diary, 'There was a time when I thought that [a] film… is going to be perceived in one and the same way by everyone who sees it… But I was wrong. One has to work out a principle that allows for film to affect people individually. The "total" image must become something private. The basic principle… is, I think, that as little as possible has actually to be shown, and from that little the audience has to build up an idea of the rest.'[141]

Although Tarkovsky had been adhering to this rule of showing as little as possible long before he wrote that diary entry, *Mirror* marks a new phase in his narrative technique, as it requires the viewer to be more active than usual in trying to work out what exactly is going on. One critic described *Mirror* as the nearest anyone had come to filming the soul.[142]

Poetry, Memory and Dreams

A brief overview of the apparently loose structure of the film will go some way to orientating the viewer on this, the supposedly most difficult of Tarkovsky's films. Although plotless in conventional terms, the film does in fact have a remarkably coherent form. The film has three time periods – the present day, the mid-1930s and the Second World War – and combines real time with dreams, memories, visions and newsreel. The colour coding generally acts as a guide: the present-day scenes are usually in colour and the dreams and visions are often in black and white or sepia, although this is not always the case. Lack of colour stock meant that Tarkovsky had to film certain scenes, such as Alexei and Natalya's last conversation in the flat, in monochrome, while the first scene after the credits, clearly a memory, is in colour. This lack of clarity over what we are watching was one of the main criticisms Tarkovsky faced when the film was being completed, but it also adds considerably to the film's richness and mystery.

Mirror's prologue is the curing of the stutterer, which, being placed at the start of the film, acts as a metaphor. When the boy says 'I can speak', this is clearly also Tarkovsky speaking as well. The fact that we are witnessing an actual curing makes the scene immeasurably more moving (like many things in Tarkovsky, the scene becomes more powerful the more one rewatches it). The scene also establishes that the film is 'happening' in the present. The Bach prelude used in the opening titles, 'Das alte Jahr vergangen ist', was intended for use at the New Year, perhaps suggesting that now that Tarkovsky could 'speak', what is to follow is a new beginning.

The first scene proper shows Alexei's mother sitting on the fence, waiting for her husband, Alexei's father, to return from the war. Alexei's voice-over establishes this as a memory, although is it his mother's or his own imagined recollections of the event? (It cannot be Alexei's own direct memory, as we see him and his sister Marina as small children, asleep in a hammock nearby.) The doctor's arrival (written especially to get Tarkovsky's favourite actor, Anatoly Solonitsyn, into the film) is both a memory of yearning for the father and, in the mysterious wind that gets up at the end of the scene, a celebration of the natural world.

The use of Arseny Tarkovsky's poem 'First Meetings' at this point not only offers a comment on the mother's desire for her husband (the poem celebrates physical love), but also on the way Tarkovsky (junior) has attempted to capture his material: 'Every moment... / was a celebration, like Epiphany/ ... Ordinary objects were at once transfigured.'[143] By presenting moments like the mysterious wind which blows up as the doctor leaves (and which will recur throughout the film, coming out of/going along the edge of the forest), and the subsequent barn fire without any conventional narrative context, they are, as the poem suggests 'at once transfigured' into epiphanies.

The other three poems in the film also serve to transfigure the apparently mundane world and also to comment upon either the events or Alexei's feelings towards those events. The second poem, 'From morning on I waited yesterday'[144] is full of foreboding about the disintegration of a relationship; it is aptly placed, as the printing works, where the poem is quoted, is a place full of foreboding. Although this, like the other poems, is read by their author, Tarkovsky's father, they raise the question as to whose 'voice' it is: are they Maria's thoughts, or those of her eternally absent husband? (The same can be said of the first poem, too. Is it his longing for her? Or hers for him? The fact that Maria is seen crying at the end of the sequence could suggest the latter, but Tarkovsky, as ever, lets us make up our own minds.)

The last two poems move away from the strictly personal, dealing with the poet's duties in the context of the wider world. 'Life, Life'[145] is read over newsreel footage of the Red Army crossing Lake Sivash in the Crimea in 1943, and reveals the poet to be conscious both of history and his own role within it: 'All of us are standing on the seashore now,/And I am one of those who haul the nets/When a shoal of immortality comes in'. There is an irony here, too, in that the poem announces 'On earth there is no death/All are immortal', while we are looking at men who may well have been killed the very same day (as was the cameraman who shot the sequence). In placing various generations of the family at the same table, the poem uses the same kind of collapsing of epochs that the film employs, while the final lines see the poet leaving the family in the service of his calling, which Tarkovsky, his father and Alexei all do.

The final poem, 'Eurydice',[146] continues this idea of the artist restlessly pursuing his muse, while acknowledging the limitations of both his art and the frailty of the body. It is, in effect, a celebration of the transitory, an interpretation reinforced by the fact that we see the young Alexei in his grandfather's house while the poem is being read, and we know from the voice-over that this is a recurring dream that the adult Alexei experiences, a doomed attempt to recapture the paradise lost of childhood.

Following on from the barn sequence is the first of the film's three dreams, presumably being dreamt by the adult Alexei. The camera tracks along the edge of the forest as the mysterious wind returns, blowing along its edge (or even out of it?). The young Alexei then wakes up and makes his way to his parents' room. A shirt is thrown across the doorway of their room, suggesting hurried disrobing, but rather than show the act of love, Tarkovsky gives us the striking metaphor of Maria (the mother) washing her hair as plaster falls from the ceiling.[147] This celebrated sequence shows Tarkovsky's affection for fire and water to great effect, but also his concern for surfaces: watching it, one can almost feel the weight of the plaster as it falls in slow motion, or the dampness of the wall down which the water courses. For Tarkovsky, there was no such thing merely as 'backdrop' or 'scenery'; everything, even an old wall, has an important part to play in helping to shape his poetic universe. A shot of a hand shielding a burning branch concludes this, the first 'movement' of *Mirror*. The musical analogy is apt, as Tarkovsky acknowledged that he 'used the laws of music as the film's organising principle'.[148]

The second and third dreams are also Alexei's. The former shows the dacha, together with a voice-over from Alexei saying that he has the dream with 'amazing regularity', and that in the dream he never succeeds in entering the house. Coming as it does after Natalya's complaint that nothing miraculous ever seems to happen to her (the story of Moses and the burning bush having come up in conversation), Alexei's admission that he can't enter his grandfather's house suggests that he is as lost as Natalya, although this would seem to be a fact that he has managed to keep hidden from her.

The final dream has the poem 'Eurydice' laid over it. The poem suggests that, although Alexei in the dream has now managed to enter the dacha, the world of his childhood is as lost as Eurydice herself.

The film moves into the present-day after 'First Meetings' has been read, in which the ever-offscreen Alexei talks on the phone with his mother. She tells him that Liza, her colleague from her printing works days, has just died. This leads into the printing works sequence, which must either be the mother's memory, or Alexei's imagining of it, as he wasn't present. This device establishes one of the organising tools of the film, namely that the present-day scenes act as precursors to scenes set in the past. For instance, the next scene in the flat shows Alexei telling Natalya that she looks like his mother; 'apparently that's the reason we divorced', she replies, and this takes us into a shot of Maria carrying a pail of water towards the dacha with the unidentified man from the fire scene.

The printing works marks the beginning of *Mirror*'s central movement, which will conclude with the firing-range sequence. The era of Stalin's terror is hinted at through the use of sepia and the numerous fences, doorways and drab corridors that Maria has to negotiate before she can reach the office.[149] Again, things happen in slight slow motion, with Maria's breathing prominent in the mix. This, a device Tarkovsky would come to use more in his later films, immediately makes us close to the character, sharing in their interior experience. The other striking aspect of this introduction to the printing works scene is its beauty: it is as if Tarkovsky were content just to watch Margarita Terekhova running through the rain, down steps, across yards, into corridors. Here, Tarkovsky reveals the presence of beauty in something that is apparently mundane and, para-doxically (given the period), also potentially fatal for Maria if the mistake she thinks she's made has gone to press. Showering afterwards, Maria recalls a fire in the field; a shot of the fire closes this movement of the film.

The clash between Maria and Liza (the woman whose death prompts the whole flashback) shows two typically Tarkovskian characters, in that, when they fail to communi-cate properly with each other, they fall back on literary quotations to articulate themselves. Liza tells Maria she reminds her of Maria Timofeyevna from Dostoyevsky's *The Devils.* Literary allusions occur frequently in the film: Maria asks the country doctor whether he knows Chekhov's story *Ward 6*; Liza quotes Dante after Maria refuses to come out of the shower; and Alexei disparagingly calls Natalya's new partner – an unpublished writer – 'Dostoyevsky'.

The Newsreels: History as Film

The following sequence (or movement, to retain the musical analogy), is one of the most remarkable in the film. While Alexei urges Natalya to remarry, a group of Spanish friends in the next room takes us into the first of the film's newsreel sequences. Unlike the rest of the film, the newsreel sequences are placed in chronological order, beginning with the Spanish Civil War in the mid-1930s. Tarkovsky sought long and hard for newsreel images that were fresh, not over-exposed in the historical consciousness. The shots of the Spanish children being evacuated to the Soviet Union are remarkably poignant: a line of children march down the street carrying their suitcases, almost autonomous already from their parents; a father kisses his daughter repeatedly; a little girl looks towards the camera as a train's whistle blows.

We then cut to one of the most beautiful sequences of the film, that of the record-breaking Soviet balloon ascent of 1934. As we have noted, balloons had previously appeared in Tarkovsky, most notably in the prologue to *Andrei Rublev* and in the dacha scenes in *Solaris*. But here Tarkovsky's love of flight is given free reign: the shots take on a strange life of their own, almost as if Tarkovsky sees in the footage something not merely of historical or national interest, but rather something eternal, a feeling heightened by the use of Pergolesi's *Stabat Mater* on the soundtrack. The poignancy of the sequence is underscored by the fact that the balloonists all died in the ascent. The flight theme is continued with shots of the aviator Chkalov's triumphant return to Moscow after his flight over the North Pole in 1937. A sense of loss attends the celebrations, as all Soviet viewers would have been aware that Chkalov, a Soviet national hero, died in a plane crash 18 months later. In using these particular newsreels, Tarkovsky is subtly equating history, both personal and national, with loss and a sense of sadness.

The subsequent newsreel sequences bring Soviet history almost up to the time the film was made. The Great Patriotic War is represented by the Lake Sivash sequence; the liberation of Prague; the body of Hitler's double lying in the ruins of Berlin; a man on crutches (perhaps an acknowledgement that when Tarkovsky's father returned from the war, he was on crutches due to losing a leg); and fireworks in Moscow celebrating the end of the war in Europe. The euphoria is short-lived, as this almost immediately cuts to a shot of the atomic bomb destroying Hiroshima. Post-war history is captured with newsreel of Mao's Cultural Revolution in the China of the 1960s and the Sino-Russian border conflict of 1969.

Unlike the earlier sequence, these wartime and post-war newsreels are cut into the film in such a way that the orphan Asafiev seems to 'see' them (or at least somehow be aware of them) from where he is standing, either in the firing range, or at the top of the hill where the bird lands on his head. This is simply achieved by having the boy suddenly look to his left, for instance, and then Tarkovsky cuts to Soviet tanks liberating Prague. It is a simple, but effective, device and one that brilliantly brings together the spheres of the personal and the historical. Tarkovsky seems to be suggesting that we are somehow *connected* to history, that we are always a part of it. Indeed, the sense of unseen – perhaps even uncanny – connections between people, history and nature is one of *Mirror*'s finest accomplishments.

The historical context provided by the newsreels is also present in the strange scene of the dark-haired woman who mysteriously appears in the flat and asks Ignat to read Pushkin's letter to Chaadeyev. The letter speaks of Russia's role in saving Europe from the Mongol hordes and fore-shadows the newsreel of Damansky Island. The continued threat from the East suggests that history is not over, but is still going on around us.[150]

Art as Mirror

The first newsreel sequence ends with the young Alexei looking at a monograph of Leonardo's paintings and draw-ings. Art functions in the film in a way similar to the newsreels and the poems, to comment on the action and to provide both a cultural context and to suggest that the characters are linked to this tradition. The works we see most prominently in the film are a self-portrait and the portrait of Ginevra de Benci. The first needs no comment – the film, after all, is a self-portrait – but the use of the second is slightly more ambiguous, as it is presented without a context (in other words, it's not shown to be a close-up of a page from the monograph, although the painting would have probably been in it). Tarkovsky explained that he always found the painting highly ambiguous: one minute the woman looks attractive, the next repellent or sinister, feelings intended to mirror the experience of the young Alexei upon his father's return.

The monograph scene also suggests a simultaneity of periods: Leonardo's own time and the present day somehow existing at the same time. Tarkovsky was apparently inspired to introduce this element into the film after studying a photograph of his sister Marina and her son, which, due to an accidental double exposure, also shows their mother, Maria Ivanovna.[151] The following scene, of Ignat helping his mother to pick up coins that have fallen from her purse, continues this theme. Ignat suffers a small electric shock from one of the coins. He then tells Natalya that he feels 'as if it had already happened', but then adds 'but I've never been here [i.e., on the floor picking up coins] before.' There are other instances in the film: during the first dream, Maria sees herself as an old woman reflected in the mirror; the ending shows her as an old woman but with the children as they were when young; while the firing range scene, cut as it is against the Lake Sivash newsreel, suggests that the boys are already men.

The film also contains scenes that are not dream, memory or present day. The mysterious woman who appears in the flat and asks Ignat to read Pushkin's letter to Chaadeyev was put into the film to add more historical context, but Tarkovsky never explains who she is, or how she so mysteriously appears and then disappears, leaving only a heat mark on the table from her cup of tea. Likewise, Tarkovsky does not explain the scene which portrays Alexei either on his deathbed or sickbed; the woman and her maid are present again. The dialogue here is extremely ambiguous: the doctor says that 'it's a common case' and that the man's wife and child have died suddenly. The woman denies this, saying that no one in his family has died. Other mysteries: Maria's levitation; the old Maria failing to recognise Ignat when she calls at the flat; the bird that lands on Asafiev's head; and the final marriage of past and present, memory and dream when the old Maria leads the two children across the field, being watched by Maria's younger self as she was before the children were born.

Tarkovsky's Confession

The childhood memories that Tarkovsky drew on for *Mirror* fall into three groups: the pre-war scenes set at the dacha; the wartime scenes; and the dreams. The first scene after the opening credits shows Maria waiting on a fence. Alexei describes in voice-over how she would wait for passers-by to reach the bush in the middle of the field: if they turned towards the house, it meant that it was father, returning home; if they carried straight on, it meant that they were not father and that he would never return. This would appear to be one of Tarkovsky's own memories, as he writes that his enduring memories of childhood were of waiting for the war to end and for his father to come home. The barn burning down is also an actual event: it happened when the son of a family friend accidentally started a fire while playing with matches. The dacha itself is taken from Tarkovsky's childhood and was reconstructed on the same foundations as the original. Both its exterior and interior are faithfully reproduced from Tarkovsky's memory and the photographs of Lev Gornung, Tarkovsky's godfather, who photographed the dacha between 1932 and 1935; he also took pictures of Tarkovsky's parents during their summer stays in the country and of Tarkovsky and his sister Marina as small children.[152] In the film, the narrator identifies it as his grandfather's house.

The episode where Maria tries to sell a pair of earrings to a rich doctor's wife takes place in wartime, when Alexei is 12 years old. In reality, Maria Ivanovna apparently went across the Volga one day to sell her earrings, but, unlike Maria in the film, successfully concluded business and returned with a sack of potatoes. Despite this bit of poetic licence, the hardships of Tarkovsky's family, to say nothing of the country as a whole, were real enough, and they remained financially straitened even after the end of the Great Patriotic War. Another wartime episode, that of Alexei's father returning home, was based on Arseny's unexpected return from the Front in the summer of 1943, when Maria was working at a children's camp in Peredelkino, the writer's retreat near Moscow. Again, the hardships of wartime are encapsulated in the briefly glimpsed interior of the dacha, when Maria is chopping wood. Outside, Marina threatens that she'll tell on Alexei for stealing the Leonardo monograph. Tarkovsky's sister once made a similar threat to her brother during their wartime stay at Peredelkino, when the young Tarkovsky apparently cut pictures out of a book.[153]

The dreams mainly concern themselves with the dacha and the young Alexei's attempts to enter it. The one dream in which the location is ambiguous is the first one, which shows Alexei's parents together when his mother washes her hair. The sense here is of Alexei's exclusion from his parents' conjugal bed. As has been noted, Tarkovsky was haunted for years by dreams of the house where he was born, and we can assume that the dreams of the dacha in the film are faithful to the spirit of the dreams that he experienced.

The present-day scenes in Alexei's flat chronicle the aftermath of his marriage to Natalya and his relationship with his mother. Alexei tells Natalya that she looks like his mother and that he always remembers his mother with Natalya's face. 'Apparently that's the reason we divorced,' she quips in response. In reality, Irma Rausch bore a strong resemblance to Maria Ivanovna as she was when she was younger and the two women remained close, even after Tarkovsky left her. 'You only know how to demand,' Natalya accuses him. 'That's because I was brought up by women,' Alexei replies, echoing Tarkovsky's own upbringing.

Alexei and Natalya later discuss custody of Ignat, who lives with his mother, as did Tarkovsky's and Irma's son Arseny (also known as Senka). Natalya tells Alexei that he should visit his son more often, as Ignat is missing him. Alexei wants Ignat to live with him, which Ignat seems reluctant to do and the conversation ends inconclusively. Tarkovsky's own situation was similar. 'What's going on with Senka?' he writes in his diary. 'Ira has done everything she can to stop us seeing each other... Will things ever be all right between Senka and me?'[154] Ignat wanders outside and sets fire to a bush in the yard, which annoys Alexei; furthermore, the boy is not doing well at school, which troubles Alexei: 'If he doesn't finish school he'll end up being drafted.' Compare this with Tarkovsky's diary entry for 13 June 1970: 'I took Senka to school. My impression was that he had failed [his exams].'[155] And on 1 September that year, Tarkovsky complains that Senka is 'dreadfully scatterbrained, doesn't concentrate, doesn't pay attention'.[156]

There are problems, however, with a straight autobiographical reading of *Mirror*. Although Tarkovsky claimed that 'everything happened, nothing was invented', his friend and collaborator Olga Surkova remarked[157] that the film was in fact pseudo-autobiography, as it said nothing about Tarkovsky's relationship with his second wife and second son. (Perhaps the poster for *Andrei Rublev* that can be seen in Alexei's flat is a hint that maybe *Mirror* is Tarkovsky's life up until his second feature?) The dacha is likewise a collage of two separate locations. Alexei tells us in the film that the house, in which he was born, belongs to his grandfather. However, the dacha we see in the film is not the house in which Tarkovsky was born, but the villa where the Tarkovskys summered at Ignatievo, which belonged to the Gorchakovs, who would become family friends. Tarkovsky was indeed born in his grandfather's house, but that was in Zavrazhie. To be fair to Tarkovsky, though, we must note that the reasons for choosing Ignatievo over Zavrazhie for the film may well have been practical, as the house of his birth had been submerged when the area was flooded during the development of a hydroelectric project in 1950.[158] The fence on which Maria sits when she talks to the country doctor and the well from which she drinks when the shed burns down are also taken from Zavrazhie and transplanted to Ignatievo.

One major scene cannot be classed as autobiographical in the strict sense, as Tarkovsky was not present when it took place, namely the printing works episode. While it is possible that Tarkovsky chose to have Liza recite the opening lines from Dante's *Inferno* during this sequence – 'Halfway through this earthly life I awoke to find myself in a dark wood' – as a possible reference to his own perceived midlife crisis, the sequence is more properly described as a cross between a scene from his mother's life and a Soviet urban legend, in that the printing error is something Maria Ivanovna heard about as happening to someone else (the mistake supposedly being a misspelling of 'Stalin' as 'Sralin', meaning 'shitting man').

There are other scenes in the film where the autobiographical element has been subordinated to the fictive or poetic process. The pre-credits scene of the healing of the stutterer, while a mock documentary scene staged by Tarkovsky, is actually a real healing – the boy and the hypnotist are not acting – and its purpose in the film is metaphorical. When the boy says 'I can speak', it is clearly Tarkovsky himself talking. The end of the first dream, where Maria sees herself as an old woman, is one of the ways in which Tarkovsky links the two timeframes of the film, while echoing his father's poem 'I only need my immortality for my blood to go on flowing from age to age', recited over the Lake Sivash newsreel. The same device recurs at the end of the film, where Alexei's father asks Maria if she wants a boy or a girl and Maria looks away, to see herself as an old woman again, but with her as yet unborn children.

The 'Pushkin' scene, in which a mysterious woman gets Ignat to read Pushkin's 1836 letter to Chaadeyev, was added, according to Tarkovsky, in order to provide a historical dimension to the film. (This was also the reason for the addition of the newsreel sequences.) The mysterious woman reappears in what is perhaps the film's least explicable scene, that of Alexei on either his sickbed or deathbed. The doctor (played by Tarkovsky's co-screenwriter, Alexander Misharin) says that 'a mother dies suddenly, then the man's wife and child. A few days, and the man is no more,' to which the woman replies, 'But no one died in his family.' Is the doctor being rhetorical here, not referring to Alexei specifically? It would seem so, as one of the women asks Alexei (played by Tarkovsky himself, although only his chest and arm are seen)[159] what will happen to his mother if he doesn't get up. The conversation then moves on to discuss conscience, memories and guilt, which would seem to point to Tarkovsky's own position. '*Mirror* was not an attempt to talk about myself,' he wrote on *Sculpting in Time*. 'It was about my feelings towards people dear to me; about my relationship with them; my perpetual pity for them and my own inadequacy – my feeling of duty left unfulfilled.'[160] Whether Alexei is dying in this scene is highly ambiguous. Tarkovsky wrote that the film was comprised of episodes that the narrator remembered 'at an extreme moment of crisis [which] causes him pain up to the last minute'.[161] If the scene is indeed a deathbed one, then it takes on a prophetic air, as would *Stalker* and *The Sacrifice* after it.

Stalker (1979)

Triptych I

Alternate Title: *The Wish Machine* (Working title)
Production Company: Mosfilm, Unit 2
Production Supervisor: Alexandra Demidova
Director: Andrei Tarkovsky
Screenplay: Arkady and Boris Strugatsky [and Andrei Tarkovsky, uncredited], based on their novel, *Roadside Picnic*
Director of Photography: Alexander Knyazhinsky (1978), Georgy Rerberg (1977, uncredited), Leonid Kalashnikov (1977, uncredited)
Production Design: Andrei Tarkovsky, Alexander Boym (1977, uncredited), Shavkat Abdusalamov (1977, uncredited)
Editor: Ludmila Feiginova
Assistant Directors: Larissa Tarkovskaya, Maria Chugunova
Music: Eduard Artemyev, Beethoven: *Symphony No.9*, Ravel: *Bolero*, Wagner: *Meistersinger*
Musical Direction: Emil Kachaturian
Costumes: Nelly Fomina
Make-Up: V Lvova
Sound: V Sharun
Cast: Alexander Kaidanovsky (Stalker), Anatoly Solonitsyn (Writer), Nikolai Grinko (Professor), Alissa Freindlikh

(Stalker's Wife), Natasha Abramova (Monkey), F Yurna, E Kostin, R Rendi
Shot: February–September 1977, June–November 1978
Running Time: 161 mins
First Screening: Moscow, May 1979
USSR Release: May 1979
First Screening in West: Cannes Film Festival, 1980
Release in West: 1980
Awards: Special Jury Prize, FIPRESCI Prize, Ecumenical Jury Prize, Cannes Film Festival, 1980; Luchino Visconti Prize (awarded at the 1980 Taormina Festival)

Storyline

Part One

The opening credits play over a shot of a down-at-heel bar, filmed in sepia. A caption then appears, explaining the mysterious appearance of 'The Zone' in the small country in which the film takes place. We then see Stalker, his wife and their daughter asleep in a big brass bed in a dingy flat. A train passes. A fragment of Wagner's *Meistersinger* can be heard. Stalker gets up and dresses. His wife argues with him in the kitchen, but he leaves.

He meets Writer in the docks, who is drinking and talking to a smartly dressed young woman about the lack of mystery in modern life. Stalker sends Writer's lady friend away. The two men go to the bar, where Professor is waiting for them. Writer says that he wants to go to the Zone for the sake of inspiration, while Professor claims to be motivated by scientific curiosity.

The men leave the bar and drive in a jeep to an abandoned industrial area, avoiding the police as they go. They follow a train into a heavily guarded floodlit area, where they are shot at by the police. They journey into the Zone on a railcar. Writer asks if they will be followed, but Stalker reassures him that the authorities fear the Zone 'like the plague'.

The film cuts to colour. Stalker refers to the Zone as 'home' and goes off to be by himself for a while. Professor tells Writer that Stalker is an ex-convict and that his daughter is some kind of mutant. He mentions that another stalker, Porcupine, became fabulously wealthy and hanged himself after a trip into the Zone. He then describes the Zone – how it mysteriously appeared 20 years earlier, possibly as the result of a meteorite, and that it contains a room where one's innermost wishes can come true. The authorities have been guarding it ever since, allowing access to none.

Stalker returns and the three men continue on their journey. Stalker throws nuts attached to bits of cloth in order to navigate through the Zone's booby traps. Writer wants to walk straight towards the building that contains the Room. Stalker warns him not to. A voice calls out, telling him to stop. Writer returns to the other two. None of them can explain the voice. Stalker tells the two men that people have died in the Zone. They bicker. Professor decides to stay put and wait for the other two to return, but Stalker forbids it.

Part Two

Stalker calls for the other two to join him and creeps along a wall. In voice-over, we hear 'Stalker's Prayer', which asks for Writer and Professor to be given faith, and which goes on to paraphrase the Tao Te Ching celebrating the virtues of weakness and flexibility. Professor wants to go back and collect his rucksack, which he has left behind. Stalker tells him to forget it and they set off again.

They come to a waterfall, nicknamed 'the Dry Tunnel'. Writer notices that Professor has disappeared. They emerge from the Dry Tunnel to find Professor waiting for them. Stalker thinks that they have walked into a trap and urges them to rest. Writer and Professor exchange insults, then discuss art between dozing.

A dream sequence follows, which contains a voice-over (read by Stalker's wife?) from Revelation 6:12–17 as the camera tracks over industrial and military detritus submerged in shallow water. Also visible is a fragment of the Van Eyck brothers' Ghent Altarpiece.

The men arrive in a dark tunnel known as 'the Meat Grinder'. They draw lots to see who will go first. Writer draws the short straw. At the far end of the tunnel, he finds a door. He produces a pistol, but Stalker shouts at him to drop it. Writer goes through into a flooded room. He wades across it. Professor and Stalker follow.

Writer goes ahead into a room containing small sand dunes. Stalker shouts at him to stop. Two birds fly across the room: one vanishes in mid air, while the other lands on one of the small dunes. Writer collapses, suffering a sharp pain to the head. When he recovers, he delivers a monologue about his disgust with his profession and himself.

Stalker recites a poem written by Porcupine's brother (who died in the Meat Grinder). (The poem is 'But there has to be more', actually by Tarkovsky's father.)

The three men argue in a small room that contains a telephone. It rings. Writer answers it. It's a wrong number. Professor then dials the laboratory where he works and speaks with a colleague, saying that he has found something hidden in bunker number four and that he is now on the threshold of 'that place'. His colleague tells Professor that his career is over; he can see Professor hanging himself in jail once they return from the Zone.

Professor thinks that the Room will be misused by both politicians and those bent on saving the world. Writer believes that the world cannot be saved.

Stalker leads them to the threshold of the Room. He tells them to get ready for the most important moment in their lives. Writer declines to go in, as he feels he would be humiliating himself. Professor takes a bomb out of his bag, declaring that the Room will never make anyone happy and that it is better to destroy it than have it fall into the wrong hands. Stalker tries to snatch the bomb from Professor. Writer breaks up the tussle, accusing Stalker of being only interested in money and the fact that he can play God in the Zone. Stalker denies these are his motives. Writer announces that the real reason why Porcupine hanged himself was that he realised his deepest wish was for money, not the desire to save his brother.

The three men sit down outside the Room. Professor dismantles his bomb and throws the parts into the Room, where it begins to rain inside. The sound of a train passing can be heard, along with a fragment of Ravel's *Bolero*.

The film cuts back to sepia: Stalker's wife meets the men at the bar. Stalker accompanies her and their crippled daughter, Monkey, back to their flat.

The film cuts back to colour to show Monkey apparently walking. It is revealed that she is riding on her father's shoulders.

Back at the flat, and again in sepia, Stalker laments exhaustedly that no one has any faith any more. His wife addresses the audience, telling us about the hardships of life married to a stalker. But she has no regrets, for, if there were no sadness in life, then there would be no happiness either.

Cut to colour: Monkey is reading. She puts the book down; in voice-over, we hear her recite the poem, 'How I Love Your Eyes' by Fyodor Tyuchev. She then seems to move three beakers across the tabletop telekinetically. She rests her head on the table. Outside, a train rattles past, and a snatch of Beethoven's 'Ode to Joy' is heard.

Production History

Tarkovsky first read *Roadside Picnic*, the novel by Arkady and Boris Strugatsky on which *Stalker* is based, in early 1973. He noted in his diary that a 'tremendous' screenplay could be made out of the novel.[162] It is not clear whether he himself wanted to direct the film, but once *Mirror* had been completed and a proposal to film Dostoyevsky's novel *The Idiot* had been turned down, Tarkovsky's thoughts began to return to the Strugatsky brothers' novel. By March 1975, he was in talks with the brothers over the script, and by the autumn, when the proposal was submitted to Mosfilm, it seemed as though the film would go ahead the following summer. At this stage, the project was called *The Wish Machine*.

The usual bureaucratic delays meant that the film did not actually start shooting until February 1977, by which time Tarkovsky was also directing a stage adaptation of *Hamlet* in Moscow. The scenes set in the Zone were originally to have been shot in Isfara, in the Soviet Republic of Tajikistan, but an earthquake there just before shooting was scheduled to begin scuppered the plan and Tarkovsky instead chose to shoot in Estonia. By July 1977, when all the exteriors had been shot, it had become apparent that there was a fault with the film stock and everything had to be scrapped. Tarkovsky started again from scratch, but the production ran into further trouble when the state of the equipment was found to be wanting. Tarkovsky's relationship with Georgy Rerberg, his Director of Photography, was also deteriorating and Rerberg was fired. Although Leonid Kalashnikov took over almost immediately, there was now a major problem in that two-thirds of the budget had already been spent, but they still had very little usable footage. Yermash tried to persuade Tarkovsky to drop the film, but Tarkovsky refused, instead seeking permission to make *Stalker* as a two-part film.[163] This would provide both more money and extend the delivery date. While this application was going through, the film closed down.

Tarkovsky used this opportunity to rewrite the script. In the new version, the Stalker underwent a radical change, from being 'some kind of drug-dealer and poacher... to... a slave, a believer, a pagan of the Zone'.[164] Tarkovsky continued to rewrite the script, even during postproduction, to such an extent that the Strugatskys claimed 'We are not the scriptwriters, he [Tarkovsky] did it all – alone.'[165]

Filming was further delayed when Tarkovsky, perhaps not surprisingly, suffered a heart attack in April 1978, which forced him to spend two months in a sanatorium. Finally, in June, shooting on the film started for the third time. Tarkovsky was also onto his third cameraman, as Kalashnikov had refused to continue working on the film. His replacement was Alexander Knyazhinsky. Shooting was difficult, mainly because the money they had been given for the hypothetical second part of the film had to be used to fund the entire production, and so Tarkovsky was constantly forced to cut corners and pare down the film as much as possible. Filming lasted until November, by which time Tarkovsky had started editing. He became ill again in

February 1979 and at one point thought he was going to die. To Tarkovsky's surprise, *Stalker* was accepted with relatively few changes. The film was completed by May, when it had its first industry screening, and went on release in the Soviet Union the same month. The film was first shown in the West a full year later, at Cannes in May 1980, where it met with an overwhelming response.

Tarkovsky's Triptych

Stalker is the first film in Tarkovsky's 'late' period, which would see his films become pronouncedly more philosophical in tone, and also more minimal in terms of plot and art direction. These last three films are also marked by an ever-lengthening take, as well as by the use of almost imperceptibly slow zooms and an ever greater difficulty in determining whether events portrayed on-screen happen externally or internally. In essence, *Stalker*, and the two films that follow it, are closely linked enough to be said to form a triptych in which Tarkovsky's main theme is the catastrophic state of the world and the desire to avert the looming apocalypse.

As with *Solaris*, Tarkovsky faced problems with the science fiction genre of the Strugatsky's original novel. In *Roadside Picnic*, there are six Zones, to which the various Stalkers go to forage alien equipment (the Zones being perhaps the result of an alien visitation, or 'roadside picnic', 20 years before). In the film, this was whittled down to one, but a number of other elements remain, namely the 'Plague Quarter' (the deserted industrial area where the three men steal the trolley car); mention of the Zone being full of abandoned military vehicles and equipment; the use of the nut-weighted ribbons; the idea that to progress one needs to make significant detours; that the Stalker has a crippled daughter; that the Zone is a place where normal rules of empirical space–time do not apply; and that there is something in the Zone that grants one's innermost wishes.

In the novel and the original script, this was called the 'Golden Ball', which would be one of the principal victims of Tarkovsky's reductionism. He would further strip away the violent deaths and supernatural occurrences of the original novel to be left with what he termed a 'philosophical parable'. In another departure both from the novel and his earlier films, Tarkovsky wanted to observe the three classical unities of space, time and action, and also deliberately to omit some of his signature motifs, such as horses and apples. There is very much a sense that *Stalker* is, for Tarkovsky, a new beginning.

The Landscape of the Soul

Stalker is frequently described as being an allegory. The characters, for instance, do not have names; instead, they are labelled for what they are: Stalker, Writer and Professor. By having characters from what was called the 'Two Cultures' by the Soviet intelligentsia, Tarkovsky was aiming to portray two different approaches to life: Professor is rational, while Writer is intuitive. Between them stands Stalker, a man of faith to whom Tarkovsky said he felt closest of the three.

But is the film an allegory of faith, or of life in the Soviet Union, a combination of the two, or something else altogether? Typically, the setting is not identified as the Soviet Union, but, according to the opening title, as 'our little country'. With its drab look, military guards and general air of pollution, *Stalker* could easily pass for a contemporary Eastern Bloc country. Maya Turovskaya memorably described the film as 'far from being something from the world of tomorrow [a reference to the film's nominal science fiction status], this looks more like today, or rather the day before yesterday.'[166] The unseen threats of the Zone call to mind the phantom presence of the secret police, while Stalker's comment that he is imprisoned everywhere also suggests that Tarkovsky is making a comment on life in the USSR. It should be noted, too, that the Gulag camps were known as 'the Zone', a fact that would not have been lost on a Russian audience. Mark Le Fanu notes that, 'When the film was shown in front of a native audience, no aspect of it was perceived as more allegorical than Stalker's whirling of bolts in different oblique directions. The making of a detour of several miles to progress a mere hundred paces. "Of course," said my friend, "that's *exactly* what life is like in the Soviet Union!"'[167]

And yet it would not do justice to the film to read it in entirely this way. The men, although nameless, are fully rounded characters whose constant barrage of arguments and insults makes them both three-dimensional and ultimately sympathetic. Tarkovsky, in concentrating on their lined, anxious faces, imbues each of them with a quiet dignity. Indeed, *Stalker* is one of the great films of the human face – principally Kaidanovsky's, but Solonitsyn's world-weary visage is almost as equally compelling, such as in the approach to the Dry Tunnel, or in the Meat Grinder – and it is here that we can perhaps detect the film's deeper meaning than that of mere allegory. Alexander Kaidanovsky's shaven-headed Stalker is as iconic as Falconetti in Dreyer's *The Passion of Joan of Arc*, and it is Joan's suffering and saint-hood that reveal the bedrock of *Stalker*. It is ultimately a film about the search for faith and the difficulties the seeker encounters on the path. Viewed this way, the Zone becomes a landscape of the soul.

The film also makes great – and daring – use of silence and stillness. Often nothing 'happens' in conventional terms for minutes on end. The sequence where the men journey into the Zone on the trolley car is perhaps the most celebrated example: for over three minutes, Tarkovsky's camera patiently looks at the faces of the three men as they head towards the unknown. Eduard Artemyev's score and the hypnotic clanking of the railway tracks bolster the sense of a threshold about to be crossed. But perhaps even more radical is the shot of the three men sitting outside the Room at the end of their journey. For over four minutes, they simply sit huddled in the dirt, gazing into the enigma of the Room: the light fluctuates; Professor dismantles the bomb and throws parts of it into the water; it starts to rain within the Room; the rain ceases; the men continue to sit. Finally, when we cut back to the bar, nothing is said. The three of them are by now exhausted and dishevelled, and yet the silence conveys the possibility that all three have learnt something about themselves. As Stalker and his wife leave the bar, Writer looks on, contemplatively smoking a cigarette. Again, there is no dialogue. There is no need for any. (The shot is, in retrospect, even more moving when one realises that it is the last time we are to see Anatoly Solonitsyn in a Tarkovsky film. He was to die in June 1982.[168])

The Wasteland and the Grail

If *Stalker* is a film about faith, then its basic narrative structure could be compared with the narrative of the Grail Quest. Traditionally, the knights who set out to find the Grail would traverse a strange landscape full of magical encounters. 'Here begin the terrors, here begin the marvels', as one Grail text puts it,[169] a phrase perfectly apt for *Stalker*.

The terrors and marvels of the Zone are depicted in a more restricted colour palette than usual: greens, greys and blacks dominate. The characters, with their superstitions and beliefs, could easily be straight out of the Middle Ages, a feeling reinforced by the absence of many of the trappings of modernity once the men reach the Zone.

The strangeness of the Zone is made most manifest in Tarkovsky's handling of space and time. Space is frequently non-representational and ambiguous, especially in the film's second part. For instance, in the scenes shot around the tiled wall, Tarkovsky does not show all three characters together at the same time; it is up to us to determine how the characters are positioned in relation to each other. Stalker is shown alternately looking apparently towards Writer and Professor, yet at other times, he appears to be facing away. In some shots, he is lying on his back, in others, on his front. When Stalker and Writer approach the Dry Tunnel, we see Writer look around, and then move out of frame to the right. The camera then begins to track right, but does not pick up Writer again almost immediately where we would expect him to be, but only after it has passed the arches through which cascading water can be seen. Writer looks puzzled, as if he is aware that he has managed to cover all that ground in the blink of an eye. A similar effect occurs during the dream, where we see Stalker sleeping on the ground, and the camera then tracks away from him to examine the various detritus that lies in the shallow water. The track finishes when it picks up Stalker's hand lying semi-clenched at the opposite end of the water, as if he is in both places at once. In this way, Tarkovsky adheres to the three classical unities of space, time and action, but also subverts them.

Stalker comments that the Zone seems to change by the minute: 'I don't know what's going on here in the absence of people, but the moment someone shows up, everything comes into motion. Old traps disappear and new ones emerge. Safe spots become impassable. Now your path is easy, now it's hopelessly involved. That's the Zone.'[170] He then adds significantly [emphasis added] 'It may even seem capricious. But it is *what we've made it with our condition.*' This implies that the Zone's true nature is something akin to the mind, which also changes by the minute unless one has learnt to master it. That the film has such a slow pace (Tarkovsky said he wanted to convey the idea that the film had been made in a single take) makes watching it a meditative experience. It suggests that what the Room grants is in fact the discovery of the Grail – to continue with this metaphor for a moment – within oneself, perhaps with the aid of meditation or contemplation. In other words, if faith is rediscovered, then the self is also, and vice versa.

Tarkovsky is not merely concerned with the salvation of individual seekers in the film, but also of society as a whole. He laments the secularisation of the world, but does not offer an explicitly Christian solution: the voice-over known as 'Stalker's Prayer', with its praising of weakness, is actually paraphrasing the Tao Te Ching. Faith, for Tarkovsky, is ecumenical; it matters not what God or Goddess one serves, as long as one has the capacity to believe, and to love. If there is a miracle at the end of the film, it is not Monkey's apparent telekinetic abilities, but Stalker's wife's continuing love for her husband. Human love, for Tarkovsky, is the miracle, especially in a world as bereft of spiritual values as the world of *Stalker* seems to be.

Ecology and Prophecy

Stalker's distinctive look was the work of no fewer than three separate production designers: Alexander Boym, Shavkat

Abdusalamov[171] and finally Tarkovsky himself. It is one of the first films to feature a post-industrial aesthetic, which would later recur in films from directors as diverse as Terry Gilliam and David Fincher. It is a world of decay and debris where what truly matters has been forgotten. The dream captures this with great simplicity: the camera, in one of the tracks over shallow water that punctuate the film, moves over a variety of industrial and military debris that lie abandoned beneath it. At one point, we glimpse a detail of the Van Eyck brothers' Ghent Altarpiece, surrounded by algae and rusting coins. A more succinct – and cinematic – portrayal of the neglect of spiritual values would be difficult to imagine.

As Mark Le Fanu has noted, with *Stalker* Tarkovsky becomes 'one of the great contemporary artists of *poverty*, understood in its true spiritual sense.'[172] It is the poverty not only of a materialist world bent on self-destruction, but also of the 'poor in spirit' – people such as Stalker – who will eventually find the Grail and redeem the wasteland. And yet such optimism is somewhat tentative. While Tarkovsky clearly yearned for a better world, he realised that it would take a colossal effort and the signs for this did not look good. It is this despair that gives *Stalker* its power, and is what prompted the Polish director Andrzej Wajda to describe the film as Tarkovsky's 'throwing down the gauntlet' to all of us who live in the developed world.

The film's spiritual wasteland is also an actual wasteland caused by pollution. Although the film is one of Tarkovsky's most waterlogged, much of the water appears filthy and stagnant. The decay evident everywhere seems not so much to be the result of an alien visitation (which was thought to have caused the Zone to appear), but of a man-made catastrophe. This threat is made much more real and urgent by the fact that the film uncannily pre-empts the disaster at the VI

Lenin Nuclear Power Station in Chernobyl in April 1986. Not only was a zone created around the facility and the nearby town of Pripyat (where many of the power station's staff lived), into which people were forbidden to enter, but also the explosion itself happened in the Fourth Reactor: in the film, Professor finds the nuclear device with which he hopes to destroy the Room in the 'fourth bunker'. That Tarkovsky also quotes from Revelation during the film only adds to the sense of prophecy. The name Chernobyl in Ukrainian means 'Wormwood', which many took to mean 'The Star Wormwood', which falls from Heaven in Revelation to make a third of the Earth's waters fatally bitter.[173]

The bitter waters in the film may have even led to Tarkovsky's own death and to the deaths of most of the principal cast and crewmembers. Sound engineer Vladimir Sharun believes that the power station visible at the end of the film, when Stalker, his wife and Monkey walk back to their flat, was pouring out chemicals into the water. He noted 'white foam floating down the river. In fact, it was some horrible poison. Many women in our crew got allergic reactions on their faces. Tarkovsky died from cancer of the right bronchial tube. And Tolya [Anatoly] Solonitsyn too. That it was all connected to the location shooting for *Stalker* became clear to me when Larissa Tarkovskaya [Tarkovsky's wife and the film's assistant director] died from the same illness in Paris.'[174] Other fatalities from the film include Professor, Nikolai Grinko, who died in 1989, Alexander Kaidanovsky who, unlike the others, did not die of cancer, but suffered a heart attack in 1995 at the age of 49, and the film's brilliant Director of Photography, Alexander Knyazhinsky, who died in 1996. Tellingly, Alissa Freindlikh, all of whose scenes as Stalker's wife were shot at Mosfilm, is still alive (a double was used in the power station shot at the end).[175]

Autobiographical Elements

After *Mirror*, Tarkovsky's childhood dreams stopped. 'Childhood memories, which for years had given me no peace, suddenly vanished, as if they had melted away, and at last I stopped dreaming about the house where I had lived so many years before.'[176] He 'felt as though he had lost himself in a certain sense'.[177] If that is the case, then it is no surprise to find Tarkovsky filling this apparent void in his life by working on a stage production of *Hamlet* – perhaps the greatest work on the ethics of action and human purpose ever written – in Moscow during 1976–7. Shakespeare's philosophical enquiries are echoed by those of *Stalker*, which Tarkovsky began shooting while the play was still running.

The film that *Stalker* most closely resembles is *Rublev*. In the earlier film, Tarkovsky identified with the artist-monk and his mission; in the latter, it is Stalker's faith that proves to be one of the film's main centres of gravity. *Stalker* is, if anything, an autobiography of the spirit: in it, Tarkovsky's own aspirations and fears are allowed full reign. It could be argued that, once his childhood phantoms had been laid to rest, Tarkovsky, as he had done in *Rublev*, once more turned his gaze outward, only to find a world bereft of faith and hope. *Stalker*, like all of Tarkovsky's work, occupies an indeterminate position with regard to 'inner' and 'outer': the film is simultaneously a record of Tarkovsky's own inner landscape at the time it was shot, but at the same time, it is also reaching out, wondering if a better world can be made. The address made directly to the audience by Stalker's wife at the end of the film exemplifies this position perfectly. It is a cry from the heart, but one that acknowledges a tension, if not a dialogue, between the outer and inner aspects of human experience.

If the film as a whole can be seen more as 'the soul's landscape, after confession',[178] rather than 'straight' autobiography, two incidents in the film are, in fact, taken from Tarkovsky's own experience. Once the three men are in the Zone, Writer becomes tired of the 'nuts and bandages' that the Stalker is throwing ahead of them to detect the Zone's booby traps, and decides to make straight for the ruined building across the meadow that contains the Room. When he is nearly at the threshold of the building, a mysterious wind blows up, more sinister than the one in the 'country doctor' scene in *Mirror* (both the doctor and Writer are played by Anatoly Solonitsyn). A male voice commands: 'Stop! Don't move!' Writer retreats back to where Stalker and Professor are anxiously waiting; all three men deny uttering the command and, in a state of uncertainty and unease, move on. Compare this with something Alexander Gordon remembers Tarkovsky once telling him about an incident that took place when Tarkovsky was in Siberia: 'Andrei… was lying in a hunter's hut all alone one windy night… the trees were rustling and a storm was coming. Suddenly he heard someone say: "Get out of here!" It was a clear, quiet voice; Andrei didn't move a muscle. Then he heard it again: "Get out of here!" Andrei ran out of the hut, either in response to the command, either out of fear, or for some other reason he couldn't explain himself. Right then an enormous larch, cracked like a match by a powerful gust of wind, fell on the hut right over the place where he had been lying just a minute before… we were sceptical about his story. Andrei kept insisting that it really happened to him.'[179]

The film's final scene owes its origins to something less

dramatic, but, again, something directly from Tarkovsky's own experience. The scene shows Monkey, Stalker's daughter, apparently moving some beakers across the tabletop by telekinesis. It is based on a scene from one of the films of Eduard Naumov, who made documentaries about the paranormal. In one film, Naumov shows the psychic Ninel Kulagina moving items across a tabletop while under the scrutiny of a panel of scientists. As Vladimir Sharun recalls, 'Tarkovsky attentively watched Naumov's film and after it was finished he immediately exclaimed: "Well, what do you say, here is the ending for *Stalker!*"'[180]

Despite his nominally Orthodox upbringing, Tarkovsky was interested in paranormal phenomena of all kinds. It is relatively well known that in the late 1960s he attended a séance in Moscow, at which the spirit of Boris Pasternak predicted that Tarkovsky would only make seven films, a prediction that Tarkovsky refers to on a number of occasions in his diary. In another diary entry (7 February 1976) – while discussions were under way to get *Stalker* made – he mentions going to see a clairvoyant. At one point, Tarkovsky even took his dog to see one (health problems in the hind paws were diagnosed). *Stalker*, along with *The Sacrifice*, is perhaps the most 'supernatural' of Tarkovsky's films. That events which defy rational explanation came to appear more in these later films is a possible sign that Tarkovsky was either becoming increasingly mystical as he got older, or more convinced that only miracles can now save us.

Nostalgia (1983)

Triptych II

Alternate Title: *Nostalghia* (Italian title)
Production Company: Opera Film. RAI (Rome)/Sovin Film (Moscow)
Producer: Francesco Casati
Director: Andrei Tarkovsky
Screenplay: Andrei Tarkovsky & Tonino Guerra
Director of Photography: Giuseppe Lanci
Editor: Erminia Marani, Amedeo Salfa
Music: Verdi: *Requiem 'Requiem aeternam'*; Beethoven: *Symphony No. 9 'Choral'*; Russian and Chinese folk music
Art Director: Andrea Crisanti
Assistant Directors: Norman Mozzato, Larissa Tarkovskaya
Costume: Lina Nerli Taviani
Make-Up: Giulio Mastrantonio
Sound: Remo Ugolini
Special Effects: Paolo Ricci
Cast: Oleg Yankovsky (Andrei Gorchakov), Domiziani Giordano (Eugenia), Erland Josephson (Domenico), Patrizia Terreno (Maria, Gorchakov's wife), Laura De Marchi (woman with towel), Delia Boccardo (Domenico's wife), Milena Vukotic (Municipal employee), Alberto Canepa

(peasant), Raffaele Di Mario, Rate Furlan, Livio Galassi, Piero Vida, Elena Magoia
Shot: Autumn 1982
Running Time: 126 mins
First Screening: Cannes Film Festival, May 1983
First Screening in USSR: April 1987
Release in West: 1983/4
Awards: Grand Prix de Création, Ecumenical Jury Prize, FIPRESCI Prize, Best Director, Cannes Film Festival 1983

Storyline

The opening credits roll over a sepia shot of some women (whom we later learn are Gorchakov's family in Russia) and a child in a misty landscape. The music is an Italian folk song that is replaced by Verdi's *Requiem*.

Gorchakov and his interpreter, Eugenia, drive to visit Piero della Francesca's *Madonna of Childbirth*. Gorchakov refuses to go into the church. Eugenia witnesses a fertility ceremony, but finds herself unable to kneel to pray. She has a brief conversation with the sacristan, who tells her it is a woman's duty to bear children.

Gorchakov and Eugenia wait in the hotel lobby, discussing Arseny Tarkovsky's poetry, translation and the difficulties of understanding another culture. Gorchakov feels that the only way for people to get to know one another is to abolish borders between states. Eugenia asks Gorchakov why Sosnovsky, the composer whom Gorchakov is in Italy to research, returned to his native Russia. Gorchakov tells her that he began to drink, eventually taking his own life. Eugenia tells him of a maid from the south who burned down the house of her master, out of nostalgia for her home town. The hotelier appears and they are shown to their separate rooms.

Gorchakov dreams of Russia (shown in black and white). He loiters in his room. Eugenia knocks and asks him if he wants to call his wife in Moscow; he declines. Gorchakov dreams of his pregnant wife, who appears to levitate above his hotel bed, and also of Eugenia.

Gorchakov and Eugenia visit St Catherine's Pool. Eugenia tells bathers taking the waters that Gorchakov is a Russian poet researching the life of the Russian composer Sosnovsky. The bathers also comment on Domenico, a mad recluse who can be seen nearby, saying that he has locked his family up for seven years to await the end of the world. Eugenia tells Gorchakov that everyone thinks Domenico mad; his latest obsession is to try to carry a lighted candle across the pool.

Gorchakov and Eugenia visit Domenico, who is initially reluctant to welcome Gorchakov into his home, a semi-derelict building. Once inside, Gorchakov finds a diorama laid out on the floor that mirrors the landscape which can be seen from the window. Domenico offers Gorchakov some bread and wine. He explains that he was only trying to save his family, but now the whole world must be saved. He gives Gorchakov the candle, and charges him with the task of carrying it across St Catherine's Pool. He hints that 'we' are planning 'something big' in Rome.

A sepia sequence follows in which we see the authorities liberating Domenico's family. Domenico struggles with a man in a white coat and then chases his small son. The boy looks up at him and asks, 'Papa, is this the end of the world?'

Gorchakov returns to the hotel, to find Eugenia drying her hair on his bed. Her frustrations at being unable to interest Gorchakov result in a hysterical outburst, at the end of which she tells him to go back to his wife and slaps him, causing his nose to bleed. On her way out of the hotel with her case, she stops to read a letter written by Sosnovsky in Italy about his homesickness.

Gorchakov, his nose still bleeding, lies down. We then see, in sepia, shots of his home in Russia, then in voice-over he reads Arseny Tarkovsky's poem, 'As a child I once fell ill'.

Gorchakov wades through a flooded, ruined church. He gets drunk on vodka and talks to a little girl who appears in the church. Another poem, 'Sight grows dim', is read in voice-over. Gorchakov is seen lying on a wall next to the nearly empty vodka bottle; the book of poems is burning.

A sepia sequence shows Gorchakov in a street littered with rubbish. He goes up to a cupboard that has a mirror on its door. He sees Domenico's reflection instead of his own.

In black and white, Gorchakov walks through a ruined abbey. In voice-over, St Catherine asks God why He doesn't make Himself known to Gorchakov. God replies that He does, but Gorchakov is unaware of His presence.

We cut back to colour, and Gorchakov lying by the now-burnt stub of the book of poems.

Gorchakov waits for his taxi at the hotel. He is told there is a phone call for him. It is Eugenia. She tells him that she is going to India with her new boyfriend and that Domenico is in Rome, taking part in some kind of demonstration. Domenico asked her whether Gorchakov had done what he had asked him to do. When the taxi arrives, Gorchakov tells the driver not to go to the airport, but to St Catherine's Pool.

Domenico, standing atop the equestrian statue of Marcus Aurelius in Rome, gives a speech to a crowd, which is made up largely of what appears to be inmates from a psychiatric hospital. His words are a call for a new way of living and the establishment of a new world.

Gorchakov arrives at the pool, which has been drained. A

woman is cleaning it out and places the various objects retrieved from the pool – a bottle, a broken doll, an old lamp – on the parapet surrounding it. Gorchakov swallows a pill.

Domenico's speech reaches its climax; he calls for music. A man runs across the piazza with a tape recorder. A petrol can is passed up to Domenico, who empties its contents all over himself. He sets fire to himself and falls from the statue as the tape recorder plays a snatch of Beethoven's *Ode to Joy* before it breaks down completely, leaving Domenico's screams the only sound that can be heard. He crawls a short distance, then dies.

Back at St Catherine's Pool, Gorchakov attempts to carry the lighted candle across the pool. The wind blows it out halfway across and he starts again. The wind blows it out for a second time. Gorchakov makes a third attempt. This time he makes it, and places the candle on a ledge at the far end of the pool. The Verdi is heard again on the soundtrack, while Gorchakov collapses and dies off-screen. A man comes running across the pool, while the woman who had been cleaning the pool looks on.

A sepia shot of Gorchakov's son and his wife (although we do not see her face).

A black and white shot of the dacha. The camera pulls back to reveal that the house stands inside a ruined Italian cathedral. Gorchakov and the dog are seen sitting by a pool. It begins to snow.

A caption appears, dedicating the film to Tarkovsky's mother.

Production History

The English version of Tarkovsky's diaries charts the development of *Nostalgia* better than any of his other projects. The film grew out of *Tempo di Viaggio*, which Tarkovksy had been planning as far back as 1976 (*see* the 'Works in Other Media' chapter). While in Italy in April 1979, Tarkovsky noted down an idea for a screenplay idea entitled 'The End of the World', in which a man, believing the apocalypse to be imminent, incarcerates his family for 40 years. They are eventually found by the authorities and taken away. As they are being helped into an ambulance, the man's small son asks him 'Papa, is this the end of the world?'[181] By this time, Tarkovsky had also sketched out the 'Voice of God' scene.[182] By 17 July 1979, the title, *Nostalgia*, had been decided upon, and Tarkovsky knew that the hero would be a translator (a musicologist and poet in the final film) and that the themes of the film would be 'Loneliness. Giotto, Assisi. He doesn't notice anything and doesn't look at anything.'[183] By the last week of July, Tarkovsky and his co-writer, Tonino Guerra, were incorporating 'The End of the World' into *Nostalgia*, while Tarkovsky was pondering the reason for hero's journey to Italy.[184] It would seem that they did not stumble upon the idea of Gorchakov, the film's protagonist, going to Italy to research the Russian serf composer Maxim Berezovsky (*c.*1745–77) until the following spring, as Berezovsky is not mentioned in the diary until 27 May 1980.[185]

If Gorchakov was not noticing the beauties of Italy, Tarkovsky evidently soaked up the country himself: 'We did some shooting [for *Tempo di Viaggio*]. The 'goat pass' in Pozzo d'Antullo, next to Collepardo, and a little monastery, the church at Dituralti, and the chemist's shop, which is old and astonishingly beautiful… The situation and the view are unbelievable.'[186] A few days later he notes, 'Harvested corn fields with burnt stubble. Black hills, with trees scattered over the black fields. Straw burning on the fields.'[187] Diary entries for the summer of 1979 show Tarkovsky in good spirits, and

168

working well: 'In less than two months we have written a screenplay [*Nostalgia*], done a *scaletta* [shooting script] of the second draft, worked out how we are going to work on 'The End of the World' [*Nostalgia*] and filmed the 'Special' [*Tempo di Viaggio*]. Unbelievable! That's the way to live! Working with sheer delight.'[188]

Tarkovsky returned to Italy in April 1980. *Tempo di Viaggio* and the script for *Nostalgia* were both completed at this time, with negotiations to make *Nostalgia* getting under way. RAI, which had put up the money for the documentary, asked Tarkovsky to cut the budget, which he was reluctantly forced to do. By the time Tarkovsky returned to Moscow in August, the budget had been cut, with Tarkovsky scrapping all the studio scenes. Everything would have to be shot on location.

After more than a year of delays, Tarkovsky was allowed to return to Italy in March 1982. The part of Gorchakov had been written for Anatoly Solonitsyn, but he was by this time too ill to take the role. Tarkovsky then offered it to Alexander Kaidanovsky, who accepted, but was not allowed to travel abroad. Tarkovsky was finally able to secure Oleg Yankovsky – who had played the role of the father in *Mirror* – for the part.

The film was shot in the autumn and was completed in time for the Cannes Film Festival in 1983. The screening turned out to be another scandal, with the festival jury wanting to give Tarkovsky the Palme d'Or, but the official Russian delegation, led by veteran director Sergei Bondarchuk, worked overtime to persuade the jury not to give Tarkovsky the prize. Instead, Tarkovsky shared a new prize invented for the occasion, the Grand Prix de Création, with Robert Bresson, whose film *L'Argent* was also in competition.

SEAN MARTIN

A Great Park Filled with Statues

'I wanted to make a film about Russian nostalgia,' Tarkovsky wrote in *Sculpting in Time*, 'about the particular state of mind which assails Russians who are far from their native land.'[189] However, Tarkovsky's reasons for being far from his native land are intimately bound up with his feelings about the impossibility of continuing to live and work in it. Hence *Nostalgia* is, in many respects, not just a film about nostalgia for the past, but also of the search for home and a place of belonging on a wider scale.

Nostalgia continues Tarkovsky's refining of his new minimal style that had begun in *Stalker*. The film is dominated by slow camera movements and spartan art direction (made all the more remarkable by the fact that the whole film was shot in found locations). In many respects, it is Tarkovsky's most 'minimal' film all round: it is essentially a three-hander revolving around the characters of Gorchakov (a supremely world-weary Oleg Yankovsky); his strained relationship with his interpreter, Eugenia; and the mad recluse Domenico. These latter two characters are played by newcomers to Tarkovsky's films, Domiziani Giordano and Erland Josephson. New actors often represent new feelings or new themes in Tarkovsky, and Giordano and Josephson are no exception. Although Eugenia starts out as being one of a number of unsympathetic or remote women in Tarkovsky's films (one thinks of the rich doctor's wife and Liza from *Mirror*), her fieriness and independence are something new (perhaps attributable to Tarkovsky's co-writer, Tonino Guerra). Domenico, although a man of faith like Stalker, differs from the earlier character in that he is not just a man of sorrows, but also a man of action, ready to take drastic steps to redeem a world heading for the abyss.

The plot – never a foremost concern of Tarkovsky's – is also minimal and quickly thwarts any sense of traditional dramatic development. It is as if Tarkovsky is heeding the advice of Robert Bresson in this film – more so than in any of his previous work – 'Be sure of having used to the full all that is communicated by immobility and silence.'[190] If *Stalker* was one of the great films of silence, then *Nostalgia* is one of the great films of immobility: Gorchakov, in particular, is frequently photographed standing still, turning to look into the camera, or sitting facing away and turning back. This static quality of the film, together with Yankovsky's enigmatic, tired gazes into the camera, draws the viewer in and implies complicity with what is happening on screen. Through this technique, Tarkovsky deepens the film, rather than extending it in the linear sense of a forward-moving plot, calling to mind a statement he once made in his diary: 'in the end it is important to confine yourself within a framework that will deepen your world, not impoverish it'.[191]

Immobility is, in fact, an element that does more than deepen the film. Sosnovsky's letter, describing a dream in which he is a statue in a park, is the meeting place of the film's concerns: Russia and Italy, past and present. These ideas suffuse the characters themselves. Russia appears in Gorchakov's dreams, as well as being embodied in the person of his wife, Maria. She is contrasted with Eugenia, who represents the attractions of Italy (although her apparent shallowness and Tarkovsky's showing of Italy as a strangely deserted, austere place temper her attractiveness). Gorchakov himself is contrasted with Domenico, who, although Italian, represents the redemption theme. Gorchakov's identification with the recluse becomes the way out of his personal crisis, and also unifies the film: Russia and Italy, the past and the present, madness and sanity, faithlessness and the rediscovery of faith are all embodied in Gorchakov by the time he fulfils his promise to Domenico to carry the candle across St Catherine's Pool.

The Dreams

Doubling is one of *Nostalgia*'s cornerstones, and one of the main instances of this technique is in the dream sequences, which differ from those in the previous films in a number of interesting ways. Tarkovsky's colour coding in the past had been inconsistent. In *Andrei Rublev* and *Stalker*, colour signifies a mysterious, living reality, with black and white being reserved for the mundane. In *Solaris* and *Mirror*, the use of monochrome sequences seems largely to have been the result of insufficient colour stock; as a result, the colour coding of those films is rather arbitrary. In *Nostalgia*, however, black and white is reserved solely for memories and dreams. The one small exception to this rule is when Domenico's son looks into the camera and asks, 'Papa, is this the end of the world?' That this has been shot in colour brings it onto the same plane as the external plot of the film, and suggests that, for Domenico, and perhaps later for Gorchakov as well, apocalypse is not something that is merely a dream or fantasy, but something that has already begun. Colour makes this short dream active in the sense that it seems to be as real as the waking world, a world it has the ability to affect.

Tarkovsky had used this device before, most memorably in *Mirror*, where the characters seem to be able to 'see' the past and the newsreel sequences, and uses it again to great effect throughout *Nostalgia*. When Gorchakov and Eugenia are talking in the darkness of the hotel lobby near the beginning of the film, the sound of running water can be heard. Gorchakov looks over his shoulder, almost back towards the camera as if he has heard the water; we then cut to a brief sepia shot of Maria cleaning a wine glass. At the end of the scene, when the hotelier appears, Eugenia asks Gorchakov if she has the keys to the other hotel. He replies that they are the keys to his house back home. Gorchakov walks towards the camera and the running water can be heard again. He looks into the camera; we cut to the sepia shot of Maria again, only this time she is looking at the camera as well and smiling, almost as if she has seen Gorchakov. She turns away and the camera tracks right to reveal the dacha and the children playing with the dog.

When Gorchakov falls asleep on his bed, we cut to a sepia sequence showing Maria comforting Eugenia, who, when we first see her, is looking off-screen to the right, as if she is looking at Gorchakov as he slumbers. The scene changes to show a pregnant Maria supine on what appears to be Gorchakov's hotel bed. Gorchakov leaves her, and she turns towards the camera and calls his name. As the lighting changes and the image fades – making her appear almost to be levitating over the hotel bed – we hear Eugenia calling for Gorchakov from outside in the corridor.

Another interesting feature of this first dream sequence is the role of Domenico's dog, which trots out of the bathroom to settle by the side of the bed only shortly after Gorchakov has lain down. Here the dog, like the one in *Stalker*, acts as a mediator between two worlds – in this case the world of Gorchakov's imagination and the 'real world' in which Gorchakov (as well as Domenico) will ultimately make his decisive act. But what is interesting here is that the dog is not shown in sepia, as it sometimes is in *Stalker*. Here, the dream walks right into the room, suggesting the possible influence of the Greek director Theo Angelopoulos, who often used the same technique.[192]

After Sosnovsky's letter has been read, Gorchakov lies down in one of the hotel's corridors nursing the bloody nose that Eugenia has given him. We then cut to a sepia shot of Maria in bed. We can hear Gorchakov call her name gently. She seems to hear, waking up and rising to draw back the curtains. This leads into one of the most beautiful shots in the film, a track showing Maria, their son and the two other women[193] in two incompatible spaces outside the dacha as a radio plays on the soundtrack. At the end of the shot, the moon rises over the dacha. We then cut back to the hotel, where we hear Maria calling for Gorchakov again. He looks into the camera, as though he can hear her.

The sepia sequences associated with Domenico likewise seem to be in communication with the sequences in full colour. Upon entering Domenico's house, Gorchakov seems to see a diorama beneath a window. This is shot in sepia and, oddly enough, the artificial landscape on the floor seems more 'real' than the view out of the window. The diorama is the microcosm to the macrocosm outside, suggesting that the drama that took place in Domenico's house is being played out in the wider world. When Gorchakov leaves the house, it is intercut with sepia shots of the liberation of Domenico's family after their seven years' incarceration in such a way as to suggest that either Domenico is remembering it as he shows Gorchakov to his taxi, or that Gorchakov is trying to picture the scene as he leaves. The final sequence involving the two men is perhaps the most crucial. After getting drunk in the flooded church, Gorchakov dreams of or envisions himself in a deserted, littered street. The debris in the street suggests war, or some other epochal crisis. He passes an abandoned cupboard and stops, looking back. At this point we hear Gorchakov speaking lines that could have been said by Domenico 'My God, why did I do it? They're my children, my family, my own flesh and blood.' Looking into the mirror on the cupboard door, Gorchakov is met not with his own reflection, but Domenico's. Their merging is now complete. This sequence, and all the preceding sepia sections, suggests that the real drama of *Nostalgia* is internal, not external.

The Search for Home

Nostalgia is Tarkovsky's most 'internal' film after *Mirror*, and it is in some respects a companion piece to the earlier film. If *Mirror* is Tarkovsky's own 'in search of lost time', then *Nostalgia* is a quest for a lost homeland or place that is both actual and metaphorical. It is Tarkovsky's most eloquent depiction of alienation.

Gorchakov is adrift from the very beginning of the film. At the pool, he doesn't know what time of day it is (rather like Alexei not knowing what time of day it is when he talks to his mother in *Mirror*), and he and Eugenia face away from each other when talking both there and in the darkness of the hotel. They don't so much as engage in dialogue, but rather deliver monologues. In fact, the whole film could be interpreted as Gorchakov's interior monologue. Real communication seems to be possible only in the sphere of actions, not words.

Unlike *Stalker*, where space was frequently enigmatic, time is puzzling in *Nostalgia*, adding to the sense of Gorchakov's dislocation. It is difficult to tell over how many days the film takes place. It could be one or two, with the day of Domenico's protest and the candle scene taking place a few days or weeks later, but Tarkovsky keeps the time period vague. Nature, too, is depicted in such a way as to make it seem cold. Stone dominates, with Tarkovsky indulging his love of old walls and ruins. His appreciation for the Japanese concept of *saba* – or 'natural rustiness' – suggests that both Gorchakov and Eugenia have lost contact with nature, for, although the many walls are worn and lichen-covered, they are beautiful in terms of *saba* (age and wear being seen as inherently desirable), a fact which seems to be lost on the characters.[194]

Estrangement from nature – both our own and that of our surroundings – is perhaps the ultimate theme of the film, for, during the final 20 or so minutes, Tarkovsky moves away from mere nostalgia for home to address this global problem. As Peter Green has noted, 'To limit the identity of these yearnings [of nostalgia] specifically to Russia would be to reduce the dimensions of the film. For, on the one hand, loss of habitat has now become a worldwide ecological problem, with man fast destroying his own natural environment; and on the other, home is also a place within the heart.'[195] Domenico's despair is clearly Tarkovsky's: 'The eyes of all mankind are looking at the pit into which we are all plunging,' Domenico declaims during his speech in Rome. 'It's the so-called healthy who have brought the world to the verge of ruin.' He suggests that the only way to salvation is for 'Great things [to] end, small things [to] endure… Just look at nature and you'll see that life is simple, that we must go back to where we were, to the point where you took the wrong turning.' He then acknowledges the near-futility of his protest and also makes a comment that calls up the images of the filthy chemical water in *Stalker*: 'We must go back to the main foundations of life without dirtying the water. What kind of a world is this if a madman has to tell you to be ashamed of yourselves?'

ANDREI TARKOVSKY

In the context of Domenico's protest, the final sequence in St Catherine's Pool takes on a redeeming significance. That Gorchakov might finally *do* something has been hinted at earlier, when he tells Eugenia that he thinks he knows why Domenico locked up his family. His dream of St Catherine imploring the Almighty to make Himself known to Gorchakov suggests that the Russian is yearning for salvation. In a daring sequence worthy of the men sitting outside the Room in *Stalker*, Tarkovsky's camera patiently follows the ailing Gorchakov across the pool with the candle in an unbroken take lasting nearly nine minutes. Twice the wind blows it out. He nearly trips. His breathing, prominent in the mix, accentuates his inner struggle to be redeemed and reborn. It is this scene that Krzysztof Kieślowski described as a 'miracle', for, by the time Gorchakov reaches the far end of the pool, the candle he is carrying is no longer just a candle.

'A spectacle of unrelieved gloom.'

When Tarkovsky finally saw the material he had shot, however, he noted with surprise that it was 'a spectacle of unrelieved gloom.'[196] He goes on to explain that gloom had not been his intention: 'I had been worn down by my separation from my family and from the way of life that I was used to, by working under quite unfamiliar conditions, even by using a foreign language.'[197] In the process of negotiating to live and work in Italy, during which time the Soviet authorities refused to allow Tarkovsky's young son to join him, the director's own experience began to inform the film: 'irrespective of my own theoretical intentions, the camera was obeying first and foremost my inner state during filming.'[198] Russia and Tarkovsky's own life are present in the film in the monochrome sequences; in Gorchakov's reading of Arseny's poems; in the 'Moonrise' scene, which was based on Tarkovsky's own moon-watching of 15 September 1976[199]; in the fact that Gorchakov and Tarkovsky's father are poets; that he shares the same first name as Tarkovsky himself; and that his surname harks back to Tarkovsky's childhood – the dacha in Ignatievo where the Tarkovskys summered during the mid-1930s, and which was recreated in *Mirror*, was owned by the Gorchakov family. 'It could never have occurred to me when I started shooting,' Tarkovsky wrote, 'that my own, all too specific, nostalgia, was soon to take possession of my soul forever.'[200] After failing to get reassurance from the Soviet leader, Yuri Andropov, that he would be given work if he returned home, Tarkovsky announced his decision to remain in the West, elevating *Nostalgia* from premonition to prophecy.

The Sacrifice (1986)

TRIPTYCH III

Alternate Titles: *Offret* (Swedish Title), *Sacrificatio*

Production Company: Swedish Film Institute (Stockholm)/Argos Films (Paris); in association with FilmFour International, Josephson & Nykvist, Sveriges Television/SVT2, Sandrew Film & Teater; with the participation of the French Ministry of Culture

Executive Producer: Anna-Lena Wibom

Producer: Katinka Faragò

Director: Andrei Tarkovsky

Screenplay: Andrei Tarkovsky

Director of Photography: Sven Nykvist

Editor: Andrei Tarkovsky & Michal Leszczylowski

Assistant Director: Kerstin Eriksdottir

Music: JS Bach: *St Matthew Passion* BWV 244, No.47, 'Ebarme dich'; Japanese and Swedish Folk Music

Art Director: Anna Asp

Special Effects: Svenska Stuntgruppen, Lars Höglund, Lars Palmqvist

Costumes: Inger Pehrsson

Make-Up: Kjell Gustavsson, Florence Fouquier

Sound: Owe Svensson

Cast: Erland Josephson (Alexander), Susan Fleetwood (Adelaide), Valérie Mairesse (Julia), Allan Edwall (Otto), Gudrún Gísladóttir (Maria), Sven Wolter (Victor), Fillipa Franzén (Marta), Tommy Kjellqvist (Little Man), Per Kallman, Tommy Nordahl (Ambulancemen)
Shot: April–July 1985
Running Time: 149 mins
First Screening: Paris, April 1986 (preview); Cannes, May 1986 (Official Premiere)
First Screening in USSR: April 1987
Release in West: 1986/87
Awards: Grand Prix, FIPRESCI Prize, Special Jury Prize, Best Artistic Contribution (Sven Nykvist), Cannes Film Festival 1986; Best Film, Valladolid Film Festival 1986; British Academy Award, Best Foreign Language Film 1987

Storyline

The credits roll over a close-up of Leonardo's *Adoration of the Magi* to Bach's 'Ebarme Dich'. The Bach is replaced by the sounds of seabirds and waves. The camera holds on the Leonardo after the credits have ended.

Alexander is watering a skeletal tree on the seashore with his young son, Little Man, and telling him the story of a monk who watered a dead tree every day until it finally flowered. Alexander speculates on changing the world through simple rituals.

Otto the postman cycles up and presents Alexander with a birthday telegram. They walk inland, Otto chiding Alexander for being gloomy. He tells Alexander that he shouldn't be waiting for 'something real' to happen to him. They discuss Nietzsche's theory of the eternal return and the nature of belief. Otto quotes Mark 11:24. He falls off his bicycle, which Little Man has tied to a bush.

Alexander and Little Man continue their walk in a grove of trees. As Adelaide (his wife) and Victor (the family doctor and possibly Adelaide's lover) arrive in a car, Alexander is musing that humanity has taken the wrong turning. Victor quizzes Adelaide about Alexander's state of mental health, to which she replies that he is all right, but has been working a lot lately. Victor congratulates Alexander on his birthday and tells Little Man that he will be talking within a week. (The boy is forbidden to speak due to an operation on his vocal chords.) Adelaide and Victor drive back to the house.

Alexander continues to soliloquise. Man has violated nature and has built a society governed by fear and power. There is a dreadful disharmony between our material and spiritual development; savages are more spiritual than we are. Our civilisation is built on sin, or that which is unnecessary. He then says he is fed up with talk – quoting *Hamlet's* 'Words, words, words' – and wishes somebody would *do* something. A shepherdess's call is heard; Alexander falls to the ground.

In black and white, we see a deserted, littered street.

Back at the house, Alexander leafs through a book of icons. He thanks Victor for the birthday present. Their talk is interrupted by the arrival of Marta, apparently Alexander's daughter,[201] who can remember Alexander's time as an actor. Adelaide joins them, regretting that Alexander gave up acting. Alexander explains his dislike of acting. Victor tells him that he is thinking of emigrating to Australia. Adelaide and Marta both see someone approaching the house.

Otto arrives with a large, framed seventeenth-century map of Europe, his present for Alexander. Otto tells Victor that he has lived in the area for only two months; before that, he was a schoolmaster.

One of the maids, Maria, enters and asks Adelaide if she can go. Adelaide gives her three final tasks to do. Otto tells Victor that Maria, who is originally from Iceland, lives near him and that they are 'acquainted'. Alexander says he finds Maria 'very odd', while Adelaide confides that sometimes Maria scares her.

Alexander goes to look for Little Man. Otto tells everyone – at Victor's behest – of his interest in paranormal phenomena. He cites the case of a young soldier who appeared alongside his mother in a photograph taken 20 years after he died. He suddenly collapses at the end of his account. Recovering, he says that an 'evil angel' touched him, but he is OK.

Outside, Maria can be seen walking towards the house. Back inside, the wine glasses tremble as military jets fly overhead. Everyone runs to the windows to look. A jug of milk falls from a shelf.

Outside, in the first of the film's extremely pale, washed-out scenes, Alexander finds an exact miniature replica of the house. He mutters lines from *Macbeth*. Maria appears and tells him that Little Man made the model (with Otto's help), as a birthday present.

The Leonardo reappears. Alexander and Otto are heard discussing it. We are now shown that a reproduction hangs on the wall of Alexander's study. We can then hear fragments of a TV broadcast coming from downstairs about a crisis involving the army.

Downstairs, everyone is gathered around the TV. The news is grave: what appears to be a World War has just started. The scene alternates between black and white, normal colour and muted colour. Alexander admits that he has been waiting his whole life for this; Adelaide demands that someone 'do something'. She becomes hysterical, so

Victor sedates her. He also sedates Marta against her wishes, but Julia, the other maid, refuses.

Alexander goes outside. Otto tries the phone; it's dead. Adelaide gives a monologue in which she admits that she married the wrong man. They agree to stay put rather than go north. Adelaide decides they should eat dinner and asks Julia to wake Little Man. She refuses, saying it would only lead to the boy becoming frightened.

Alexander notices a gun in Victor's doctor's bag. He calls in on Little Man, who pretends to be asleep. Alexander then goes into his study and prays that if God will restore things to how they were that morning, he will sacrifice all he holds dear, destroy his home, give up Little Man and never speak again. He then crawls to the sofa and lies down.

The shepherdess's call is heard again, as Marta, in her room, calls for Victor and disrobes.

In black and white, we see Alexander[202] running away down a corridor, followed by a shot of him sitting in a chair, looking towards the window. Maria's house can be seen through it, and Alexander reappears outside. He walks through mud, bending to pull up a root. He wanders around in a snowy landscape with houses, trees and a statue. The camera tracks over dead leaves, mulch, dropped coins. He calls for Little Man, of whom only his feet can be seen, before he runs off. Jets fly overhead. Alexander wakes with a start.

Otto calls on him, accessing the study via a ladder. He tells Alexander that there is still one last chance: he must sleep with Maria who, he says, is a witch. Alexander goes downstairs and takes Victor's gun. Adelaide, Victor and Marta are dining outside. Alexander sneaks past and cycles off on Otto's bike. He falls off and is about to turn back when the shepherdess's call comes again, which this time he seems to hear. He gets back on and continues his journey.

Maria welcomes Alexander into her home. She washes his hands, after which he plays a piece of music on an organ. He rambles incoherently about how he once tried unsuccessfully to improve his mother's garden, before pulling out the gun and putting it to his temple, begging Maria to love him. The jets roar overhead again. Alexander and Maria embrace, then rise up above Maria's bed.

We see the littered street again, this time full of people running in panic. On the soundtrack, a woman consoles Alexander, asking him why he is so frightened.[203] The camera pans down to reveal Little Man asleep.

Alexander sleeps on a camp bed. Adelaide is with him. She turns to face him, and we can see that it is Maria, wearing Adelaide's clothes.

Back in colour, Marta, naked, chases chickens through the house. The camera tracks past Adelaide into Alexander's study, where he is still asleep on the couch.[204] He wakes up, slowly realising that things are back to normal. He calls his publishers, who tell him 'you can't imagine what things are like here today'. He puts on a robe and, in tears, goes downstairs.

Adelaide, Victor and Marta are having breakfast outside, discussing Victor's plans to move to Australia. Marta finds a note from Alexander, asking them all to go on a walk. Alexander watches them go.

He moves the cars away from the house, then piles chairs up in the porch, covering them with a tablecloth. He sets light to the cloth and watches the house burn as Adelaide, Victor, Marta and Julia run towards him. Alexander tries to evade them, running towards Maria, who has now appeared. Adelaide threatens Maria, who backs off. Adelaide and Victor lead Alexander to an ambulance as Otto cycles up.

They chase Alexander, who finally gets into the ambulance of his own accord. The ambulance takes him away as Maria commandeers Otto's bicycle and heads off in the opposite direction. The remains of the burning house collapse.

Little Man is at the tree, watering it. The shepherdess's call can be heard again. Maria cycles up to see the ambulance drive past. The Bach piece fades in. Little Man lies down beneath the tree and speaks for the first time. 'In the beginning was the Word. Why is that, Papa?'

The camera cranes up the tree until it reaches the top branches. The shot holds, and a caption appears dedicating the film to Tarkovsky's son 'with hope and confidence'.

Production History

Tarkovsky began what was to become his final film in late 1980. Again, as with *Nostalgia*, it would mirror Tarkovsky's own life without him being conscious of it, at least initially. 'The Witch', a script that he was contemplating writing in 1980/81 with Arkady Strugatsky, was to have been about a wealthy man who is cured of cancer after spending a night with a witch. Many years later, the witch appears outside the man's house and he gives up his family and possessions to go off and live with her. Tarkovsky signed the contract to make the film at Cannes in 1983, when it was still called 'The Witch', but at some point the hero's cancer was replaced with the outbreak of a nuclear conflict. The character of Maria, the witch, remained, although Tarkovsky changed the title to *The Sacrifice* when he realised that the word 'witch' – in Russian derived from the verb 'to know' – did not have the same connotations in other languages.[205]

The film was shot in Sweden in the spring and early summer of 1985. Although Tarkovsky initially had a somewhat frosty relationship with his cameraman, Sven Nykvist, the two men developed a close working relationship. But even Nykvist's considerable skills couldn't prevent the cameras jamming during the shooting of the house burning down. The set had to be rebuilt, with the scene being re-shot on the morning of the last day of principal photography.

The film was completed in January 1986. By this time, Tarkovsky was bedridden, and editing meetings were held in his hospital room. The film's first public screening was at Cannes, where it was given the Grand Prix and the Special Jury Prize.

A Dreadful Disharmony

Tarkovsky's last film is the summation of the themes begun in *Stalker*, and which continued through *Nostalgia*. *The Sacrifice* is the closing chapter in Tarkovsky's triptych and, like the two preceding films, it is driven by a sense of desperation about the state of the world. Perhaps intuiting that it would be his last film, Tarkovsky uses the film to settle accounts with the modern world and, as such, *The Sacrifice* has the unmistakable air of being a last testament. It also goes further than any of his other films in exploring the tension between the outer and inner worlds, and much of the film takes place in a world which seems to be simultaneously a dream and also real. Tarkovsky admitted that the film's events had more than one level of meaning, describing *The Sacrifice* as a parable.

Tarkovsky explains his reasons for making the film in *Sculpting in Time*. He notes 'the more clearly I discerned the stamp of materialism on the face of our planet… the more I came up against unhappy people' who were suffering from the 'inability or unwillingness to see why life had lost all delight and all value, why it had become oppressive', the more committed Tarkovsky became to making the film, describing it as 'the most important thing in my life'. For Tarkovsky, the problem that confronts us is that we have acquired 'a dreadful disharmony',[206] as Alexander says in the film. 'It seems to me that the individual stands today at a crossroads,' Tarkovsky continues, 'faced with the choice of whether to pursue the existence of a blind consumer, subject to the implacable march of new technology and the endless multiplication of material goods, or whether to seek out a way that will lead to spiritual responsibility, which ultimately might mean not only his personal salvation but also the saving of society at large.'

Such sentiments are clearly echoed by Alexander in the film. He is portrayed from the opening as something of a philosopher, musing on the story of a monk who watered a dead tree every day until it blossomed, as he himself plants a tree by the water's edge. When he is alone with Little Man in the next scene, he launches into a monologue deploring the state of the world. In many respects, this follows on from Domenico's speech in *Nostalgia* (both characters are played by Erland Josephson), but whereas Domenico was poetic and allusive, Alexander is prosaic and direct: '[Man] has constantly violated nature. The result is a civilisation built on force, power, fear, dependence. All of our "technical progress" has only provided us with comfort... savages are more spiritual than we are... As soon as we make a scientific breakthrough, we put it to use in the service of evil... some wise man[207] once said that sin is that which is unnecessary. If that is so, then our entire civilisation is built on sin, from beginning to end. We have acquired a dreadful disharmony... between our material and our spiritual development.'

With this speech, Tarkovsky could not be nailing his

colours to the mast any more explicitly. He clearly felt that
the state of the world is so dire that sermonising was called
for in order to get his urgent message across. What is so
extraordinary, though, about this scene is what we see when
Alexander is talking: Little Man, exploring on all fours the
little copse where they are, followed by a shot that simply
shows the wind blowing through the grass. It is one of the
most elegantly uncomplicated, almost Zen-like, moments in
all of Tarkovsky. Is this what our 'dreadful disharmony' has
robbed us of, the ability to appreciate something as simple as
this? Is Alexander even aware of it? Tarkovsky, as ever, lets us
make up our own minds.

Otto is the character who precipitates Alexander into
action. He is first seen delivering a birthday telegram to
Alexander, and chides him for being so gloomy, as if he were
yearning for something, or waiting. Otto admits to having
the feeling that he has spent his whole life waiting for something real to happen to him. This seems to spur Alexander
on, as in the next scene, when he is alone with Little Man,
he reproaches himself for his monologue and says 'If only
someone could stop talking and *do* something instead!' This
sets up an expectation that when something *does* happen,
Alexander will be ready to act. When the news comes that
the missiles are in the air, he says to himself, 'I've waited for
this all my life.' Realising that words are useless, Alexander
now has only one course of action left open to him: he must
do something.

A Midsummer Night's Dream?

The Sacrifice uses colour in much the same way as *Nostalgia*.
Full colour is used for everyday life, with black and white
being reserved for dreams or visions. There are three main

monochrome sequences in the film: the two shots of the city street,[208] which would appear to be a vision (or even a flash-forward); and Alexander's dream of trying to find Little Man in the snow. However, much of the film's central section takes place during one of Scandinavia's 'white nights', and the colour in this section is very muted.[209] Is this part of the film therefore a dream, or real? Has nuclear war actually broken out, or is it all in Alexander's head? Or even one of the other characters, such as Little Man?

The film's colour coding is made even more problematic, as some of the central section is photographed in something close to full colour, such as the scene where the family watch the television broadcast about the outbreak of hostilities, and the two scenes were Marta appears naked. The second of these scenes, where she chases hens down a previously unseen corridor in the house, would seem to be happening on the same plane or level of consciousness as the preceding section, the monochrome shot of the city street full of people, but the first is extremely ambiguous.

So subtle, however, is Tarkovsky's use of colour that these issues are perhaps not, on first viewing, the film's most noticeable difficulties. A more obvious hurdle is in the very nature of Alexander's sacrifice itself. During his prayer, he vows to 'give Thee all I have. I'll give up my family, whom I love. I'll destroy my home and give up Little Man. I'll be mute, and never speak another word to anyone. I will relinquish everything that binds me to life if only Thou dost restore everything as it was before, as it was this morning and yesterday. Just let me be rid of this deadly sickening animal fear!' In due course, Alexander does indeed destroy his home, but can it really be a sacrifice if it involves other people? In other words, it is not simply his own home that Alexander is destroying, but also that of his family. Furthermore, he is also depriving Little Man of a father. Is it really a sacrifice when he is inflicting such things on people he loves, his own family?

If Alexander's final action is therefore controversial, the events that lead up to the film's climax are likewise problematic. As we have noted, Alexander prays after he has watched the TV broadcast. Given that he admits to Otto at the beginning of the film that his relationship with God is 'non-existent', it is remarkable that he prays at all. But what follows is even more peculiar. After his prayer, he seems to fall into a doze on the couch and what is possibly a dream sequence follows, in which Marta offers herself to Victor. The dream of looking for Little Man then follows, with Otto appearing in Alexander's study afterwards to explain to Alexander that his servant Maria is a witch, and that if he sleeps with her, they will all be saved. Given that, come morning, everything is 'as it was this morning and yesterday', what has saved them? Is it Alexander's prayer, or his visit to Maria's? Has there even been a war at all?

The key to the film's ambiguity is the start of the dream, but Tarkovsky doesn't let us know when it begins. That Alexander falls asleep is undeniable: after he prays, he crawls to the couch and seems to fall into a slumber at once; we likewise see him waking the next morning. The black and white sequences are almost certainly dreams or visions, but as to how much of the colour sequences are, Tarkovsky leaves us on our own to decide. Recalling the narrative puzzles of *Solaris*, *The Sacrifice* constantly wrong-foots us when we think we have solved the film. What we are watching seems to be real – the ominous thunder heard at the beginning of the film; the jets screaming overhead rattling the wine glasses and breaking the milk jug; the family's watching of the broadcast; Adelaide's hysterics; Alexander's praying – but

ANDREI TARKOVSKY

there are also things in the film that have an oddness to them,
which suggests that we are now in a dream. Otto's nocturnal
visit to Alexander is a case in point. 'What is it? What's
happened?' Alexander asks when Otto knocks on the
window. 'There's still one last chance!' the postman replies,
but Alexander doesn't appear to understand. 'A chance? What
kind of chance?' One would assume that had the TV broadcast and the prayer been real, Alexander would know full
well 'what's happened'. To further complicate matters, *something* seems to have happened, as the electricity has failed, and
the two men hear the shepherdess's call. 'What was that?'
Otto asks. 'I don't know,' Alexander replies. 'I thought it
sounded like music.'

To cap it all, Alexander, despite the fact that he declares
that Otto's proposition to go to Maria is madness, does
precisely that. Cycling to the other side of the bay where
Maria lives, he falls off and is about to return to the house
when the shepherdess's call seems to stop him in his tracks.
This appears to be real, but what about the car that we can
see in this scene? Why would anyone fleeing a supposed
nuclear war abandon their car there, in the middle of
nowhere, of all places?[210]

Events at Maria's do little, if anything, to help matters.
Alexander's imploring that Maria saves everyone seems real
enough. More jets fly overhead, while Maria's TV 'went dead
about 11.00 and didn't come on again', suggesting some sort
of power cut. But what of their levitation? Unlike the levitation in *Mirror*, which takes place after a voice-over,
suggesting that it is an imagined or dreamed episode,
Alexander's and Maria's floating above the bed takes place in
real time with the real sounds of their lovemaking. Yet even
this seems to be more real than the two shots that immediately follow, which show the city street now full of people

fleeing the disaster as Little Man sleeps above them, and then Maria wearing Adelaide's clothes, watching over Alexander as he sleeps on a camp bed. Not only have the two women seemed to merge in identity, but Maria is also seen gazing towards the remains of the burned-down house (its chimney stack, all that will remain of it by the end of the film, is clearly visible beyond the trees).

A more radical interpretation of *The Sacrifice* might be to suggest that, apart from the monochrome sequences, there are *no* dreams in the film at all.

'Life as a Reflection, Life as a Dream'

Despite its ambiguities, or maybe even because of them, *The Sacrifice* remains an enormously affecting film. The emotional nakedness of the film is remarkable: the prayer scene is almost embarrassing to watch, so acutely does Tarkovsky project his own personal fears into Alexander's words. Adelaide's hysteria is similarly powerful, as is her argument with Julia about waking Little Man and her monologue to Otto. The film is arguably the most beautiful of Tarkovsky's films, with Sven Nykvist's camerawork brilliantly capturing the northern light against which the action unfolds. Tarkovsky quietly celebrates the human form in showing the actors frequently full-length in long shots as the characters go about their daily business, and also nature, specifically the trees outside the house.

The soundscape is also particularly memorable. The never-seen shepherdess's calls act as both the film's leitmotif and suggest that the world of the unseen is ever-present. Likewise, the repeated soft tapping on the window conveys an air of expectancy or immanent presence. The use of Leonardo's *Adoration* seems to serve a similar purpose, almost

ANDREI TARKOVSKY

as if it is a character watching silently as the events of the
night unfold, not judging but patiently reflecting the faces of
Alexander and Otto as they peer into it, or the trees outside,
blowing in the night air.

One could even go as far as to argue that this is what the
film is really about, to 'capture pure poetic states of soul',[211]
as Mark Le Fanu puts it. In never letting us know what is
dream and what is real, Tarkovsky has found a new way of
showing the world, a perfect example of what Ingmar
Bergman called Tarkovsky's ability to show 'life as a reflection, life as a dream'.

Autobiographical Elements

It is often assumed that Tarkovsky knew he had cancer while
shooting *The Sacrifice*, which would go some way to
explaining why it comes across as his 'settling of accounts
with the West' and has the air of an eleventh-hour sermon.
But as his diaries show, he was not given the diagnosis until
December 1985. Nevertheless, Tarkovsky must have uncon-
sciously known that it would be his last film. His realisation
that it was is noted in a diary entry for 13 December:
'Pasternak was right', a reference to the prediction that he
would only make seven films. Unlike Alexander in 'The
Witch', there was to be no cure for Tarkovsky's own cancer,
and he would die just over a year after the original diagnosis,
on 29 December 1986.

Although a number of people, such as the critic David
Robinson of *The Times*, who visited the set of the film and
attested to Tarkovsky's good spirits during shooting,[212] *The
Sacrifice* contains a thinly veiled portrait of his own family
and personal circumstances at the time. Alexander's family is
modelled on his own, in particular the characters of

Adelaide, Marta and Little Man. Adelaide is surely the most unsympathetic of Tarkovsky's women; she is also the character who is most closely modelled on his second wife, Larissa, whom he was firmly convinced was a witch by the time the film was shot.[213] (One assumes he meant witch in its traditional, dark fairy-tale aspect, as opposed to the benign witches of 'The Witch' and the pagan episode in *Rublev*.) Adelaide's flowing dresses, her carefully coiffured hair and her haughty demeanour are specifically based on Larissa's own mannerisms and appearance. One cannot but help wonder if Adelaide's confession, delivered to Otto as she lies on the couch after the sedation has worn off, that she 'loved one man but married another' has any basis in reality also.

If Adelaide could be said to be a woman trapped by material needs, Marta is likewise trapped by her overpowering mother, with whom she competes for Victor's attentions. It is not made clear in the film, but Marta is Adelaide's daughter from a previous marriage. When Tarkovsky met Larissa in 1965, she already had a five-year-old daughter, Olga, who would appear in both *Solaris* and *Mirror*, and of whom Tarkovsky was apparently pathologically possessive. Tarkovsky could have transferred some of his own feelings for his stepdaughter onto Adelaide, as it is she who is possessive in the film, not Alexander; that Marta appears naked in the film on two occasions reveals another stratum of Tarkovsky's complex relationship with his stepdaughter.

Little Man is Andrei Jr, although in the film he is about half the age he actually was when *The Sacrifice* was made (14 years old). Here, the autobiographical element verges on the theatrical, in that Alexander can talk to Little Man on their afternoon walks, but Little Man cannot reply, due to a recent operation on his vocal chords. Likewise, Tarkovsky was not able to have a 'normal' conversation with his son, as Andrei

Junior had not been allowed out of the Soviet Union. The authorities had apparently hoped that this situation would force Tarkovsky to return to Russia, but it did not. Tarkovsky was as a result dependent on phone calls placed at odd hours of the day to talk to his son, who was finally allowed to join his father in January 1986, the month *The Sacrifice* was completed.[214]

Out of the other characters, Otto the postman deserves a mention. He suffers a fainting fit (which he ascribes to the touch of an evil angel), describes his hobby as 'collecting' strange events, and then proceeds to tell the family a story about a soldier who appeared in a photograph next to his mother, although he had been dead for years. While Otto's forebears are such characters as *Rublev*'s Theophanes the Greek and *Solaris*'s Gibarian, who mediate between the living and the dead, the Stalker, who mediates between the Zone and the outside world, and *Nostalgia*'s Domenico, who mediates between sanity and madness, normal time and eschatological time, Otto likewise stands between the normal waking world and the world of Alexander's dream. But Otto differs from these other characters in that he seems to have been based on someone Tarkovsky knew personally in the Soviet Union. On 7 February 1976, Tarkovsky mentions going to visit a clairvoyant, whom he then, correcting himself, describes as a 'collector' of psychic phenomena, as Otto does in the film.

Several other episodes come directly from Tarkovsky's own experience.[215] The monologue that Alexander delivers to Maria when he makes his night-time visit to her house is based on Tarkovsky's diary entry for 31 December 1978, where Tarkovsky mentions an argument about improving the garden until it became an eyesore.[216] Finally, the decision Adelaide takes that the family should stay put once the news broadcast has announced that the missiles are in the air seems to be derived from a rather strange diary entry for September 1975, when a UFO was spotted over Tarkovsky's dacha at Myasnoye. Tarkovsky himself was not present (he may have been inside at the time, working on the script for *Hoffmaniana*), but Larissa was, and she told Tarkovsky that the district prosecutor, who witnessed the object with her, made a comment as to whether the appearance of the craft signalled the outbreak of a nuclear war, and remarked that 'it would be better to die at home than somewhere on the road'.[217] Ironically, Tarkovsky was not able to do the same. He died in a Parisian hospital, far from his adopted home in Italy, and even further from the land of his birth. But *The Sacrifice* is, amongst other things, a call to courage. 'There is no such thing as death,' Alexander tells Little Man, 'only the fear of death.'

Works in Other Media

Tempo di Viaggio (1980)

Alternate Titles: *Journey In Time* (US DVD release)
Literal Title: *A Time of Travel*
Production Company: RAI/Genius
Production Supervisor: Franco Terilli
Directors: Andrei Tarkovsky & Tonino Guerra
Screenplay: Andrei Tarkovsky & Tonino Guerra
Director of Photography: Luciano Tovoli
Editor: Franco Letti
Sound: Eugenio Rondani
Mix: Romano Checcacci
2ⁿᵈ Unit Photography: Giancarlo Pancaldi
Cast: Andrei Tarkovsky (Himself), Tonino Guerra (Himself)
Shot: July/August 1979
Running Time: 63 minutes
First Screening: Rome, 9 June 1980 (Industry screening)
First Screening in West: Italian Television, 1980
Release in West: February 2003 (DVD release)

Storyline

The opening credits roll over a black screen in silence. A
view of Rome from the roof terrace of Tonino Guerra's
apartment. Guerra is shown on the terrace. Tarkovsky arrives;
the two men talk. Tonino recites a new poem to Tarkovsky,
who praises it. They discuss a screenplay they are writing,
only to be interrupted by a phone call from Antonioni. We
see a still life of a birdcage and a book. On the terrace,
Tarkovsky talks of his impressions of Italy.

A flashback shows them visiting a location near Amalfi.
Guerra speaks of his enthusiasm for Lecce, church architec-
ture and whether they should make their protagonist an
architect. Tarkovsky feels that Lecce is 'too beautiful' for their
film. They are seen visiting Otranto Cathedral, where a priest
explains the symbolism of a mosaic. A tracking shot from a
car takes us into the town of Locorotondo. A still life of a
bird in a tree. Tarkovsky and Guerra discuss Piero della
Francesca's *Madonna of Childbirth*, with Guerra expressing the
view that no reproduction could ever do the painting justice.

Inside the apartment, Tarkovsky talks about his favourite
directors, citing Dovzhenko, Bresson, Antonioni, Fellini,
Vigo, Parajanov and Bergman. They visit a villa famed for its
ornate floor commissioned by a Russian princess, but are
denied access.

Back on the terrace, Guerra asks Tarkovsky what advice
he would give young directors. Tarkovsky replies that they
should not separate their work from their lives and should be
morally responsible. Visiting another church, Tarkovsky
complains that all they are seeing are tourist sites, which the
hero of the screenplay probably wouldn't visit. Tarkovsky eats
with some Italians.

Back at the apartment, Tarkovsky speaks of his dislike of

science fiction, and then about using Bagno Vignoni as a location. He stresses the importance of their protagonist's inner journey. We then see the steam baths at Bagno Vignoni, followed by a brief interview with an elderly bell ringer.

Returning to the terrace, Tarkovsky speaks about unrealised projects and describes two ideas. Over a shot of the open French windows, Guerra speaks of death and parting, now that it is time for Tarkovsky to return to Moscow. He asks Tarkovsky what he will do when he gets home. Tarkovsky replies that he will go back to the village where he has a house. Over several long landscape shots, the two men discuss nature and the countryside. Guerra recites another poem. Sheep shelter beneath a tree. Tarkovsky contemplates in a doorway. A close-up of the *Madonna of Childbirth*.

Once more on the terrace, Guerra asks Tarkovsky if he likes his house. We see a series of still lifes inside the house, including the screenplay of *Nostalgia*. Tarkovsky blows out a candle. He asks Guerra to read the first poem again. Tarkovsky stands at the window, looking out. We cut to a close-up on an old photograph of a Russian village in the snow. The image fades to white. The end credits roll over a white screen in silence.

Production History

Tarkovsky was noting in his diary as early as 20 January 1976 about the possibility of making a film in Italy,[218] and by 22 August he had a title, echoing Goethe: *Italian Journey*. His collaborator on the project was to be his friend, the screenwriter Tonino Guerra, and the idea was to convey Tarkovsky's impressions of Italy as he travelled around. The first draft of the script was completed in October, and Tarkovsky spent the next two years hoping to be allowed to make the film once the nightmare of making *Stalker* was finally over.

Tarkovsky visited Italy in April 1979, when he and Guerra had the idea for a film they called 'The End of the World', which would eventually be incorporated into *Nostalgia*. He returned in July, and *Tempo di Viaggio* – 'A Time of Travel' – was shot over the summer, with editing beginning in August, while they were still filming. To judge from Tarkovsky's diary, shooting went well, and it was evidently something of a liberation for him to be working in the West (although his enthusiasm for working in the West would wane). Editing continued into September, when Tarkovsky returned to Moscow. By now, he planned to return to Italy to make *Nostalgia*, as well as finish *Tempo*. He was allowed to return the following spring, and *Tempo di Viaggio* was completed in April and May 1980, whilst he and Guerra were also working on the script for *Nostalgia*, which was completed at the same time. The first screening of *Tempo* was held at RAI – which was one of the backers of *Nostalgia* – in Rome on 9 June 1980. The film was later broadcast on Italian television.

An Italian Journey

Tempo di Viaggio is Tarkovsky's only documentary. Originally, the film was to have shown Tarkovsky soaking up the sights of Italy and giving his impressions. In calling the film *Italian Journey*, Tarkovsky was obviously echoing Goethe and would have probably wished to appear as an inheritor of the Romantic tradition (he had a deep interest in the German Romantics and for many years wanted to make a film about ETA Hoffmann – *see* Appendix II). However, as Goethe revised his Italian diaries before publishing them, so Tarkovsky's original idea had changed somewhat by the time he was finally able to make the film. Shortly before

Tarkovsky began shooting, he and Guerra had had an idea to which they gave the working title 'The End of the World', which quickly became subsumed into *Nostalgia*; *Tempo di Viaggio* shows Tarkovsky and Guerra visiting possible locations for the planned feature.

Although a documentary, *Tempo di Viaggio* contains many of Tarkovsky's signature devices. The film has a measured pace, and is composed of many long, slow pans. The film's opening is a case in point. We see a wooded hilltop; the camera then pans right slowly, reaching a building that may be an observatory, before zooming out to reveal that our point of view is from a roof terrace of a city apartment. This is followed by a shot of a busy city street, and another slow zoom out reveals one of the roof terrace's walls. A doorbell sounds and we cut back to the previous angle, now showing Tonino Guerra standing on the terrace. The camera pans right with him as he enters the apartment, saying that the caller must be Tarkovsky. We then hold for nearly 30 seconds on some shutters before they are rolled up, revealing French windows that lead inside. Another ten seconds elapse before we hear the muffled voices of Tarkovsky and Guerra, and then, after another 20 seconds or so, Tarkovsky himself emerges through the windows and sits down on a deckchair.

Guerra tells Tarkovsky that they need to decide which parts of their journey they are going to keep for the script-in-progress of *Nostalgia*. This then sets up the film's storyline. Tarkovsky admits that his impressions of their journey are confused, and when discussing Amalfi, we then cut to a shot of the town, followed by their visit to a steep gorge. The film then returns to Tarkovsky and Guerra on the terrace, continuing their discussion. In this way, *Tempo di Viaggio* relates Tarkovsky's journeys around (mainly) Southern Italy.

Guerra's apartment acts as the film's centre of gravity, with his frequent questioning of Tarkovsky being the reason either for conversations – Tarkovsky's favourite directors, advice to young filmmakers – or for flashbacks of their travels.

One such flashback is to the cathedral of Otranto, which is one of the film's most interesting sequences. After discussing whether Gorchakov should be an architect, Tarkovsky, Guerra and their interpreter enter the cathedral to look at the celebrated twelfth-century floor mosaic. A priest is on hand to explain the symbolism of the floor. In a speech that could well have played a part in influencing Domenico's sermon in Rome, he explains the diverse cultures represented on the mosaic (of the tree of life) and that 'in all cultures there is something true... to enrich themselves... human beings take whatever they need from other cultures... today we can have a dialogue with all cultures. Without any obstacles. Without any ideology.'[219]

Nostalgia is further foreshadowed in a number of other scenes. Tarkovsky feels a location is 'too beautiful' for the film, a sentiment that would resurface in *Nostalgia* as Gorchakov's comment that he is 'tired of seeing these sickeningly beautiful sites'. At another location, Tarkovsky complains that Guerra is only showing him tourist sites and, in the nearest the film gets to some humour, admits 'I am a bit worried as I feel like I am on holiday.'

The theme of Russians in exile occurs during the episode where Tarkovsky and Guerra attempt to view a trompe l'œil floor in a villa, while back at the apartment Tarkovsky tells Guerra of his attraction for Bagno Vignoni, where much of *Nostalgia* would eventually be shot. We see shots of steam rising from the spa pool and what is possibly Tarkovsky's own hotel room there, which served as the inspiration for Gorchakov's room in the film. Already Tarkovsky feels that

Nostalgia will be largely concerned with Gorchakov's inner state: 'I think it is important to pay attention to the journey that our character makes inside himself. This is the most important [thing].'

Tempo di Viaggio does, however, contain elements that are not typically Tarkovskian, and which could possibly be attributed to Guerra, who was the film's co-director. There are several sequences using a hand-held camera – the visit to Flore, the mosaic scene, the drive into Locorotondo – which are the first in a Tarkovsky film since *Ivan's Childhood*. The film's soundtrack is also particularly spare; in addition, there are several moments where the film is completely silent, such as during the trip to the gorge at Flore, or just before the priest explains the mosaic in Otranto cathedral. Bagno Vignoni is the only location from *Tempo* to find its way into *Nostalgia*, and the shots of the pool in both films highlight the differences in the use of sound: in the feature, the pool is always bubbling, and we also hear the voices of the bathers and Domenico, but in the documentary, the shots of the pool are completely unadorned.

Despite its occasional stylistic variations, *Tempo di Viaggio* is thoroughly Tarkovskian in most other respects. There are some striking still lifes, such as the bird and the cage, the birdcage and the book, the typewriter on the chair on the roof terrace, and some distinctive landscape shots, especially towards the end of the film (Bagno Vignoni, the trees in the meadow). The narrative, too, is typical of Tarkovsky, with its frequent flashbacks and uncertain timescale. It is not possible to gauge how long Tarkovsky and Guerra spent on their travels, but the framing device, that of the two men's conversations in the apartment and on the terrace, is revealed to have taken place in a single day when Tarkovsky asks Guerra to read his poem about the house again, which Guerra had read to Tarkovsky at the beginning of the film. Guerra wonders which poem Tarkovsky is referring to, and then he remembers 'Ah! The one I told you this morning.' The frequent conversations between Tarkovsky and Guerra reflect Tarkovsky's belief that 'an artist is only justified in his work when it is crucial to his way of life',[220] which is also the advice he gives to young directors when questioned by Guerra. As such, *Tempo di Viaggio* is not so much a film about the early stages of making *Nostalgia*, but a film about art as daily life, and anticipates films such as Victor Erice's *The Quince Tree Sun*.

Stage

Hamlet (1977)

Cast: Anatoly Solonitsyn (Hamlet), Margarita Terekhova (Gertrude), Inna Churikova (Ophelia), Nikolai Karachentsev (Laertes), Vsevolod Larionov (Polonius)

Production History

Tarkovsky first saw *Hamlet* – the most popular of Shakespeare's plays in Russia – while he was at VGIK. He seems to have begun thinking about mounting a production of his own in March 1975, when he wanted to stage it at the Alexander Theatre in Moscow. This did not prove to be possible and, by June, he was hoping for the Lenin Komsomol Theatre instead, which is where the play was eventually staged. He noted that he was planning to start rehearsals in November 1975,[221] and a first read-through was held in January 1976.

The production was beset with difficulties with the cast:

Oleg Yankovsky quit early on when it became apparent Solonitsyn was going to play the Dane, while Inna Churikova (Ophelia) angered Tarkovsky by taking unannounced holidays during rehearsals. Tarkovsky was also not happy with any of the existing translations of the play, finding Lozinsky's 'inarticulate and clumsy' and Pasternak's 'appalling, opaque'.[222] In the end, he settled for a prose version, finding that it captured Shakespeare's meaning better.

Rehearsals finally began in November 1976, by which time Tarkovsky was also in pre-production on *Stalker*. A dress rehearsal in front of an audience was held on 24 December 1976, with the general consensus being that the acting was bad. The management of the theatre even wanted Tarkovsky to replace Solonitsyn and Terekhova, but he refused. Things seem to have improved by the time of the official first night on 18 February 1977, with Tarkovsky noting that 'Tolya [Solonitsyn] has started to act' and that 'the play might work'.[223]

The 'Unsolved' Play

Unfortunately, no record of the play seems to exist, apart from two scenes that were filmed for television on 24 February 1977, after which Tarkovsky, Solonitsyn and Terekhova were also interviewed. As such, it is difficult to gauge how much of a success the production was. Tarkovsky makes few references to it in *Sculpting in Time*, only noting that when Polonius is murdered, he clutches the red turban he had been wearing to his chest, to signify blood.[224] Perhaps the most controversial aspect of Tarkovsky's adaptation was the ending, where the dead Hamlet comes back to life and one by one resurrects all of the dead characters.

Tarkovsky notes in his diary that, by early 1978, *Hamlet* 'has been laid to rest'.[225] He later quotes some positive audience feedback – 'your version of *Hamlet* is the most modern production I have ever seen on stage... Could that production be put on again?'[226] – but in general, the play seems not to have been a total success. Tarkovsky wrote that '*Hamlet* is the one play in world literature that has not been solved',[227] and the fact that he continued to entertain ideas about making a film version of the play right up until the end of his life suggests Tarkovsky felt he still had unfinished business with it.

Boris Godunov (1983)

Cast: Paul Hudson (Nikitich), John Gibbs (Mitukha), Jonathan Summers (Andrei Shchelkalov), Philip Langridge (Prince Vasily Ivanovich Shuisky), Robert Lloyd (Boris Godunov), Gwynne Howell (Pimen), Michel Svetlev (Grigory Otrepiev – The Pretender Dmitri), Elizabeth Bainbridge (The Hostess of the Inn), Francis Egerton (Missail), Aage Haugland/Anton Diakov (23 & 25 Nov) (Varlaam), Donald Adams (Frontier Guard), Joan Rogers (Xenia), Fiona Kimm (Fyodor), Marta Szirmay (Xenia's Nurse) Anthony Smith (The Boyar in attendance), Eva Randova (Marina Mniszek), John Shirley-Quirk (Ragoni), Patrick Power (The Simpleton), John Kerr (Khrushchov), John Gibbs (Czernikowski), William Mackie (Lavicki)
Director: Andrei Tarkovsky
Conductor: Claudio Abbado
Libretto: Modest Mussorgsky, based on Pushkin's play and Karamzin's *History of the Russian State*
Music: Modest Mussorgsky
Designs: Nikolai Dvigubsky

Lighting: Robert Bryan
Choreography: Romayne Grigorova
Company: The Royal Opera

Performance dates: 31 October, 4, 7, 10, 15, 19, 23, 25 November 1983 Royal Opera House, Covent Garden, London

DVD Version

Cast: Yevgeny Fedotov (Nikitich), Grigory Karasyov (Mitukha), Mikhail Kit (Andrei Shchelkalov) Yevgeny Boitsov (Prince Vasily Ivanovich Shuisky), Robert Lloyd (Boris Godunov), Alexander Morosov (Pimen), Alexei Steblianko (Grigory Otrepiev – The Pretender Dmitri), Ludmila Filatova (The Hostess of the Inn), Igor Yan (Missail) Vladimir Ognovenko (Varlaam), Olga Kondina (Xenia), Larissa Dyatkova (Fyodor), Eugenia Perlassova (Xenia's Nurse), Olga Borodina (Marina Mniszek), Sergei Leiferkus (Rangoni), Vladimir Solodovnikov (The Simpleton)
Directors: Stephen Lawless (Stage), Humphrey Burton (Television)
Conductor: Valery Gergiev
Company: Kirov Opera
Performance Date: April 1990 Mariinsky Theatre, St Petersburg
Revivals: Vienna 1991; Tokyo 1994; London 2003

Production History

Tarkovsky's involvement with a production of Mussorgsky's opera goes back to 1981, when the producer Daniel Toscan du Plantier approached Tarkovsky with a view to directing it. The 'suggestion threw them all into a trance,' Tarkovsky noted in his diary. '"But why not Bondarchuk?" was their reaction; the answer to which was: "Because the director has to be a religious man and a poet."'[228] When Claudio Abbado was asked to stage the opera at the Royal Opera House in London in 1983, he was given the choice of director. Tarkovsky was his only choice.

Tarkovsky was delighted to be able to begin work on *Boris* at last, and preparations began in October 1983, a few months after the furore surrounding *Nostalgia* at Cannes. He was still in the West, still trying to attain assurances that, if he were to return home, he would be guaranteed work. He was also trying to get the Soviet authorities to allow his son, Andrei Jr, to join him. He made no headway with either appeal. 'I am lost!' he wrote in his diary on 25 May 1983, 'I cannot live in Russia, nor can I live here.'[229] This sense of ambivalence about the West, begun in *Nostalgia*, continues in *Boris Godunov*. The opera also makes reference to nearly all of his films, and could almost be said to form, along with *Nostalgia* and *The Sacrifice*, a kind of 'Trilogy of the West', reflecting Tarkovsky's own personal predicament as much as his ongoing artistic concerns.

Conscience and Exile

Tarkovsky saw *Boris Godunov* as being about conscience (an echo of *Solaris*?), with Boris himself being a man tormented by 'a terrifying premonition that his own son will have to pay for his sins'.[230] (Boris had ordered the death of the Tsarevich Dmitri in order to secure his own accession.) In *Mirror*, Tarkovsky himself was the son, aware that he was repeating his father's mistakes. In *Boris*, his sympathies are rather more with the father – Boris – and, whereas the film looked back to the past, the opera looks both ways, to the past and to the ever-uncertain future. (It could almost be said that Tarkovsky was wishing for his son a better life than the one he himself had had.)

With its subject matter being concerned with Russian history, it cannot help but recall *Andrei Rublev*, although here the tone is darker. As the last scene fades out, a bloody axe remains illuminated in a spotlight, a reminder, if one were needed, that Russia's history is very much far from over, and anticipates the chaos and bloodshed of Mafia-dominated post-Soviet Russia. Russian history also forms the *cantus firmus* of *Mirror*, and Pushkin's letter to Chaadeyev, quoted in that film by Ignat to the ghostly woman in black, is here dramatised in the Polish act. The enemy is not the Mongols, this time, but the West, as personified by the sinister Jesuit Rangoni, who schemes to get Marina to convert Russia to Roman Catholicism once she becomes Tsarina. We must recall that not only is the opera based on Pushkin's play, but that his letter to Chaadeyev sparked the Slavophile-Westerner controversy, which dominated nineteenth-century Russian intellectual life. (For proselytising Roman Christianity, Chaadeyev was thrown into a mental asylum.) The opera's Poland is, for Tarkovsky, the same as Italy was for Gorchakov and Sosnovsky in *Nostalgia*, and the garden of statues that Sosnovsky dreams about here appears in the grounds of the castle of Sandomir.

Boris Godunov employs a range of traditional Tarkovskian motifs: a huge bell, icons, candles, mist and dreams. It is here that the opera is at its most filmic: as the monk Grigory confides in the *staretz* Pimen that he has had 'that dream' again, we see the dream – the murder of the Tsarevich Dmitri – being enacted at the back of the stage, bathed in a spectral green spotlight, which is here the equivalent of the filmic device of cutting from colour to monochrome. The boy reappears during Boris's delirium when he is sitting on the great map of Russia, again bathed in the green light, and finally at Boris's death. This penultimate scene in the opera is perhaps its most powerful. As with the axe at the very end, the scene has an air of unwitting prophecy about it: as Boris lies dying, the ghost of the young Tsarevich reappears and, seeing that Boris is about to expire, turns to face the huge pendulum that swings under the arch at the back of the stage until it finally comes to a standstill as Boris dies. The boy is normally lit this time, as if to suggest that the past and present are now in some kind of harmony that defies logic but recalls the 'impossible' endings of *Ivan*, *Solaris*, *Mirror* and *Nostalgia*. The fact that the dead Tsarevich is, in his nightshirt, very reminiscent of Ivan, gives the scene deeper meaning, almost as if Tarkovsky were coming to terms and peace with his own work. One cannot help but see the stopping of the pendulum as Tarkovsky's unconscious acknowledgement that his own time had nearly run its course.

Radio

Turnabout (1965)

Tarkovsky's only radio drama, *Turnabout*, is based on William Faulkner's 1932 short story about First World War fighter pilots. (It was filmed in 1933 as *Today We Live*, directed by Howard Hawks.) The play, which Tarkovsky directed and adapted, was recorded when he was working for the all-Soviet radio station during 1964 and 1965. However, *Turnabout*'s anti-war tone did not sit well with the Party, resulting in the play being pulled from the broadcast schedules at the last minute. It was not broadcast until 26

September 1987, when Gorbachev's *glasnost* was in full swing. In 1990, it was broadcast in Germany, and later in the UK and Sweden.

In addition to *Turnabout*, there exists an original script for a radio play called *The White Crow*, apparently a science fiction story, but which seems to have never been recorded, let alone broadcast.

BOOKS

Sculpting in Time (1984)

Tarkovsky's book of film theory and autobiographical reminiscences was a long time in the making. The first mention of the book in his diary is on 7 September 1970, when it bore the title *Juxtapositions*. His then collaborator, Lenya Kozlov, was later replaced by Olga Surkova, who suggested that the book should take the form of a dialogue between filmmaker and critic, and also came up with *Sculpting in Time* as a title. The book continued to gestate throughout the 1970s. By 1980, Tarkovsky was convinced that it would never get published at home, and so began to think about getting it published abroad. This eventually happened, with the book being first published in German in 1984 and in English in 1986. A revised version, including a chapter on *The Sacrifice*, appeared in 1989.

Unfortunately, there are small textual discrepancies between all three of these editions and a definitive text has yet to appear. This is all the more regrettable, as *Sculpting in Time* has become something of a cult book since its first appearance, ranking alongside Bresson's *Notes on Cinematography* as being one of the best books ever written by a director about filmmaking.

SEAN MARTIN

The Diaries (1989)

As with *Sculpting in Time*, the diaries were also first published
in German, in 1989. An English edition appeared as *Time
Within Time* two years later. Whereas the differences between
the various editions of *Sculpting* were generally small, the
differences between the various editions of the diaries are
quite large, with whole sections being omitted from certain
translations. The English edition is perhaps the worst of
them, with very few entries for the last few years of
Tarkovsky's life. A complete edition was not published until
2001, when the Italian edition appeared.

Andrei Rublev (1991)

The screenplay of *Rublev* published in 1991 is apparently
Tarkovsky's original *kino roman*, and it differs from the
version of the script as published in *Iskusstvo Kino* in 1964 in
the ordering of its episodes (the balloon flight, for instance,
was at the beginning of Part II in the 1964 version).
Nevertheless, it gives a good impression of how Tarkovsky
originally intended the film to be and includes all of the
episodes that were cut from the shooting script, such as 'The
Hunt' and 'Indian Summer'.

Collected Screenplays (1999)

Intended as a follow-up to the *Andrei Rublev* script, this
collects most of Tarkovsky's remaining screenplays together.
Like the published *Rublev*, most of the scripts are written as
kino romans and read well. All feature details that were subsequently changed or omitted in the finished films, and as such
this collection forms a useful companion to the films.

Unfortunately, it does not include the scripts for the student films (assuming they still exist), the early *Antarctica, Distant Land, Tempo di Viaggio* (a script for which was originally written in 1976), or any of the films that Tarkovsky reportedly wrote or co-wrote, such as the relatively late potboiler *Lookout, Snake!* (directed by Zakir Sabitov in 1979).

Instant Light: Tarkovsky Polaroids (2002)

The only example of Tarkovsky's work as a photographer yet to appear, *Instant Light* is a collection of Polaroids taken by Tarkovsky in Russia during 1980 and 1981, and in Italy between 1979 and 1984. Rather than being rehearsals for film compositions, the photographs often employ angles that Tarkovsky would never have used in a film (such as the photograph of the tree outside his dacha at Myasnoye from September 1981)[231] and work independently of the films. They frequently employ the same restricted palette, and could perhaps be thought of as being both instances of 'imprinted time' and examples of Tarkovsky's dictum that 'my function is to make [the viewer] aware of his need to give his love, and aware that beauty is summoning him'.[232]

NOT CURRENTLY AVAILABLE IN ENGLISH

Lectures on Film Directing (1989)

Edited by one of Tarkovsky's cinematic 'heirs', the director Konstantin Lopushansky, this is divided into five chapters: 'Film as Art', 'The Film Image', 'The Script', 'The Concept and its Realisation' and 'Editing'. In this book, Tarkovsky is apparently 'more specific and somewhat less theoretical and philosophical than *Sculpting in Time*'.[233]

Récits de jeunesse (2004)

Youth Stories is a collection of Tarkovsky's prose and poetry dating from his VGIK years up to 1962. Some of the pieces are inspired by Tarkovsky's time in Siberia. Currently only available in French, from Éditions Philippe Rey.

PAINTINGS AND POEMS

Writing about their collaboration on *Boris Godunov*, Claudio Abbado describes Tarkovsky as 'just as I had imagined him from his films – an artist of immeasurable range, a visionary director, a painter and a poet'.[234] In 1991, Abbado was instrumental in reviving *Boris* at Vienna, which formed the centrepiece – along with the films – of a Tarkovsky festival that included two exhibitions of Tarkovsky's paintings. This is, to date, one of the few occasions when Tarkovsky's paintings have been publicly exhibited. A number of his drawings, however, appear in the diaries, and they reveal Tarkovsky to have been a gifted draftsman, with a fine, well-judged line.

Tarkovsky's poetry has likewise been somewhat neglected, with only a handful of rough verses being included in the English edition of the diaries. The French *Youth Stories* contains poems written in Tarkovsky's twenties, but they have yet to be translated into English.

Endnotes

1. Natasha Synessios, *Mirror*, IB Tauris, 2001, p.4.
2. Peter Green, *Andrei Tarkovsky: The Winding Quest*, p.1.
3. Synessios, p.118.
4. This is possibly due to the fact that North American prints of Tarkovsky's films were frequently cut by distributors. An uncut version of *Solaris*, for instance, was not released in the USA until 1990. In Europe, the films were usually distributed uncut, although there were one or two exceptions, the most notorious of which being the Italian *Solaris*, which was cut so heavily and even re-edited by its distributor, Dino de Laurentiis, that Tarkovsky sued him.
5. Ingmar Bergman, *The Magic Lantern*, Penguin Books, 1988, p.73.
6. Marina Tarkovskaya interview, Vida T Johnson and Graham Petrie, *The Films of Andrei Tarkovsky: A Visual Fugue*, p.18.
7. Mark Le Fanu, *The Cinema of Andrei Tarkovsky*, British Film Institute, 1987, p.16.
8. Natalia Baranskaya, *About Andrei Tarkovsky* (Editor: Marina Tarkovskaya), Progress Publishers, 1990, p.25.
9. Johnson & Petrie, p.19.
10. Tarkovsky's sister Marina believes there to be no truth to this legend. Johnson & Petrie, p.20.

11. Maya Turovskaya, *Tarkovsky: Cinema as Poetry*, Faber and Faber, 1989, p.17.

12. Alexander Gordon, *About Andrei Tarkovsky*, pp.39–40.

13. Johnson & Petrie, p.21.

14. The complete article, originally published in the Italian newspaper *L'Unita* in 1963, is reproduced on nostalghia.com.

15. Ingmar Bergman, *The Magic Lantern*, Penguin, 1988, p.??.

16. Wajda quote cited in Johnson & Petrie, p.15.

17. Andrei Tarkovsky, *Time Within Time: The Diaries 1970–1986*, Seagull Books, 1991, diary entry for 10 April 1979, p.180.

18. The film did, however, win the FIPRESCI Prize, the Ecumenical Jury Prize, Best Director and shared with Bresson's *L'Argent* the Grand Prix de Création.

19. *Kieślowski on Kieślowski*, Danusia Stok (Editor), Faber and Faber, 1993, p.195.

20. Diary entry for 3 July 1975, *Time Within Time*, p.111.

21. *Sculpting in Time*, University of Texas Press, 1989, p.132.

22. *Sculpting in Time*, p.126.

23. Johnson & Petrie, p.51.

24. Their first script together was the unproduced *Antarctica, Distant Land* of 1959.

25. Johnson & Petrie, p.52.

26. Misharin's participation in the editing of *Mirror* is perhaps ascribable to the fact that he and Tarkovsky were friends, and he was also on good terms with Tarkovsky's mother.

27. Arkady Strugatsky, *About Andrei Tarkovsky*, p.260.

28. Diary, 25 March 1985. The English translation includes it in the entry for 9 March 1985, *Time Within Time*, p.343. Tarkovsky here is actually quoting Tolstoy.

29. Johnson & Petrie, p.48.

30. Giuseppe Lanci, press conference 19 January 1987. Reproduced on nostalghia.com.
31. The whole of this fascinating scene appears on Disc Two of the Criterion DVD edition of the film.
32. *Sculpting in Time*, p.158.
33. Owe Svensson, *Sound in Tarkovski's Sacrifice*, article on Filmsound.org.
34. Johnson & Petrie, p.96.
35. *Sculpting in Time*, p.212.
36. Johnson & Petrie, p.38.
37. *Sculpting in Time*, p.200.
38. *Sculpting in Time*, p.200.
39. *Sculpting in Time*, p.223.
40. *Sculpting in Time*, p.108.
41. *Sculpting in Time*, p.50.
42. 'The Apocalypse', *Temenos*, Issue 8, 1987, pp.14–15.
43. From an interview with Charles de Brantes in *La France Catholique*, 20 June 1986. Reproduced on nostalghia.com.
44. *Sculpting in Time*, p.212.
45. In the 1985 Stockholm interview, Tarkovsky is quite unequivocal: 'I feel very close to pantheism.' The whole interview is reproduced on nostalghia.com.
46. De Brantes interview.
47. The pale horse in the latter film only appears in the close-ups of the Leonardo (it is to the right of the Carob tree). The dream sequence where Alexander is lying on a camp bed with Maria wearing Adelaide's clothes originally also showed Little Man leading a pale horse past them. This was cut from the final version of the film, although it can be seen in the documentary, *Directed by Andrei Tarkovsky*.
48. Diary entry for 3 January 1974, *Time Within Time*, p.89.

49. Diary entry for 15 September 1976, *Time Within Time*, p.131.

50. The filming of this shot can be seen in Donatella Baglivo's documentary, *Andrei Tarkovsky in Nostalgia*, which clearly shows Patrizia Terreno and the little boy running around the back of the camera once it has tracked past them in order to reach their second marks.

51. *Sculpting in Time*, p.138.

52. *Sculpting in Time*, p.138.

53. The strange whistlings in *Mirror* almost suggest that the film is not merely poetic, but psychic, as if the sound was the means by which Tarkovsky could communicate with the past and his ancestors.

54. Surkova was furious that Tarkovsky wanted to be credited as sole author and took legal proceedings against him.

55. *Sculpting in Time*, p.38.

56. Alexander Pushkin, 'The Prophet', quoted in *Sculpting in Time*, pp.221–2. The version quoted here is the Ted Hughes translation, from *Collected Poems*, p.1,194, Faber & Faber, 2003.

57. Nick James, 'Icon', *Sight and Sound*, March 2005, p.30

58. *Sculpting in Time*, p.29.

59. *Sculpting in Time*, p.20.

60. *Sculpting in Time*, p.20.

61. The tune was often broadcast by Voice of America and came to be seen as a symbol of freedom.

62. Shukshin (1929–74) went on to have a successful career as both actor, writer and director. He died of a heart attack after completing what is perhaps his best-known film, *The Red Snowball Tree* (1973).

63. Gordon, *About Andrei Tarkovsky*, p.44.

64. Gordon, *About Andrei Tarkovsky*, p.44.

65. The film was shot in the Russian city of Kursk.
66. Mark Le Fanu, *The Cinema of Andrei Tarkovsky*, pp.17–18.
67. Maya Turovskaya, *Tarkovsky: Cinema as Poetry*, p.19.
68. Marina Tarkovskaya, interview with Gonzalo Blasco, Zaragoza, Spain, 10 November 2003. Originally published in Spanish on andreitarkovski.org, an English translation appears on nostalghia.com. Marina and Alexander Gordon did later adapt the story into a script, parts of which were actually shot (but not directed by Gordon) for the 1994 Russian television documentary *Andrei Tarkovsky's Taiga Summer*.
69. The film faced competition from a professional Lenfilm production which was adapting the same story at the same time. The Lenfilm version lost out to Tarkovsky's and Gordon's film, which was the one that Soviet television broadcast.
70. Alexander Gordon, interview with Gonzalo Blasco, Zaragoza, Spain, 10 November 2003. Originally published in Spanish on andreitarkovski.org, an English translation appears on nostalghia.com.
71. *Sculpting in Time*, p.136.
72. c.f. diary entry for 24 January 1973:'… it isn't a question of details, but of what is hidden'. *Time Within Time*, p.65.
73. The Iranian director Abbas Kiarostami also uses this technique, although he seems to have arrived at it independently of Tarkovsky.
74. It may simply be a quality of the Facets DVD edition of the film – from which this dialogue quotation comes – but the music teacher almost seems to be in black and white in an otherwise colour scene.
75. Johnson & Petrie, p.68.
76. Evgeny Zharikov, Interview, *Ivan's Childhood*, Artificial Eye DVD.

77. *Sculpting in Time*, p.27.
78. Tarkovsky used back-projection on only five occasions: in this dream; in the scene in the car after Galtsev and Kholin pick Ivan up after he runs away; during Berton's drive into the city in *Solaris*; and twice in *The Steamroller and the Violin*.
79. *Sculpting in Time,* p.193.
80. Natasha Synessios, *Mirror*, p.64.
81. Turovskaya, p.35.
82. *Sculpting in Time*, p.29.
83. Before this scene was shot, Anatoly Solonitsyn took a month-long vow of silence in order to make Rublev's return to speech more convincing.
84. Scholarship now puts Rublev's date of birth at 1370, not 1360. He died in 1430.
85. Robert Bird, *Andrei Rublev*, BFI Film Classics, British Film Institute, 2004, p.23.
86. Bird, p.23. The film was eventually made in 1975 by Mikhail Shveitser, starring Donatas Banionis, who, by that time, had worked with Tarkovsky on *Solaris*.
87. Turovskaya, p.48.
88. Diary entry for 17 June 1973, *Time Within Time*, p.77.
89. Tarkovsky, quoted in Bird, p.37.
90. *Sculpting in Time*, p.50.
91. Robert Bird argues that it is Foma's imagining, pointing out that the sequence begins with a shot of a piece of cloth floating in the river and ends with a shot of Foma washing some brushes in a river which echoes the shot of the cloth. See Bird, pp.77–9.
92. Tarkovsky's portrayal of the pagans is sympathetic enough – their candle-lit rituals are perhaps the most visually beautiful things in the film – to suggest that he admired their way of life and beliefs. This feeling is

borne out by Marfa's refuting of Rublev's charge that their celebrations are bestial, 'Isn't all love the same? It's just love.'

93. These appear in the 205-minute version only.

94. Bird, p.78.

95. Guy Gauthier, pp.34–7.

96. Tarkovsky defended the cruelty of the original edit by pointing out that the horse was destined for the abattoir the next day anyway and the cow was covered in asbestos, so it didn't actually suffer any burns. Given that Tarkovsky was an animal lover, especially of horses, one is left wondering why, after having saved the horse from the abattoir, they couldn't simply have pretended to kill it and let the poor beast live out its dotage in pasture. One also wonders what distress the cow suffered. Needless to say, Tarkovsky would have been in considerable trouble from animal welfare organisations had the film been shot today.

97. Michel Ciment, *Dossier Positif*, Issue 79.

98. Jacques Demeure, *Dossier Positif*, Issue 81.

99. Andrei Tarkovskii, 'Iskat' i dobivat'sia', *Sovetskii ekran* 17 (1962), pp.9, 20. Translation by Robert Bird. Cited on nostalghia.com.

100. E.g. in the diary entry for 11 July 1970, Tarkovsky mentions both women, writing that Bibi Andersson had visited him in Moscow and was very keen to be in the film and that he had also shot tests with Irma Rausch. *Time Within Time*, p.5.

101. Diary entries for 12 July, 10 & 11 August 1971, *Time Within Time*, p.39.

102. Diary entry for 6 September 1971, *Time Within Time*, p.42.

103. Turovskaya, p.57.

104. Johnson & Petrie, p.29.

105. In summarising Bradbury's masterpiece, *The Martian Chronicles*, John Clute and Peter Nicholls draw attention to the book's qualities, which are positively Tarkovskian: 'The mood is of loneliness and nostalgia… throughout the book appearances and reality slip, dreamlike, from the one to the other… [it has an] anti-technological bias, the celebration of simplicity and innocence as imagined in small-town life, the sense of loss as youth changes to adulthood.' *The Encyclopedia of Science Fiction*, Orbit, 1993, p.151.

106. The character is called Rheya in the novel (and in the Soderbergh version).

107. Lem, *Solaris*, p.147.

108. Diary entry for 24 May 1981, *Time Within Time*, p.280. Tarkovsky quotes widely in the diaries: the Church Fathers, the Bible, Zen and Taoist masters, plus his beloved Tolstoy and Dostoyevsky, among others, frequently recur.

109. Lem, p.76.

110. At the end of the Crucifixion scene, where Foma is washing brushes in the river, the camera pans down to dwell on the fronds undulating below the surface of the water.

111. Le Fanu, p.64. This quote is reminiscent of Bresson's dictums: 'Be sure of having used to the full all that is communicated by immobility and silence' and 'Build your film on white, on silence and on stillness.' Bresson, *Notes on the Cinematographer*, pp.20, 126.

112. Mysterious layouts of dachas and flats would continue in all of Tarkovsky's remaining films.

113. All translations of dialogue are taken from the Criterion DVD edition of the film.

114. Apparently Tarkovsky's second wife Larissa occasionally suffered fits, which may well have inspired the 'Resurrection' scene. Stalker's wife and Adelaide in *The Sacrifice* also suffer similar fits.

115. Montaigne, 'On Experience', *Essays*, III.13.

116. Diary entry for 17 March 1971, *Time Within Time*, p.37.

117. Andrei Tarkovsky, *Collected Screenplays*, Translated and edited by William Powell and Natasha Synessios, Faber & Faber, 1999, footnote 4, p.131. See also the diary entries for 15 June and 15 August 1970, *Time Within Time*, pp.5–6.

118. Diary entry for 12 September 1970, *Time Within Time*, p.21.

119. Diary entry for 12 September 1970, *Time Within Time*, p.19.

120. Diary entry for 12 September 1970, *Time Within Time*, p.21.

121. Painted in the early 1660s, the work now hangs in the Hermitage in St Petersburg.

122. Johnson & Petrie, p.19.

123. Johnson & Petrie, pp.22–3.

124. Most synopses of the film identify the boy as Ignat, but a close examination of the costume – a tatty coat with a wide collar – reveals that it is definitely the young Alexei.

125. Pushkin was responding to the first of Chaadayev's *Philosophical Letters*, published that year, which attacked Russian institutions such as the Church, autocracy and serfdom. He urged Russia to embrace Roman Catholicism, and was declared insane.

126. Andrei Tarkovsky, *Uroki rezhissury* [Lectures on Film Directing], Moscow 1993, p.28, quoted in Synessios, p.11.

127. Synessios, p.11.

128. Diary entry for 7 September 1970, *Time Within Time*, p.13.

129. Diary entry for 12 July 1971, *Time Within Time*, p.39.

130. Diary entry for 11 August 1971, *Time Within Time*, p.40.

131. Synessios, p.21. Yermash's 'thaw', which also saw Elem Klimov's *Agony* greenlit, was sadly short-lived.

132. Diary entry for 23 March 1973, *Time Within Time*, p.74.

133. Synessios, p.27.

134. Film title quotes from diary entry for 4 February 1973, *Time Within Time*, p.69.

135. Diary entry for 17 March 1974, *Time Within Time*, p.93.

136. Synessios, p.38. 'Mysticism' was a charge levelled at Tarkovsky throughout his career.

137. Letter sent to the Central Committee of the Communist Party, quoted in Synessios, p.116.

138. Diary entry for 31 December 1978, *Time Within Time*, p.161.

139. *Sculpting in Time*, p.10. Tarkovsky quotes the 'baffled' letters on the preceding pages.

140. *Sculpting in Time*, p.29.

141. Diary entry for 24 January 1973, *Time Within Time*, p.65.

142. I have not been able to locate the source of this quote. If any reader knows, please get in touch via Pocket Essentials, and I will rectify this in further editions.

143. Arseny Tarkovsky, 'First Meetings', translated by Kitty Hunter-Blair, *Sculpting*, p.101. The translations of the poems in *Sculpting in Time* are far superior to the mildly excruciating subtitles on the Artificial Eye DVD of the film.

144. The Kitty Hunter-Blair translation can be found on p.123 of *Sculpting*.

145. The Kitty Hunter–Blair translation can be found on p.143 of *Sculpting*.

146. The Kitty Hunter–Blair translation can be found on p.157 of *Sculpting*.

147. This doesn't appear to be the dacha. It more resembles Alexei's flat in the present day scenes, suggesting he has perhaps inherited it from his parents.

148. Synessios, p.48.

149. The sequence also anticipates the desolate, post–industrial landscapes of *Stalker*.

150. An idea that is given further weight by the fact that Damansky Island was not ceded to China until 1991. The other islands that were also a focus of the 1969 dispute were ceded to China in 2004. The transfer was finalised as this book was being written, in June 2005.

151. The photograph, taken in 1962 by Marina's husband, Alexander Gordon, is reproduced in Synessios, p.78.

152. A selection of Lev Gornung's photographs can be found Synessios, *Mirror*.

153. Synessios, p.76.

154. Diary entry for 20 August 1971, *Time Within Time*, p.41.

155. Diary entry for 13 June 1970, *Time Within Time*, p.5.

156. Diary entry for 1 September 1970, *Time Within Time*, p.7.

157. Johnson & Petrie, p.115.

158. One scene deleted from the script has Alexei dreaming that he is swimming around the submerged remains of Zavrazhie. Elem Klimov's masterly *Farewell* (1981) deals with the impact of a hydroelectric project on a small Siberian community.

159. A contemporaneous trailer for *Mirror*, included as an Easter Egg on the Artificial Eye DVDs of both *Andrei Rublev* and *Solaris*, contains material that did not appear

in the final film, including a shot from this scene that clearly shows Tarkovsky's face. Likewise, a still showing Tarkovsky holding the bird that he releases into the air appears on p.128 of *Instant Light: Tarkovsky Polaroids* (London: Thames & Hudson, 2004)

160. *Sculpting in Time*, p.134.

161. *Sculpting in Time*, p.134.

162. Diary entry for 26 January 1973, *Time Within Time*, p.66.

163. Two-part films were generally the longer ones and were subject to different bureaucratic rules than 'one-part films'. *Andrei Rublev*, *Solaris* and *Stalker* – Tarkovsky's three longest films – were all two-part films. Despite having an intertitle saying 'Part II' around the halfway point, two-part films were always shown without an intermission.

164. Diary entry for 26 August 1977. *Time Within Time*, p.147.

165. Cited in Johnson & Petrie, p.138.

166. Turovskaya, p.111.

167. Le Fanu, p.103.

168. Incidentally, the day after Rainer Werner Fassbinder died.

169. The 'Lancelot Grail', quoted in Malcolm Godwin, *The Holy Grail*, Bloomsbury, 1994, p.10.

170. Dialogue taken from the Artificial Eye DVD of the film.

171. Sacked for, respectively, 'being drunk' and 'behaving like a bastard.' Diary entry for 15 April 1978. *Time Within Time*, p.154.

172. Le Fanu, p.105.

173. 'And the third angel sounded, and there fell a great star from heaven, burning as it were a lamp, and it fell upon the third part of the rivers, and upon the fountains of

waters; and the name of the star is called Wormwood: and the third part of the waters became wormwood; and many men died of the waters, because they were made bitter.' Revelation 8:10–11.

174. 'In *Stalker* Tarkovsky Foretold Chernobyl', Vladimir Sharun interviewed by Stas Tyrkin, 2001. Interview reproduced on nostalghia.com.

175. Another prophetic instance in the film occurs in the dream. Shortly after we have seen the Ghent Altarpiece, we see a page torn from a diary. The date is 28 December which, in 1986, was Tarkovsky's last full day alive. (He died at 02:00 on the 29th.)

176. *Sculpting in Time*, p.128.

177. Synessios, p.110.

178. The subtitle of Maya Turovskaya's chapter on *Stalker* in *Tarkovsky: Cinema as Poetry*, pp.105–16. The 'confession' is, of course, *Mirror*.

179. Gordon, *About Andrei Tarkovsky*, p.42.

180. 'In *Stalker* Tarkovsky Foretold Chernobyl' Vladimir Sharun interviewed by Stas Tyrkin, 2001. Interview reproduced on nostalghia.com.

181. Diary entry for 10 April 1979, *Time Within Time*, p.180.

182. Diary entry for 11 April 1978, *Time Within Time*, p.152.

183. Diary entry for 17 July 1979, *Time Within Time*, p.188.

184. Diary entry for 18 July 1979, *Time Within Time*, p.189.

185. Berezovsky's life story as recounted by Gorchakov to Eugenia is the traditional one, in which the composer's nostalgia for Russia drives him to return home, where he ultimately takes to drink and hangs himself. Recent research on Berezovsky suggests, however, that he enjoyed some success upon his return home and died of a fever.

186. Diary entry for 19 July 1979, *Time Within Time*, p.189.

187. Diary entry for 23 July 1979, *Time Within Time*, p.191.

188. Diary entry for 11 September 1979, *Time Within Time*, p.206.

189. *Sculpting in Time*, p.202.

190. Robert Bresson, *Notes on the Cinematographer*, Quartet Books 1986, p.20. It is not known whether Tarkovsky ever knew of Bresson's book, which was first published in French in 1975.

191. Diary entry for 7 July 1980, *Time Within Time*, p.261.

192. For instance, in the scene in *The Hunters* (1977), where the characters are reminiscing about the elections of 1957, the actors freeze and the election officials walk into the room and the past is played out in front of the contemporary characters. In 1980, Tarkovsky co-edited a TV documentary on Angelopoulos directed by one of *Nostalgia*'s assistant directors, Norman Mozzato.

193. Their ages suggest they may be Gorchakov's step-daughter and mother-in-law, reflecting Tarkovsky's own domestic arrangements in Russia.

194. Tarkovsky discusses *saba* in *Sculpting in Time*, p.59.

195. Green, p.108.

196. *Sculpting in Time*, p.203.

197. *Sculpting in Time*, p.203.

198. *Sculpting in Time*, p.203.

199. Diary entry for 15 September 1976, *Time Within Time*, p.131.

200. *Sculpting in Time*, p.216.

201. The script actually identifies her as Adelaide's daughter by her first marriage, but this is not made apparent in the film. *Collected Screenplays*, p.526.

202. It's impossible to tell who the man is in the film, as his face is turned away, but the implication is that it is Alexander. The published screenplay confirms that

Alexander sees himself in the dream, although the dream sequence, as originally written, was quite different from the one Tarkovsky later shot. *Collected Screenplays*, p.544.

203. Actually Adelaide, not Maria. It is taken from a scene in which Adelaide comforts Alexander after a nightmare. In the published script, this comes after the 'snow' dream, *Collected Screenplays*, p.545. The scene was cut from the film, although part of it can be seen in the documentary, *Directed by Andrei Tarkovsky*.

204. The original version of this scene was much longer and also included Otto cycling through the house – a possible homage to Bunuel – and mourners gathered at Alexander's bedside. (He is dreaming of his own death.) The scene is included in the documentary, *Directed by Andrei Tarkovsky*.

205. In fact it does, at least in English, Welsh, Slavonic and Icelandic, all of which are derived from the Indo-European root *wid*, 'to know, to be wise'.

206. The dialogue is from the Swedish Film Institute DVD of the film. All other quotations in this paragraph are from *Sculpting in Time*, p.218.

207. The wise man is GI Gurdjieff. Tarkovsky notes the saying in his diary on 9 April 1981, *Time Within Time*, p.275.

208. The city scenes were shot on the exact spot where the Swedish Prime Minister Olof Palme was assassinated six months later.

209. The colour in these scenes was achieved by marrying colour and black and white prints and then bleeding as much colour out of the final print as possible; most of this part of the film is therefore literally colour and black and white at the same time.

210. The car looks similar to Victor's BMW, but Victor's car is a saloon, while the abandoned car appears to be a hatchback.

211. Le Fanu, p.127.

212. In his introduction to the Channel 4 broadcast of the film in February 1989 – its first screening on UK television – Robinson remarked that Tarkovsky 'was in better spirits than I'd ever known him'.

213. Ebbo Demont in *About Andrei Tarkovsky*, p.357.

214. Tarkovsky's interpreter on the film, Layla Alexander-Garrett, also remembers him talking on the phone to Dakus, his dog.

215. One scene that was shot but did not make it into the final cut was Alexander's dream of his own death. It had its origins in a diary entry for 27 June 1974 (*Time Within Time*, p.95), where Tarkovsky talks about how light and joyous he felt to have departed his earthly body. In the scene, we see mourners paying their respects as Alexander lies dead on the couch. The scene is included in Michal Leszczylowski's documentary, *Directed by Andrei Tarkovsky*. See note 204.

216. Diary entry for 31 December 1978, *Time Within Time*, p.161.

217. Diary entry for 26 September 1975, *Time Within Time*, p.116.

218. *Time Within Time*, p.126. The entry is erroneously dated 13 November 1976.

219. The translation comes from the Artificial Eye DVD of the film released in 2003, which is notorious for its poor subtitling. In other scenes, 'science fiction' is rendered as 'fiction', Antonioni's *L'Avventura* as 'adventures' and *Stalker* as 'Stalkin'.

220. *Sculpting in Time*, p.189.

221. Diary entry for 26 September 1975, *Time Within Time*, p.116.

222. Diary entry for 27 January 1976, *Time Within Time*, p.121.

223. Diary entry for 24 February 1977, *Time Within Time*, p.143.

224. *Sculpting in Time*, p.154.

225. Diary entry for 7 April 1978, *Time Within Time*, p.151.

226. Quoted in a diary entry for 12 December 1979. The comment comes from a talk Tarkovsky gave in Kazan. *Time Within Time*, p.216.

227. *On 'Hamlet'*, *Time Within Time*, p.383.

228. Diary entry for 23 June 1981, *Time Within Time*, p.282.

229. *Time Within Time*, p.328.

230. Irina Brown, DVD notes.

231. P.29 of the Thames & Hudson edition.

232. *Sculpting in Time*, p.200. Tarkovsky is speaking about his films, *Stalker* in particular, but the sentiment could just as easily apply to his Polaroids.

233. Johnson & Petrie, p.300, n.7.

234. Claudio Abbado, booklet notes in *Hommage à Andrei Tarkovsky* CD, p.1.

235. At the time of writing (2005), Marina has just finished writing a second memoir.

236. The CD omits two pieces that feature in *Stalker*, albeit briefly: excerpts from Ravel's *Bolero* and Wagner's *Meistersinger*.

Appendix I: Complete Filmography

FILMS DIRECTED BY TARKOVSKY

As Director

The Steamroller and the Violin (1960)
Ivan's Childhood (1962)
Andrei Rublev (1966/69)
Solaris (1972)
Mirror (1974)
Stalker (1979)
Nostalgia (1983)
The Sacrifice (1986)

As Co-Director

The Killers (1956) Co-directed with Alexander Gordon and Marika Beiku
There Will Be No Leave Today (1959) Co-directed with Alexander Gordon
Tempo di Viaggio (1980) Co-directed with Tonino Guerra

FILMS NOT DIRECTED BY TARKOVSKY

As Writer

The First Teacher (1965) Director: Andrei Mikhalkov-Konchalovsky (uncredited, with Andrei Mikhalkov-Konchalovsky and Chingiz Aitmatov)
Sergei Lazo (1968) Director: Alexander Gordon (uncredited)
Tashkent the Bread City (aka *Tashkent, City of Plenty*) (1968) Director: Shukhrat Abbasov (uncredited, with Andrei Mikhalkov-Konchalovsky)
One Chance in a Thousand (1969) Director: Leonid Kosharjan, Bagrat Oganisian
The End of the Chieftain (aka *The End of Ataman*) (1971) Director: Shaken Aimanov
The Ferocious One (1973) Director: Tolomush Okeev
Lookout, Snake! (1979) Director: Zakir Sabitov

The French edition of the diaries also lists a short TV film called *Le Rêve* [The Dream] that Tarkovsky apparently wrote for Araïk Agaranian, but gives no date.

As Artistic Adviser

One Chance in a Thousand (1969) Director: Leonid Kosharjan
Sour Grapes (1973) Director: Bagrat Oganisian

As Artistic Director

Fortune-Telling by a Daisy (1978)

As Editor

Sergei Lazo (1968) Director: Alexander Gordon (uncredited)
Theo Angelopoulos (1980) Director: Norman Mozzato (co-editor)

As Actor

The Killers (1956) Director: Tarkovsky, Gordon and Beiku; Whistling Customer
I am Twenty (1964) Director: Marlen Khutsiyev; Party Guest
Sergei Lazo (1968) Director: Alexander Gordon; Soldier (uncredited)
Mirror (1974) Director: Tarkovsky; Alexei on his deathbed/sick bed (uncredited)
The Road to Bresson (1984) Director: Leo De Boer & Jurriën Rood; Himself

Films About Tarkovsky

Andrei Tarkovsky in Nostalgia (1984) Director: Donatella Baglivo (Italy), 90 mins
A Poet in the Cinema (1984) Director: Donatella Baglivo (Italy), 60 mins
Film is a Mosaic of Time (1984) Director: Donatella Baglivo (Italy), 65 mins
Andrei Tarkovsky (1987) Producer: Charlie Pattinson, BBC Television, 53 mins
Behind the Scenes on The Sacrifice (1987) Channel 4 Television
Moscow Elegy (1987) Director: Alexander Sokurov (Russia), 88 mins
The Exile and Death of Andrei Tarkovsky (1987) Director: Ebbo Demont (West Germany), 131 mins

Directed by Andrei Tarkovsky (1988) Director: Michal Leszczylowski (Sweden), 101 mins

Andrei Tarkovsky's Taiga Summer (1994) (Russia)

Tarkovsky: A Journey to His Beginning (1996) Director: Tomoko Baba (Japan), 45 mins

The Recall (1996) Director: Andrei Tarkovsky Jr (Russia), 25 mins

One Day in the Life of Andrei Arsenevich (2000) Director: Chris Marker (France), 55 mins

Student Andrei Tarkovsky (2003) Director: Galina Leontieva (Russia), 29 mins

After Tarkovsky (2003) Director: Peter Shepotinnik (Russia), 59 mins

In addition, there exist some VGIK student shorts about the making of *Andrei Rublev* and several hours of footage were shot on the set of *Stalker*, but apparently never edited. A 1978 Finnish documentary, *The Responsibility of the Artist* (Director: Risto Mäenpää), contains footage from the first shoot of *Stalker* and interviews with Tarkovsky during the same period.

Appendix II:
Unrealised Scripts and Projects

UNFILMED SCRIPTS

Extract (1958) (AKA *Konsentrat / The Concentrate*)

Not actually a script, but a short story written as part of Tarkovsky's VGIK entrance examination, inspired by his time in Siberia, concerning the head of a geological expedition who waits on a foggy jetty for some samples to be delivered to him. Marina Tarkovskaya and Alexander Gordon later adapted the story into a script, parts of which were actually shot (but not directed by Gordon) for the 1994 Russian television documentary, *Andrei Tarkovsky's Taiga Summer*.

Antárctica, Distant Land (1959/63)

(with Andrei Mikhalkov-Konchalovsky and Oleg Osetinsky)

Originally entitled *The Smile, or Antarctica, Land of Miracles*, this was apparently Tarkovsky's first attempt at a feature-length script. It was about a group of Russian scientists on an expedition in the Antarctic. Director Grigory Kozintsev read it, but turned it down. The script was revised in 1963 for Edmond Keosayan, but he turned it down also. The original version was published in the magazine *Moskovsky Komsomolets* in January/February 1960.

Ariel (aka *Light Wind* aka *The Renunciation*) (1971)

(with Friedrich Gorenstein)

Loosely based on the science fiction novel by Alexander Beliaev, *Ariel* is set in 1900 and concerns a young monk, Filipp, who is given the power to fly as the result of a scientific experiment. The local postman tries to set him up as a messiah figure, but it does not work out and Filipp returns to the monastery. The ending sees him as a military chaplain at Verdun, where he dies.

Hoffmaniana (1975/84)

Various real and imagined episodes in the life of the German writer ETA Hoffmann: a ghostly encounter at the opera; Hoffmann's unrequited love for a young music student; a drunken wedding celebration; magic mirrors; a sinister sojourn in a castle; Hoffmann meeting his double at a banquet; and his final deathbed delirium. Dreams, memories and visions intermingle in what is perhaps the best of Tarkovsky's unfilmed scripts. Originally published in *Iskusstvo Kino* in 1976, he revised it slightly in 1984, and resumed work on the project in 1986, intending it to be his next film after *The Sacrifice*.

Sardor (1978)

(with Alexander Misharin)

A 'Tadjik Western' – the Soviet equivalent of Spaghetti Westerns which were usually shot in the Soviet Asian republics – *Sardor* is set in Kazakhstan in 1915. The family of the hero, Mirza, have contracted leprosy and been evacuated to the island of Borsa–Kelmes in the Aral Sea. Mirza decides to buy the island to safeguard the remainder of his family's lives, and spends many years panning for gold in the desert. An old rival, Sha-Mukhamed, tries to steal the gold, but is ultimately killed. Mirza is oblivious to the outside world, not even noticing the Russian Revolution. In a climactic battle on the island, all of the main characters perish. Mirza expires trying to collect water for his leprous family.

UNREALISED PROJECTS

These are projects that never got as far as the script stage; only proposals and outlines exist. Tarkovsky's two most cherished projects that he never lived to realise were film versions of Dostoyevsky's *The Idiot* (to be told twice over, from two different viewpoints), which recurs throughout his diaries from the very first entry in April 1970 until the early 80s, and a virtually silent adaptation of *Hamlet*. His last diary entry (15 December 1986) mentions *Hamlet*, lamenting the fact that he is too weak to work on it.

The diaries also mention numerous other projects, perhaps the most noteworthy of which being adaptations of Thomas Mann (principally *Joseph and His Brothers*, *The Magic Mountain* and *Doctor Faustus*) and Bulgakov's *The Master and Margarita*, all of which recur throughout entries for the 1970s.

On several occasions, Tarkovsky compiled lists of possible projects in his diaries, which are reproduced below.

List of 7 September 1970

Kagol (Bormann's trial)
Physicist Dictator
The House with a Tower (based on the story by Friedrich Gorenstein)
Echo Calls
Deserters
Joseph and his Brothers (Thomas Mann)
Matryona's House (Solzhenitsyn)
A film about Dostoyevsky
A White, White Day (eventually filmed in 1973–4 as *Mirror*)
A Raw Youth (Dostoyevsky)
Joan of Arc, 1970 (presumably a modern-day version of Joan's story. Tarkovsky was familiar with Bresson's version and Dreyer's also.)
The Plague (Camus)
Two Saw the Fox

List of 29 July 1974

(films for Television)

Oblomov (Goncharov)
The Life of Klim Samgin (Gorky)
Seminary Sketches (Nikolai Pomyalovsky)

List of 14 April 1978

(films that Tarkovsky wanted to make in the West)

The Horde
Doctor Faustus
Hamlet (both screen and stage adaptations)
Crime and Punishment
The Renunciation (*Ariel*)
'Latter day' *Joan of Arc*
Two Saw the Fox
Joseph and His Brothers
Hoffmaniana
Italian Journey (which was to become *Tempo di Viaggio*)

List of 3 December 1979

Nostalgia (which was finally shot in 1982)
The Idiot
The Escape (a projected original screenplay about Tolstoy's last years)
The Death of Ivan Ilyich
The Master and Margarita (based on Bulgakov's novel)
The Double (not simply Dostoyevsky's story, but a film about his life)

The French edition of the diaries (*Journal 1970–1986*, Cahiers du cinéma 1993) mentions several additional projects that it lists as scripts. These are: *La Derniere chasse* [The Last Hunt]; *La catastrophe* [The Catastrophe]; and an adaptation of the Estonian writer Jaan Kross's 1978 novel, *Le Fou du Tzar* [The Tsar's Madman]. Several other titles are listed as projected films (as opposed to scripts). They are *L'apocalypse*

240

ou Saint Jean à Patmos; *Le Golgotha*; *Le loup des steppes* (Hesse's *Steppenwolf*); *Le pauvre Jean ou Le Grand Inquisiteur* and *La via après vie* ('un film-documentaire').

Tarkovsky also entertained ideas about making a film about Carlos Castaneda; a version of Ibsen's *Peer Gynt*; *The Country*, a quasi-documentary about Tarkovsky's dacha, which was to have featured Alexander Kaidanovsky as Tarkovsky; a short film about Rudolph Steiner (to be made with Alexander Kluge) (1984–6); and a Life of St Anthony (1984–6).

At various times, Tarkovsky planned stage versions of *Julius Caesar*, *Macbeth* and Ostrovsky's *Last Love*. He was also due to start work on a production of Wagner's *The Flying Dutchman* at Covent Garden in January 1986, but which was postponed due to Tarkovsky's ill health.

Suggestions for Further Reading

BOOKS BY TARKOVSKY

In English

Sculpting in Time, University of Texas Press, 1989
Andrei Rublev, Faber & Faber, 1991
Time Within Time: The Diaries 1970–1986, Faber & Faber, 1994
Collected Screenplays, Faber & Faber, 1999
Instant Light: Tarkovsky Polaroids, Thames & Hudson, 2004

Not in English

Uroki rezhissury [Lectures on Film Directing], Lenfilm, 1989 (Russian)
Diari: Martirologio, Edizioni della Meridiana, 2002 (The complete edition of the diaries, Italian)
Récits de Jeunesse [Youth Stories], Éditions Philippe Rey, 2004 (French)

Books About Tarkovsky

In English

Robert Bird, *Andrei Rublev*, BFI Film Classics, British Film Institute, 2004

Peter Green, *Andrei Tarkovsky: The Winding Quest*, Macmillan, 1993

Vida T Johnson and Graham Petrie, *The Films of Andrei Tarkovsky: A Visual Fugue* Indiana University Press, 1994

Mark Le Fanu, *The Cinema of Andrei Tarkovsky*, British Film Institute, 1987

Natasha Synessios, *Mirror*, Kino Files Film Companion #6, IB Tauris, 2001

Marina Tarkovskaya (Editor), *About Andrei Tarkovsky*, Progress Publishers, 1990

Maya Turovskaya, *Tarkovsky: Cinema as Poetry*, Faber & Faber, 1989

Not Currently in English

Tatyana Elmanovits, *The Mirror of Time: The Films of Andrei Tarkovsky*, 1980 (Estonian)

Seweryn Kusmierczyk, *The Tolstoy Complex*, 1989 (Polish)

Olga Surkova, *A Book of Comparisons: Tarkovsky–79*, 1991 (Russian)

   Tarkovsky and I: A Girl Scout's Diary, 2002 (Russian)

   With Tarkovsky and About Tarkovsky, 2005 (Russian)

Larissa Tarkovskaya (as Larissa Tarkovski), *Andrei Tarkovski*, Calmann-Lévy, 1998 (French)

Marina Tarkovskaya, *Pieces of the Mirror*, 1999 (Russian)[235]

About Andrei Tarkovsky (expanded, two-volume edition),

2002 (Russian)
Maya Turovskaya, *7½, or the Films of Andrei Tarkovsky*, 1991 (Russian)

In addition, there are several hard-to-find but well-produced books in Japanese, edited by Hironobu Baba. *The Book of Andrei Tarkovsky's Mirror* (Libro Port, 1994) is lavishly illustrated and includes Tarkovsky's workbooks for the film, his diary and the shooting script. *The Book of Tarkovsky's The Killers* (Seidosha Publishers, 1997) is a companion book to the 1996 documentary, *Tarkovsky: A Journey to His Beginning*. It includes early writings and drawings by Tarkovsky and contributions from Marina Tarkovskaya, Alexander Gordon, Yuli Fait, Andrei Mikhalkov-Konchalovsky and Mikhail Romadin. Finally, there is a book solely of photographs – the editor's name is not given – simply called *Andrei Tarkovsky*, published in 1989.

RELATED INTEREST

Robert Bresson, *Notes on the Cinematographer*, Quartet Books, 1996
Pavel Florensky, *Iconostasis*, St Vladimir's Seminary Press, 1997
Rainer and Rose-Marie Hagen, *Bruegel: The Complete Paintings*, Taschen, 2000
Stanislaw Lem, *Solaris*, Penguin Books, 1981
Vittorio Sgarbi, *Carpaccio*, Abbeville Press, 1995
Arkady and Boris Strugatsky, *Roadside Picnic*, Gollancz, 1978
Arseny Tarkovsky, *Life, Life: Selected Poems*, Crescent Moon Publishing, 2000
Frank Zöllner & Johannes Nathan, *Leonardo da Vinci: The Complete Paintings and Drawings*, Taschen, 2003

ANDREI TARKOVSKY

The Swedish book of Russian icon paintings that Alexander
receives as a gift in *The Sacrifice* is Michail Vladimirovic
Alpatov's *Ryskt Ikonmåleri* [*Russian Icon Painting*], published in
1984 by Gidlunds Förlag.

RESOURCES

The Andrei Tarkovsky Institute – based in Moscow, Florence
and Paris – exists to preserve Tarkovsky's papers and memory.
Its founding members were Larissa Tarkovskaya, Krzysztof
Zanussi, Mstislav Rostropovitch and Robert Bresson. There
appears to be a significant amount of unpublished material
in their archives, which, it is hoped, will see the light of day
at some stage. The institute can be contacted at 6, Rond-
Point des Champs Elysées 75008 Paris. E-mail: tarkovski@
wanadoo.fr.

DVD RECOMMENDATIONS

The Killers, Criterion
There Will be No Leave Today, Currently unavailable on DVD
The Steamroller and the Violin, Facets
Ivan's Childhood, MK2
Andrei Rublev, Criterion (205-minute version); at the time of
writing, there is no acceptable version of the 185-minute cut
currently available on DVD in the West. In Russia, the best
DVD version is that distributed by Lizard, which features
Mosfilm's 2004 restoration of the film
Solaris, Criterion
Mirror, Artificial Eye
Stalker, Artificial Eye
Tempo di Viaggio; at the time of writing, there is no accept-
able version currently available on DVD

Nostalgia; at the time of writing, there is no acceptable version currently available on DVD
Boris Godunov, Phillips
The Sacrifice, Swedish Film Institute

COMPACT DISCS

Claudio Abbado, *Hommage à Andrei Tarkovsky*, Deutsche Grammophon 437-8402;
Abbado conducts musical tributes by Luigi Nono, György Kurtág, Beat Furrer and Wolfgang Rihm, recorded live at the 1991 Tarkovsky Festival in Vienna.

Eduard Artemyev, *Solaris, The Mirror, Stalker*, Electroshock Records ELCD 012
Artemyev's music from Tarkovsky's 1970s films. Unfortunately, some tracks have been re-recorded for this album (originally released on vinyl in 1990), but it does contain as compensation Artemyev's own tribute, *Dedication to A Tarkovsky*.

Cinema Classics: Andrei Tarkovsky, London POCL-4336
Japanese CD that contains most[236] of the classical music used in the films:
Solaris: JS Bach, 'Ich ruf zu dir, Herr Jesus Christ' BWV 639, from *Orgelbüchlein*
Mirror: JS Bach, 'Das alte Jahr vergangen ist' BWV 614, from *Orgelbüchlein*
Pergolesi, 'Quando corpus morietur' from *Stabat Mater*
JS Bach, *St John Passion* BWV 245, No. 33, 'Und siehe da, der Vorhang im Tempel zeriß'
Purcell, 'They tell us that your mighty powers' from *The Indian Queen*

JS Bach, *St John Passion* BWV 245, No.1, 'Herr, unser Herscher'
Stalker/Nostalgia: Beethoven, Symphony No.9, *Choral*,
   Fourth Movement
Nostalgia: Verdi, 'Requiem aeternam' from *Requiem*
The Sacrifice: JS Bach, *St Matthew Passion* BWV 244, No.47,
   'Ebarme dich'

The works of Maxim Berezovsky, whom Gorchakov
researches in *Nostalgia*, are available on the CDs *Sacred
Ukrainian Music Vol.1* (available from www.claudiorecords.
com) and *Maxim Berezovsky – Secular Music* (available from
www.marecordings.com).

WEBSITES

www.nostalghia.com is the pre-eminent Tarkovsky site on
the web in English. Curated by Trond Trondsen and Jan
Bielawski, the site contains a wealth of information, some of
it unavailable in English elsewhere. The site also contains
many articles and essays on Tarkovsky, a form in which some
of the most stimulating Tarkovksy criticism is currently being
published.

Other Tarkovsky sites include:

www.nostalghia.cz (Czech)
www.tarkovszkij.hu (Hungarian)
www.andreitarkovski.org (Spanish)
http://homepage.mac.com/satokk/news.html (Japanese)
www.nostalgiya.com (Korean)

Index

Abbado, Claudio
  (Conductor), 206, 208,
  214, 231, 246
Antonioni, Michelangelo
  (Director), 18, 198, 230
Apocalypse, The, 36, 38, 41,
  42, 63, 67
Art, 36, 46, 47, 59, 88, 98,
  111, 115, 126, 128, 133,
  148, 204
Artemyev, Eduard
  (Composer), 30, 33, 97,
  99, 120, 145, 155, 246
artists, 12, 15, 18, 37, 48, 58,
  59, 86, 88, 98, 117, 127,
  128, 133, 158, 160, 204,
  208, 214
autobiography, 12, 60, 73–5,
  98, 117–19, 139–44,
  160–62, 177–8, 193–6

Bach, Johann Sebastian, 16,
  33, 99, 120, 121, 124,
  131, 179, 185

Bergman, Ingmar (Director),
  13, 18, 19, 85, 193, 198,
  215, 216
Bogomolov, Vladimir
  (Writer), 29, 52, 61, 64,
  65, 66, 105
Bondarchuk, Natalya
  (Actor), 99, 106
Bondarchuk, Sergei
  (Director), 106, 169, 208
Bradbury, Ray (Writer), 107,
  109, 221
Bresson, Robert (Director
  and Film Theorist), 18,
  169, 171, 198, 211, 216,
  222, 227, 239, 244, 245
Breughel the Elder, Pieter,
  36, 89, 104, 116
Burlyaev, Nikolai (Actor),
  30, 61, 64, 77

camera movements, 45, 47,
  170
Cannes Film Festival, 20, 21,

24, 77, 84, 85, 98, 100,
107, 128, 146, 152, 164,
169, 180, 185, 186, 208
Carpaccio, Vittore, 36, 37,
90, 244
Chernobyl disaster, 159,
226, 227
colour coding, 46, 49, 82,
89, 97, 106, 130, 147,
149, 156, 166, 172, 174,
182, 184, 188, 210

Dostoyevsky, Fyodor, 38, 47,
59, 87, 122, 135, 150,
222, 238, 239, 240
dreams, 39, 42, 44, 46, 48,
49, 67, 68, 69, 73, 74, 87,
119, 125, 128, 129, 130,
133, 134, 139, 140, 160,
165, 172, 174, 188, 190,
192, 209
Dreyer, Carl Theodor
(Director), 154, 239

ecology, 38, 67, 116, 157, 176
Eisenstein, Sergei (Director
and Film Theorist), 13, 49
Erice, Victor (Director), 13,
204

faith, 13, 35, 36, 39, 88, 147,
149, 153, 155, 157, 160,
170, 172

family, 11, 44, 110, 117, 132
Fanu, Mark Le (Critic), 54,
109, 154, 158, 193, 215,
219, 222, 226, 229, 243
Feiginova, Ludmila (Editor),
29, 30, 31, 32, 76, 99, 120,
128, 145
Fellini, Federico (Director),
18, 198
fire, 96, 106, 122, 123, 131,
134, 140, 167
flight, 41, 68, 69, 94, 136,
212

Gordon, Alexander (Director
and AT's brother-in-law),
18, 50, 53, 55, 161, 216,
218, 219, 225, 227, 232,
233, 234, 236, 244
Gorenstein, Freidrich
(Writer), 29, 99, 105, 237,
239
Goskino (Soviet cinema
body), 22, 23, 24, 25, 83,
84, 85, 105, 126, 128
Green, Peter (Critic), 12,
176, 243
Grinko, Nikolai (Actor), 30,
61, 76, 99, 121, 145, 159
Guerra, Tonino (Writer), 21,
107, 163, 168, 170, 197,
198, 199, 200, 201, 202,
203, 204, 232

Hamlet (Paul Scofield stage production), 18

Hamlet (play), 181

Hamlet (Tarkovsky film version), 230, 238

Hamlet (Tarkovsky stage production), 150, 160, 206

history, 11, 117, 132, 135, 136, 209

Holy Fools, 34, 38, 39, 77, 83, 92, 93, 96, 97

icons, 82, 88, 93, 181, 209

Ignatievo (place), 142, 178

Iosseliani, Otar (Director), 13, 18, 24

Ivan's Childhood, 9, 13, 19, 21, 27, 28, 29, 31, 32, 36, 37, 38, 39, 41, 52, 55, 58, 61, 64, 66, 67, 69, 72, 73, 74, 82, 84, 86, 91, 98, 105, 203, 219, 232, 245

Josephson, Erland (Actor), 30, 163, 170, 179, 180, 187

Kaidanovsky, Alexander (Actor), 145, 154, 159, 169, 241

Kalatozov, Mikhail (Director), 24, 58

Khrushchev, Nikita, 13, 24, 65

Kieślowski, Krzysztof (Director), 13, 26, 177, 216

Knyazhinsky, Alexander (Cameraman), 31, 145, 151, 159

Kubrick, Stanley (Director), 107, 109

Kurosawa, Akira (Director), 18, 89

Lem, Stanislaw (Writer), 20, 29, 52, 99, 105, 108, 109, 244

Leonardo, 36, 123, 124, 137, 138, 140, 180, 182, 192, 217, 244

levitation, 39, 139, 191

long takes, 31, 45, 69, 91, 152, 157, 177

Mikhalkov-Konchalovsky, Andrei (Director), 13, 24, 28, 55, 58, 61, 76, 82, 86, 233, 236, 244

Mirror, 12, 15, 20, 23, 28, 31, 32, 35, 36, 38, 39, 41, 43, 45, 47, 49, 58, 67, 69, 117, 118, 119, 120, 125, 128, 129, 130, 131, 133, 134, 137, 139, 142, 144, 150, 160, 161, 169, 172, 175,

178, 191, 194, 209, 210, 215, 216, 218, 225, 227, 232

mirroring, 41, 110, 138, 165, 185

mirrors, 37, 58, 60, 102, 122, 138, 165, 175

Montaigne, Michel de, 108, 115, 223

Mosfilm, 23, 24, 31, 55, 61, 64, 65, 76, 83, 99, 105, 106, 120, 125, 126, 127, 128, 145, 150, 159, 245

nature, 17, 29, 39, 40, 41, 62, 72, 75, 92, 108, 109, 110, 111, 115, 137, 176, 181, 187, 192, 199

newsreel, 64, 73, 74, 122, 123, 124, 130, 132, 135, 136, 137, 138, 143, 172

Nostalgia, 9, 20, 25, 31, 32, 37, 38, 39, 40, 41, 42, 43, 44, 45, 46, 47, 58, 59, 67, 69, 163, 167, 169, 170, 171, 172, 175, 178, 185, 186, 187, 188, 195, 199, 200, 201, 202, 203, 204, 208, 209, 210, 218, 228, 232, 234, 240, 246, 247

nostalgia (as theme), 12, 178

Nykvist, Sven (Cameraman), 31, 179, 180, 186, 192

Ovchinnikov, Vyacheslav (Composer), 30, 32, 33, 56, 58, 61, 76

paganism, 40, 79, 88, 90, 92, 151, 194

pantheism, 40, 92

Parajanov, Sergei (Director, close friend of AT), 13, 18, 22, 24, 25, 198

poet, 122

poetry, 11, 14, 16, 26, 31, 36, 48, 122, 130, 132, 143, 164, 165, 168, 178, 193, 208, 214, 218

Pushkin, Alexander, 47, 48, 121, 123, 124, 137, 139, 143, 206, 209, 218, 223

Rausch, Irma (AT's first wife, actor and director), 18, 30, 105, 117, 118, 119, 141, 221

religion, 11, 36, 208

Rerberg, George (Cameraman), 20, 31, 120, 145, 151

Roadside Picnic (Novel), 145, 150, 152, 244

Romm, Mikhail (Director), 17, 18, 19, 50, 52, 53

Rublev, Andrei, 13, 19, 20, 22, 28, 29, 33, 34, 36, 38,

39, 41, 45, 46, 47, 49, 70,
73, 76, 78, 79, 80, 81, 82,
84, 85, 86, 88, 89, 90, 91,
92, 93, 94, 95, 98, 105,
114, 117, 122, 125, 136,
142, 172, 209, 212, 215,
220

Rublev, Andrei (Icon
painter), 82, 85, 98

sacrifice (as theme), 39, 44,
83, 183, 189

Sacrifice, The, 9, 12, 20, 21,
27, 31, 32, 33, 35, 36, 37,
38, 39, 40, 42, 43, 44, 45,
46, 47, 66, 67, 68, 98,
144, 162, 179, 185, 186,
188, 190, 192, 193, 194,
195, 196, 208, 211, 217,
222, 232, 237, 245, 246,
247

Sartre, Jean Paul, 13, 19, 65

Sculpting in Time, 26, 27, 36,
37, 47, 58, 59, 71, 73, 90,
129, 144, 170, 186, 205,
211, 212, 214, 216, 217,
218, 219, 220, 224, 225,
227, 228, 229, 230, 231,
242

Shakespeare, William, 160,
204, 205

Sight and Sound (Magazine),
13, 48

silence, 35, 38, 72, 81, 92,
96, 97, 155, 171, 198,
199, 222

Solaris, 9, 25, 31, 32, 33, 36,
37, 39, 41, 42, 43, 44, 45,
46, 52, 58, 66, 67, 69, 97,
99, 100, 101, 102, 105,
106, 107, 108, 109, 111,
114, 115, 117, 118, 119,
126, 136, 152, 172, 190,
194, 195, 208, 210, 215,
220, 222, 225, 232, 244,
245, 246

Solaris (Novel), 20, 29, 105

Solonitsyn, Anatoly (Actor),
30, 76, 99, 121, 131, 145,
154, 155, 159, 161, 169,
204, 205

sound, use of, 33, 34, 47, 58,
116, 149, 159, 163, 173,
191, 203

space, handling of, 36, 45,
58, 69, 111, 113, 153,
156, 174, 175

Stalker, 9, 20, 24, 29, 30, 31,
32, 33, 35, 37, 38, 40, 41,
42, 43, 45, 46, 47, 66, 67,
70, 144, 145, 146, 147,
148, 149, 150, 151, 152,
153, 154, 155, 156, 157,
158, 159, 160, 161, 162,
170, 171, 172, 173, 175,
176, 177, 186, 195, 200,

205, 222, 225, 226, 227, 230, 231, 232, 235, 245, 246, 247

Steamroller and the Violin, The, 20, 28, 32, 55, 57, 73, 98, 220, 232, 245

Strugatsky, Arkady (Writer), 185

Strugatsky, Arkady and Boris (Writers), 20, 29, 52, 145, 150, 152, 216, 244

Surkova, Olga (Critic), 44, 47, 142, 211, 218, 243

symbolism, 35, 39, 40, 198, 202

Synessios, Natasha (Critic), 11, 12, 74, 215, 220, 223, 224, 225, 227, 243

Tarkovsky Jr, Andrei (AT's younger son), 21, 194, 208

Tarkovskaya, Larissa (AT's second wife), 30, 99, 117, 120, 145, 159, 163, 194, 196, 243, 245

Tarkovskaya, Maria Ivanovna (AT's mother), 14, 15, 60, 119, 138, 140, 141, 143

Tarkovskaya, Marina (AT's sister), 14, 55, 118, 138, 140, 215, 243

Tarkovsky, Arseny (Poet, AT's father), 14, 15, 16, 60, 73, 121, 122, 131, 140, 164, 166, 178, 224, 244

Tarkovsky, Arseny (Senka, AT's eldest son), 18, 118, 141, 142

Tempo di Viaggio, 21, 107, 168, 169, 197, 200, 201, 203, 213, 232, 240, 245

Terekhova, Margarita (Actor), 36, 121, 127, 135, 204, 205

thaw (political), 13, 24, 126, 224

The Killers, 18, 50, 52, 53, 55, 57, 232, 234, 244, 245

There Will Be No Leave Today, 18, 19, 53, 54, 55, 57

Time Within Time, 212, 216, 217, 218, 219, 220, 221, 222, 223, 224, 225, 226, 227, 228, 229, 230, 231, 242

Tolstoy, Leo, 47, 59, 216, 222, 240, 243

Turnabout, 210, 211

Turovskaya, Maya (Critic), 17, 44, 54, 84, 153, 216, 219, 220, 221, 226, 227, 243, 244 unrealised projects, 199, 236, 238

Venice Film Festival, 19, 21, 62, 65, 66, 84, 85
VGIK (Film School), 17, 18, 19, 50, 52, 53, 55, 57, 58, 60, 204, 214, 235, 236
Vigo, Jean (Director), 18, 198

Wajda, Andrzej (Director), 20, 158, 216
water, 35, 40, 70, 72, 74, 133, 148, 155, 158, 159, 173, 176, 238

women, role of, 43, 44, 119, 141, 164, 170, 192, 194

Yankovsky, Oleg (Actor), 30, 121, 163, 169, 170, 171, 205
Yermash, Filip (Head of Goskino), 23, 25, 127, 129, 151, 224
Yurievets (place), 14, 15, 16, 17, 73
Yusov, Vadim (Cameraman), 20, 30, 31, 55, 58, 61, 64, 76, 99, 106, 108

Zavrazhie (place), 14, 142, 225